The Critic As Artist

THE
CRITIC
AS
ARTIST

ESSAYS ON BOOKS 1920-1970

with some preliminary ruminations by H. L. Mencken

Edited by Gilbert A. Harrison

Kbs

LIVERIGHT   NEW YORK

1.987654321

ISBN: 0-87140-544-X (cloth)
           0-87140-054-5 (paper)

LC Number: 74-162431

Manufactured in the United States of America

12-14-93

Contents

The Critic As Artist

THE CRITIC'S MOTIVE

H. L. Mencken

(1921)

Nearly all discussions of criticism, it seems to me, start off with a false assumption, to wit, the assumption that the primary motive of the critic, the impulse which makes a critic of him and not a politician or a stockbroker, is pedagogical—that he writes because he is possessed by a yearning to disseminate some specific doctrine, epistemological, psychological, historical, or aesthetic. This is true, I believe, only of bad critics, and its degree of truth increases in direct ratio to their badness. The motive of the critic who is really worth reading—the only critic of whom, indeed, it may be said truthfully that it is at all *possible* to read him—is something quite different. That motive is not the motive of the pedagogue, but the motive of the artist. It is simply a desire for self-expression, a thirst to function more broadly and brilliantly than the general, obscure in origin but irresistible in force. His choice of criticism rather than creative writing is chiefly a matter of temperament—perhaps, more accurately, a matter of hormones and intestinal flora—with accidents of education and environment to help. The feelings that happen to be dominant in him at the moment the scribbling frenzy seizes him and that move him powerfully to seek expression for them in words, are feelings inspired, not by life itself, but by books, pictures, music, sculpture, architecture, religion, philosophy—in brief by some other man's feelings about life. They are thus second-hand, and are rightly regarded by creative artists as inferior to their own first-hand reactions.

If a critic continues on this plane, if he lacks the intellectual agility and enterprise needed to make the leap from the work of art to the vast and mysterious complex of phenomena behind it, then he remains a mere reviewer of and valet to the ideas of his betters, and is of little more importance to the world than a schoolmaster, a newsmonger, or an auctioneer. But if a genuine artist is concealed within him—if his feelings are really profound and original, and his capacity for self-expression is above the average of educated men—then he moves inevitably from the work of art to life itself, and begins to take on a dignity that he formerly lacked. It is impossible to think of a man of any actual force and originality, universally recognized as having those qualities, who spent his whole life appraising and describing the work of other men. Did Goethe, or Carlyle, or Matthew Arnold, or Sainte-Beuve, or Macaulay, or even, to come down a few pegs, Lewes, or Lowell, or Hazlitt? Certainly not. The thing that becomes most obvious about the writings of all such men, once they are examined carefully, is that the critic is always being swallowed up by the creative artist—that what starts out as the review of a book, or a play, or other work of art, usually develops very quickly into an independent essay upon the theme of that work of art, or upon some theme that it suggests—in a word, that it becomes a fresh work of art, and only indirectly related to the one that suggested it. This fact, indeed, is so plain that it scarcely needs statement. What the pedagogues always object to in, say, the Quarterly reviewers is that they forgot the books they were supposed to review, and wrote long papers—often, in fact, small books— expounding ideas of their own, many of them vastly removed from the ideas in the books under review. Every critic who is really worth reading falls into this habit. He cannot stick to his task: what is before him is always infinitely less interesting to him than what is within him. If he is genuinely first-rate—if what is within him stands the test of type, and wins an audience, and produces the reactions that every artist craves—then he usually ends by abandoning the criticism of specific works of art altogether, and setting up shop as a general merchant in general ideas, i.e., as an artist working in the materials of life itself.

Mere reviewing, however conscientiously and competently it is done, is plainly a much inferior business. Like writing poetry, it is chiefly a function of intellectual immaturity. The young literatus just out of the university, having as yet no capacity for grappling with the fundamental mysteries of existence, is put to writing reviews of books, or plays, or music, or painting. Very often he does it extremely well; it is, in fact, not hard to do well for even decayed pedagogues often do it, as such graveyards of the intellect as the *New York Times* bear witness. But if he continues to do it, whether well or ill, it is a sign to all the world that his growth ceased when they made him Artium Baccalaureus. Gradually he becomes, whether in or out of the academic grove, a pedagogue, which is to say, an artisan devoted to diluting and retailing the ideas of his superiors—not an artist, not even a bad artist, but almost the antithesis of an artist. He is learned, he is sober, he is painstaking and accurate—but he is as hollow as a jug. Nothing is in him save the ghostly echoes of other men's thoughts and feelings. If he were a genuine artist he would have thoughts and feelings of his own, and the impulse to give them objective form would be irresistible. An artist can no more withstand that impulse than a politician can withstand the temptations of a job. There are no mute, inglorious Miltons, save in the hallucinations of poets. The one sound test of a Milton is that he functions as a Milton. His difference from other men lies precisely in the superior vigor of his impulse to self-expression, not in the superior beauty and loftiness of his ideas. Other men, in point of fact, often have the same ideas, or perhaps even loftier ones, but they are able to suppress them, usually on grounds of decorum, and so they escape being artists, and are respected by right-thinking persons, and die with money in the bank, and are forgotten in two weeks.

Obviously, the critic whose performance we are commonly called upon to investigate is a man standing somewhere along the path leading from the beginning that I have described to the goal. He has got beyond being a mere cataloguer and valuer of other men's ideas, but he has not yet become an autonomous artist—he is not yet ready to challenge attention with his own ideas alone. But it must be plain that his motion, in so far as he is moving at all, must be in the direction of that autonomy—that is, unless one imagines him sliding backward into senile infantilism: a spectacle not unknown to literary pathology, but too pathetic to be discussed here. Bear this motion in mind, and the true nature of his aims and purposes becomes clear; more, the incurable falsity of the aims and purposes usually credited to him becomes equally clear. He is not actually trying to perform an impossible act of arctic justice upon the artist whose work gives him a text. He is not trying, with mathematical passion, to find out exactly what was in that artist's mind at the moment of creation, and to display it precisely and in an ecstacy of appreciation. He is not trying to bring the work discussed into accord with some gaudy theory of aesthetics, or ethics, or truth, or to determine its degree of departure from that theory. He is not trying to lift up the fine arts, or to defend democracy against sense, or to promote happiness at the domestic hearth, or to convert sophomores into right-thinkers, or to serve God. He is not trying to fit a group of novel phenomena into the orderly process of history. He is not even trying to discharge the catalytic office that I myself, in a romantic moment, once sought to force upon him. He is first and last, simply trying to express himself. He is trying (*a*) to arrest and challenge a sufficient body of readers, to make them pay attention to him, to impress them with the charm and novelty of his ideas, to provoke them into an enchanted awareness of him, and (*b*) to achieve thereby for his own inner ego that agreeable feeling of a function performed, a tension relieved, a catharsis attained which Beethoven achieved when he wrote the Fifth Symphony, and a hen achieves every time she lays an egg.

It is, in brief, the "obscure, inner necessity" of Joseph Conrad that moves him: everything else is an afterthought. Conrad is moved by that necessity to write romances; Beethoven was moved to write music; poets are moved to write poetry; critics are moved to write criticism. The form is nothing; the only important thing is the motive power—and it is the same in all cases. It is the hot yearning of every man who has ideas to empty them upon the world, to hammer them into plausible and ingratiating shapes, to compel the attention and respect of his equals, to lord it over his inferiors. So seen, the critic becomes a far more transparent and agreeable fellow than ever he was in the discourses of the psychologists who sought to make him a mere appraiser in an intellectual customs house, a gauger in a distillery of the spirit, a just and infallible judge upon the cosmic bench. Such offices, in point of fact, never fit him. He always bulges over their confines. So labeled and estimated, it always turns out that the specific critic under examination is a very bad one, or no critic at all. But when he is thought of, not as pedagogue, but as artist, then he begins to take on reality, and, what is more, dignity. Carlyle was surely no just and infallible judge; on the contrary, he was full of prejudices, biles, naivetés, humors. Yet he is read, consulted, attended to. Macaulay was unfair, inaccurate, fanciful, lyrical—yet his essays live. Arnold had his faults too, and so did Sante-Beuve, and so did Goethe, and so did many another of that line—and yet they are remembered today, and all the learned and conscientious critics of their time, laboriously concerned with the precise intent of the artists under review, and passionately determined to set it forth with god-like care and to relate it exactly to this or that great stream of ideas—all these pedants are forgotten. What saved Carlyle, Macaulay and company is as plain as day. They were first-rate artists. They could make the thing charming, and that is always a million times more important than making it true.

Truth, indeed, is something that is believed in only by persons who have never tried personally to pursue it to its fastnesses and grab it by the tail. It is the adoration of second-rate men—men who always receive it at second-hand.

Pedagogues believe in immutable truths and spend their lives trying to determine them and propagate them; the intellectual progress of man consists largely of a concerted effort to block and destroy their enterprise. In the department of aesthetics, wherein critics mainly disport themselves, it is almost impossible to think of a so-called truth that shows any sign of being permanently true. The most profound of principles begins to fade and quiver almost as soon as it is stated. But the work of art, as opposed to the theory behind it, has a longer life, particularly if that theory is obscure and questionable, and so cannot be determined accurately. Hamlet, the Mona Lisa, Faust, Dixie, Parsifal, Mother Goose, Annabel Lee, Huckleberry Finn—these things so baffling to pedagogy, so contumacious to the categories, so mysterious in purpose and utility—these things live. And why? Because there is in them the delightful flavor of odd and attractive personality, because the quality that shines from them is not that of correct demeanor but that of creative passion, because they pulse and breathe and speak, because they are genuine works of art. So with criticism. Let us forget all the heavy effort to make a science of it; it is a fine art, or nothing. If the critic, retiring to his cell to concoct his treatise upon a book or play or what-not, produces a piece of writing that shows sound structure, and brilliant color, and the flash of novel and persuasive ideas, and civilized manners, and the charm of an uncommon personality in free function, then he has given something to the world that is worth having, and sufficiently justified his existence. Let him leave the exact truth to professors of aesthetics, who can no more determine it than he can, and will infallibly make it idiotic. He is an artist, not a schoolmaster.

What I preach will be labeled at once and thrust into its

pigeon-hole: it is impressionism. True. But it is impressionism that is not to be monkeyed with: it depends too much upon the impressionist.

CONRAD AIKEN

The Last of the Forsytes

Into the general characteristics, and obvious virtues, of Mr. Galsworthy's Forsyte Saga it is perhaps not necessary, at this date, to go. The book has been accepted as a "social satire of epic proportions"; as a "masterpiece of knowledge and insight"; as a "compendium of the Victorian epoch"; as a "masterpiece of form"; and as being "written with a flow and music that is found only in the work of the masters of prose." Certainly, this enormous and painstaking survey of a whole half-century of English life, the life of the propertied classes, has earned its right to a very definite place in English literature: like the Barchester series of Anthony Trollope, its sheer weight as a social document alone is almost enough to guarantee its permanence. What Trollope did for the "county family" in England in the early and middle parts of the nineteenth century—taking up the theme about a generation after the point at which Jane Austen dropped it—Mr. Galsworthy has set out to do for the second half of the century, and the early years of the next. The three authors provide us, indeed, with an almost perfect *continuum*. Not only do they deal with the same scene and with the same

11

kinds of people: they also share a common method. It is the "wholeness" of the social picture that interests them, and all three of them go about the presentation of this picture with something of the unexaggerative detachment of the sociologist. Allowing for individual differences—for the shrewder wit of Jane Austen, the generous urbanity of Trollope, the more inquisitive intellectualism of Mr. Galsworthy, and also his keener interest in the purely *dramatic* element in the architecture of fiction—the three authors are very obviously congeners.

Nevertheless, if Mr. Galsworthy resembles his two predecessors in his comprehensiveness and in his predilection for a level and cumulative realism, he has also his striking differences. He is not as "pure" a literary phenomenon as either of the others: his talent is not, like Jane Austen's or Trollope's, a single and immediately recognizable thing, but rather a kind of synthesis, whether we regard it from the point of view of style or the point of view of method. We can, and should, grant immediately his greater intellectual grasp: he assumes for his purpose a far more complex scene, and this more complex scene he handles with admirable control. Nothing is left out, everything is adequately seen and rendered. If we take the picture as a whole, we can say that it is true and rich, and that in assembling so much material on one canvas he has achieved a remarkable feat of design.

It is when we look at the thing in detail that we begin, perhaps, to be here and there a little disquieted and to feel that for all its energy his talent is not quite so fine or deep, nor so individual, as that of either of his literary forbears. Galsworthy has himself, in some degree, aimed at a style of this sort, or at all events, finding himself so inclined, he has decided to make the best of it. Mr. Galsworthy, too, is more interested in the thing said than in the manner of the saying: and if, for the most part, he succeeds in producing an effect of immediacy or actuality, by being—shall we say—rather informal in his literary manners, it must be added to this that he is often downright careless. One cannot, in fact, agree with that critic, quoted above, that he writes "with a flow and music that is found only in the masters of prose." Mr. Galsworthy's prose is an adequate prose, but it is not a distinguished one. It is frequently awkward, frequently monotonous, to the point of becoming actively and obtrusively *not* a good medium for the thing said. And again, Mr. Galsworthy has always been somewhat disposed to purple passages. There are, in other words, times when he wants something a little better than his "mere medium" for the thing said; he desires to be poetic; an emotional scene or atmosphere is to be conveyed, and accordingly he attempts a prose more charged and ornate. These attempts are almost invariably failures: Mr. Galsworthy's taste fails him. What one usually feels on these occasions is that he is simply unable to express feelings delicately; and that is, perhaps, a definition of sentimentality.

One feels, therefore, that when one accepts, as one does, Mr. Galsworthy's place in English fiction, one does so with very definite reserves as to the quality of his style. And even the "wholeness" of his picture, which is his major virtue, is not without grave faults. If he gives us admirable scenes, sharp, quick, and living, and admirable portraits, like that of Soames Forsyte, or Irene Herron, or old Jolyon, he also gives us a good many scenes which we do not believe in for a minute, and more than a handful of portraits which do not belong at all in any such gallery as this, but rather in the category of the Jonsonian or Dickensian "humour." Swithin, and the Aunts Hester and Euphemia, and such minor personages as the detective, are the flimsiest of caricatures, and are quite unmistakably out of key. In these instances, and in others, Mr. Galsworthy's taste has gone wrong; his tact has betrayed him; his perceptions have not been sufficiently deep. This result is always an immediate and fatal destruction of the unity of tone.

There are times, moreover, when even his handling of the "good" characters seems to be at fault: times when it seems as if he were not entirely to be trusted as a psychologist. Now and then this is due to his desire for a strong dramatic scene—as when he despatches Bosinney under the wheels of a horse-omnibus, in a fog, with George close behind him. This, like his repeated use of coincidence, violates one's sense of the actual, and gives one the feeling that one has strayed out of the world of Trollope or Tolstoy and into the world of Wilkie Collins. And one begins to entertain a disquieting suspicion. It is possible that Mr. Galsworthy has a kind of psychological blind-spot? Is it a perhaps tenable view that the sense of the actual he gives us is largely due to his patient accumulation of *little* scenes and actions and conversations, but that in the more important business of psychological dynamics—the business of creating characters which will function powerfully and inevitably out of their unmanageable integrities—he is sometimes helpless? One has the feeling, occasionally, that he is describing his characters rather than letting them live; that when they face a crisis, he solves it for them *intellectually:* and that again and again he fails to sound the real truth in the situations which he himself has evoked. Soames Forsyte, for example, is a real person, on the whole admirably drawn. But could Soames, granted the sensitiveness with which we see him to be endowed, possibly have lived four years with Irene in so total a blindness as to the real state of things between them? Here was a situation which could have been magnificent. A real "realism" would have luxuriated in the minute-by-minute analysis of this profound disaccord. But Mr. Galsworthy never comes to grips with it.

Something of this failure to get inside his characters shows again in *Swan Song,* the coda to the Forsyte Saga. In this charming but rather slight book, we are given the culmination of the interrupted affair of Fleur and Jon, and the death of Soames. The whole story moves toward, and is focused on, the eventual love-scene between Jon and Fleur: we look forward to it from the very beginning: but when it comes, it is quite lamentably inadequate; it is as if the author had gone into a complete psychological funk about it, and had simply

14

not *known* how two such people would have behaved on such an occasion. This scene needed to be the realest and richest and most moving in the book; and given the sufficient actuality of the two people, it could easily have been so. Mr. Galsworthy's failure to give us here anything but a stagey little scene of rhetorical melodrama suggests anew that his gravest fault is his habit of *thinking* his way, by sheer intelligence, into situations which he has not sufficient psychological insight to *feel*.

(1928)

QUENTIN ANDERSON

Despair

Nabokov, describing the work of "V. Sirin" (his pseudonym as a Russian emigré novelist) in *Conclusive Evidence,* says, "the real life of his books flowed in his figures of speech," and "his best works are those in which he condemns his people to the solitary confinement of their souls." *Despair,* the sixth of the nine novels Nabokov wrote in Russian, is neatly bracketed by these remarks. He wrote it in 1932, and translated it into English in 1936. But the text now published is a revision of the original—the reader who has no Russian, and no copy of the first translation for comparison is persuaded that important changes have been made by the virtuosity of the concise and resonant English of the present version. Single words carry more weight than they did in Nabokov's first two novels in English, and produce effects of startling distinctness, effects quite beyond the reach of the accomplished author of *The Real Life of Sebastian Knight* (1941) and *Bend Sinister* (1947).

Hermann, the central figure in *Despair,* is a Russian emigré living in Germany. He is entranced by a fantasy which he justifies to his worldly consciousness as an insurance swindle.

He will kill the tramp who appears to him to be his double, get his wife, whom he believes to be devoted to him, to collect the insurance on his life, and assume the double's identity. His absorption in the pattern he is creating is complete. He does not notice that his wife is sleeping with her cousin, and in the end he quite overlooks the walking stick the double is carrying at the time of the murder, a stick on which the double has carved his own name, and that of his town.

Hermann writes this book after having carried out the fantasy. He is waiting for the reviews of his work; that is, for the press reports of the murder to reach the little town in the Pyrenees where he is hiding. While he waits he lets his memory dictate a book of which the title is unknown until the disasterous realization that he has forgotten the walking stick overtakes him. He had thought of calling his book "Crime and Pun" and "The Poet and the Rabble." But *Despair* is the only possibility in the end—and not simply because of the stick. There is a deeper failure. The whole basis of his work of art has been ignored, nobody thinks him dead, nobody has even noticed the resemblance between the murdered man and himself. In the world's eyes he has no double, and the death he will no doubt die for murder will not even have the effect of bringing him into that final juxtaposition with his image which he had imagined while watching a leaf falling into still water as its double swam up toward it. The reader is confronted by various shifts in perspective—the account given of the whole affair by Hermann's "memory" stands for the fullness of event, for "life," while his work of art, a fantasy which he had pursued in the common light of day, has the status of art in that it is a selection of events made to serve a chosen design. Finally, the account given by memory is the work of the art of the emigré Russian novelist to whom Hermann proposes to send his manuscript!

Is the book more than a suffocating joke on its central figure and a trip to a mirrored fun house for its reader? It depends on what you think of the language, it depends on "the figures of speech" and how much you prize them. The very qualities which led Mary McCarthy to say that *Pale Fire* was "one of the very great works of art of this century" are here—not, it is true, in the same measure (the book is not so multilayered), but still they are here. For example, an extraordinary passage in which Hermann finds that the town in which he has undertaken to meet his double seems to be almost wholly built out of reminiscences of his own past; he wonders whether Felix can in fact appear there, or whether his very conception of Felix is not the product of an appetite for repetition which is growing in him. The play with resemblances is, of course, very intricate: is Felix a "minus I" in the sense that traces on a blotter are negatives, and can only be read in a mirror? Did Felix have the obstinacy, the stubborn bad taste (from Hermann's viewpoint) to read himself as the positive, Hermann as the negative?

All this is consonant with the patterned games played in certain other Nabokov novels. *The Eye,* a novella, and *The Defense* resemble *Despair* in that their chief figures are condemned as is Hermann to spin a world out of their fatally repetitive inner resources. With some qualifications, *Laughter in the Dark* and *Lolita* belong in this group.

In the light of one common assumption about the novel it would be denied that these were novels at all. In them the recording consciousness is jealous, and won't give up its world to the reader. What we are given is theme and variations, and denied any sense of cumulation or growth. We get experience of the order of a child's memories, experience deprived of temporal dimension. Each of the rendered moments is like a separate raid on the continuum of life which brings back an observation that is rendered with the tang of immediacy and yet serves as exemplary use in the web Nabokov is weaving. The life of his work does in fact lie in his figures of speech. And there is something in it which is wholly inimical to our gross appetite for stories of growth, development, sequential change.

I confess I do not believe in time. I like to fold my magic carpet after use, in such a way as to superimpose one part of the pattern upon another. Let visitors trip. And the highest enjoyment of timelessness—in a landscape selected at random—is when I stand among rare butterflies and their food plants. This is ecstasy, and behind the ecstasy is something else, which is hard to explain. It is like a momentary vacuum into which rushes all that I love. A sense of oneness with sun and stone. A thrill of gratitude to whom it may concern—to the contrapuntal genius of human fate or to tender ghosts humoring a lucky mortal.

Conclusive Evidence

Nabokov's prose medium deserves a name, partly a designation, partly frankly incantatory, as is Gerard Manley Hopkins' "sprung rhythm." We might call it the "light anthropomorphic," and find a simple and characteristic instance of it in the sentence, "Let visitors trip." In this medium the interpenetration of humanity by language, language by humanity is, moment by moment, felt as complete. Its range, its horizontal range, is very wide, gallery upon glittering gallery of the tricks by which we betray ourselves in language and language betrays us. But its scale is single; it can only tell us what we do to words and they to us; it cannot tell us what men have done. It appears to deny the possibility of saying *consummatum est* of any human action. It works minutely and reflectively: one little vaudeville of the light anthropomorphic gives way to the next, and so on until the pattern is complete. Here are some "verbal adventures," to steal a Nabokov phrase.

He felt that he loved his wife sincerely, tenderly—as much in fact as he was capable of loving a human being; and he was perfectly frank with her in everything except that secret foolish craving, that dream, that lust burning a hole in his life.

Laughter in the Dark

Occasionally, in the middle of a conversation her name would be mentioned, and she would run down the steps of a chance sentence, without turning her head.

"Spring in Fialta"

No lover of solitude, Boris Ivanovich would soon begin to get bored, and from his room Fyodor would hear the rustling growth of this boredom, as if the flat were slowly being overgrown with

burdocks—which had now grown up to his door. He would pray to fate
that something might distract Schyogolev, but (until he got the radio)
salvation was not forthcoming. Inevitably came the ominous, tactful
knock. . . .

The Gift

When at last I reached the summit I found there a few shacks standing
awry, a washing line, and on it some pants bloated with the wind's
sham life.

Despair

The effect of these passages is seldom occasional; three of
these are particular reflections of the theme of the work in
which they appear. Examples, however, cannot suggest the
intricate echoic games which are the works themselves.

Everything that threatens the games played in the group of
books to which *Despair* belongs is fiercely attacked by
Nabokov as if art were unsafe as long as anybody was
generalizing about anything in any context. This is Nabokov's
public role, and it is the only public role he permits his
characters to assume. Historical and cultural judgment, Marx,
Freud, politicians and metaphysicians, Dostoevsky, Balzac,
Stendhal, Proust, the novelist who is described as "the family
doctor of Europe"—Thomas Mann?—anyone who classifies
anything except words and butterflies is scorned. A novelist
remarks in *Laughter in the Dark*, "Well, when a literature
subsists on Life and Lives, it means it is dying. And I don't
think much of Freudian novels or novels about the quiet
countryside." The young writer of *The Gift* remarks on the
unsuitability of a theme: "I would have become enmired
involuntarily in a 'deep' social-interest novel with a disgusting
Freudian reek." (As one might anticipate, there is quite
another view of Joyce, a figure whom Nabokov says he
reveres.) John Wain has remarked that this scorn of
Nabokov's appears to be the scorn conventionally attributed
to the artist who is asked to write to somebody else's ends, or
everybody else's ends. I think it is a symptom of something
more than this.

The scornful detachment of the prefaces conceals the fact that in another group of novels Nabokov's art is—in his sense—very impure indeed. *Invitation to a Beheading* and *Bend Sinister* are novels in which all reality and value inhere in the central figure, and the environing world is condemned to act out an imprisoning fantasy which the hero and the reader see through. These novels are occasioned by their times, and reflect Nabokov's response to his sense of the idiocy of Communism and Nazi Germany. They can hardly be defended on the ground on which Nabokov habitually asserts the independence of his art from all ideological and psychological generalities. The human glory of their central figures is dependent on convictions about human worth that the reader must bring to the book, convictions on which Nabokov relies. With these two novels we may associate two more, *The Gift* (1937) and *The Real Life of Sebastian Knight*, in which the recording consciousness is that of a writer, and is quite as authoritative for the reader as are the heroes of the first two novels. I shall come to *Pnin*, *Lolita*, and *Pale Fire* in a moment; these four novels suffice to make the point that Nabokov has often ignored what he says in *Conclusive Evidence:* "in a first-rate work of fiction the real clash is not between the characters but between the author and the world." There is a quite shameless human glory about Krug in *Bend Sinister*, about the figures of the writer's parents in *The Gift*, about the hero of *Invitation to a Beheading*—with these characters our sympathy is complete. When these persons are placed beside Hermann, Luzhin of *The Defense*, the central figure of *The Eye*, these latter recede into the texture of the works in which they appear, seem mere themes for light anthropomorphic exercises. We are once more outsiders.

Why shouldn't Nabokov have written in two fictional modes, giving now one, now the other, the ascendancy? What is important is the critical significance of the divergence and final confluence of these two kinds in Nabokov's work. What we may call his naturalism is dominant in Nabokov's recorded memories of his childhood and youth in *Conclusive Evidence*. It is a fully peopled world, rather lush, even sentimental, through which move the figures of a father and mother (whose splendid worldly ascendancy is matched by inner grace and strength), a group of attendant persons, first loves, family retainers and so on. This interrelatedness, this sense of an ordered life in common with others does not of course recur in the Nabokov fiction I know. But *The Gift* offers, in the persons of the young writer's parents, characters who survive out of such a time and such a world. These characters are bordered in black, cherished, lonely and doomed, like Krug, and the lepidopterist father of *The Gift*, who has, anticipating John Shade of *Pale Fire*, a relation to cosmic patterns, "A sense of oneness with sun and stone." This strong sense of a lost sunlit world is the hidden positive in Nabokov's work; it is what such glinting constructs as *Despair* operate to hide. We are justified in saying that Nabokov's publicly stated aesthetic theory is equivalent to a historical judgment. He willed time to a stop. Certain lonely figures in his fiction survive the actual holocaust and his aesthetic assertion of its finality. The naturalism survives in his work and reemerges (somewhat attenuated) in the sentimental naturalism of *Pale Fire*. It is as if, having incautiously trusted to the persistence of the rules of the social order which had nourished his first nineteen years, he had determined never again to accept any set of rules from anyone. or write anything which could be subsumed within any order.

I shall not attempt here to deal with the complex interplay of the patterned as against the naturalist strands in Nabokov's work. I have suggested that the human glory of Krug, which is posed against a cruel and mindless society, represents a naturalism which gives way to a more sentimental strain in Nabokov's later work, in fact in the very next novel, *Sebastian Knight*. Knight, unsupported by a sense of the wholeness of a human community of the order we find in *Conclusive Evidence*, makes his lonely assertion of the generically human: "All things belong to the same order of things, for such is the oneness of human perception, the oneness of individuality, the oneness of matter, whatever matter may be. The only real number is one, the rest are mere repetition." To reinforce this we may quote Shade's poem in *Pale Fire:*

> And if my private universe scans
> So does the verse of galaxies divine
> Which I suspect is an iambic line.

A longer passage from *Sebastian Knight,* which, like Shade's poem, is concerned with a solution to the riddle of death, may make Nabokov's movement from a naturalism conditioned by the memory of community to a naturalism founded on a faith in our kinship with the order of nature somewhat plainer. Both seem to have been present from his youth onward, but the ascendancy of the latter grows as the memory of a society in being recedes.

And the word, the meaning which appears is astounding in its simplicity: the greatest surprise being perhaps that in the course of one's earthly existence, with one's brain encompassed by an iron ring, by the close-fitting dream of one's own personality—one had not made by chance that simple mental jerk, which would have set free imprisoned thought and granted it the great understanding. Now the puzzle was solved. "And as the meaning of all things shone through their shapes, many ideas and events which had seemed of the utmost importance dwindled not to insignificance, for nothing could be insignificant now, but to the same size which other ideas and events, once denied any importance, now attained." Thus, such shining giants of our brain as science, art or religion fell out of the familiar scheme of their classification, and joining hands, were mixed and joyfully levelled. Thus, a cherry stone and its tiny shadow which lay on the painted wood of a tired bench, or a bit of torn paper, or any other such trifle out of millions and millions of trifles grew to a wonderful size. Remodelled and re-combined, the world yielded its sense to the soul as naturally as both breathed.

The belief that such an awareness of nature might afford this measure of human fulfillment lies about fifty years behind us

23

in the European consciousness. It stems from an age in which science seemed to authorize wider hopes, rather than pose deeper threats. When we are thinking of Nabokov as a modernist his grounding in a sentimental naturalism must be recalled. The hardness, brightness and echoing intricacy of his patterned fiction is a culturally determined mode of coping with a world which denies the "sense of oneness with sun and stone."

But I have been speaking as if the Nabokov who willed time to a stop had in the process suppressed the world of his childhood, and this is misleading. His delight in exposing "the contrapuntal genius of human fate" is a quite logical extension of that world, or rather of the breakdown of the inter-personal hierarchic order that world represented. Luzhin, Paduk (the Hitler figure of *Bend Sinister*), Humbert, Hermann, are persons in whom the child's absorption in his play is prolonged into adulthood, prisoners rather than makers of patterns. Humbert keeps wooing the ten-year-old girl of the Biarritz beach, and our consciousness of this is the source of our sympathy, which persists together with our awareness that he has become loathsome. Such figures, like Luzhin, who also invites our sympathy, nonetheless fail to respond to the first moral value of the Nabokovian universe, a respect for the singleness of others. The mocking memoir of Chernyshevski in *The Gift* brims with venom directed at a generation which infected us all—infected Lenin himself—with the horrible smarmy presumption that we were so nearly identical that we could be understood en masse. Hermann's unforgivable spiritual vulgarity is the hunger for a resemblance that amounts to identity—something that can only be attributed to inanimate things, dead things. And *Despair* is, like all the internally echoing works, a struggle with the reader; he is being tested: if he thinks he can assimilate the pattern to his beliefs and expectations he is one more fool who doesn't know the value of singleness.

I have made it plain enough that the works in which everything is subdued to the pattern, while serially brillant, seem to me as exhaustible in their interest as reported games of chess. The hero of *Invitation to a Beheading,* while describing himself as incapable of writing says that he has an intuition of the way in which words must be combined, "what one must do for a commonplace word to come alive and to share its neighbor's sheen, heat, shadow, while reflecting itself in its neighbor and renewing the neighboring word in the process, so that the whole line is live iridescence." If you find the patterned works delightful it is such effects you delight in. If you are persuaded you are reading a full-fledged novelist you are unaware of the extent of your collaboration. The text under your eye is like a brilliant musical score, but the continuity of the performance is supplied by the reader, who fills in the curve of imagined human action. Of course this is a question of degree. *Lolita,* up to the death of the mother, has no such limitation. Thereafter it falls, on rereading, into fragments, some of which retain their lustre, like the scene in which Humbert sees his married and pregnant love for the last time, while others have lost it altogether, and in fact share with certain of the American social observations in *Pale Fire* the *fade* and dissonant quality of the marzipan hot dogs sold in fake Viennese candy shops. *Pale Fire* is at once more ambitious and less successful than *Lolita,* because, although there is much to be said for the poem, there is less to be said for the sentimental naturalism which informs it—except as a historical artifact—and the trapped and obsessed figure, Kinbote, unpacked in all his awful flatness and spiritual repetitiousness gives the book the flavor of his sterility. It is possible to be very serious, enormously talented, highly witty, and nonethess to trivialize what seems a proper outgrowth of Nabokov's career, the attempt to bring to a focus the struggle between the patterned figure, Kinbote, and a last beleaguered human being, John Shade.

But there remains one almost perfect work, *Pnin.* What I have rather clumsily described as the "naturalism" is here to be found in the implied character of the narrator, perhaps the most winning of Nabokov's persons, and the book appears to be completely patterned, yet the narrator's scrupulous and tender attention supplies exactly that continuity of human concern that the other patterned works lack. Not that the narrator has an unqualified role. Indeed his dramatic relation to Pnin is brilliantly sustained and developed. As he physically approaches Pnin must recede, because the narrator is precisely that element within whose ambience Pnin cannot exist. The book is a delight and a minor classic.

Modernism, the period of Proust, Joyce, Kafka, Eliot, is over, and the preoccupations of poets and writers of fiction are now so different that Nabokov has begun to seem remote. He tries to make language the vessel of our humanity, and supports in public the contention that art is its own excuse for being. He gives this contention away in certain works, and it becomes plain that it is actually parasitic on the memory of an ordered community. His assertion of the self-sufficiency of art will come to seem increasingly unintelligible to a generation unaware of the hidden premise of his humanism. He will go into a temporary eclipse. If the world of community were magically to be reborn the influence of the very thing he publicly denies would serve to reinstate him. But the world in which Beckett, Genet, Burroughs, and the non-novel flourish is a world in which the politics of the soul is primary, and verbal adventure has lost its invisible supporting warp of remembered human solidarity. This, I take it, is the end so often prematurely announced, of the romantic movement.

(1966)

SHERWOOD ANDERSON

Four American Impressions

I

One who thinks a great deal about people and what they are up to in the world comes inevitably in time to relate them to experiences connected with one's own life. The round, hard apples in this old orchard are the breasts of my beloved. The curved, round hill in the distance is the body of my beloved, lying asleep. One cannot avoid practicing this trick of lifting people out of the spots on which in actual life they stand and transferring them to what seems at the moment some more fitting spot in one's fanciful world.

And one gets also a kind of aroma from people. They are green, healthy, growing things or they have begun to decay. There is something in this man, to whom I have just talked, that has sent me away from him smiling and in an odd way pleased with myself. Why has this other man, although his words were kindly and his deeds apparently good, spread a cloud over my sky?

In my own boyhood in an Ohio town I went about delivering newspapers at kitchen doors, and there were certain houses to which I went—old brick houses with immense old-fashioned kitchens—in which I loved to linger. On Saturday mornings I sometimes managed to collect a fragrant cooky at such a place, but there was something else that held me. Something got into my mind connected with the great, light kitchens and the women working in them that came sharply back when, last year, I went to visit an American woman, Miss Gertrude Stein, in her own large room in the house at 27 rue de Fleurus in Paris. In the great kitchen of my fanciful world in which I have, ever since that morning, seen Miss Stein standing, there is a most sweet and gracious aroma. Along the walls are many shining pots and pans, and there are innumerable jars of fruits, jellies and preserves. Something is going on in the great room, for Miss Stein is a worker in words with the same loving touch in her strong fingers that was characteristic of the women of the kitchens of the brick houses in the town of my boyhood. She is an American woman of the old sort, one who cares for the handmade goodies and who scorns the factory-made foods, and in her own great kitchen she is making something with her materials, something sweet to the tongue and fragrant to the nostrils.

That her materials are the words of our English speech and that we do not, most of us, know or care too much what she is up to does not greatly matter to me. The impression I wish now to give you of her is of one very intent and earnest in a matter most of us have forgotten. She is laying word against word, relating sound to sound, feeling for the taste, the smell, the rhythm of the individual word. She is attempting to do something for the writers of our English speech that may be better understood after a time, and she is not in a hurry. And one has always that picture of the woman in the great kitchen of words, standing there by a table, clean, strong, with red cheeks and sturdy legs, always quietly and smilingly at work. If her smile has in it something of the mystery, to the male at least, of the Mona Lisa, I remember that the women in the kitchens on the wintry mornings wore often that same smile.

She is making new, strange and to my ears sweet combinations of words. As an American writer I admire her because she, in her person, represents something sweet and healthy in our American life, and because I have a kind of undying faith that what she is up to in her word kitchen in Paris is of more importance to writers of English than the work of many of our more easily understood and more widely accepted word artists.

II

When it comes to our Ring Lardner, here is something else again. Here is another word fellow, one who cares about the words of our American speech and who is perhaps doing more than any other American to give new life to the words of our everyday life.

There is something I think I understand about Ring. The truth is that I believe there is something the matter with him and I have a fancy I know what it is. He is afraid of the highbrows. They scare him to death. I wonder why, for it is true that there is often, in a paragraph of his, more understanding of life, more human sympathy, more salty wisdom than in hundreds of pages of, say, Mr. Sinclair Lewis's dreary prose—and I am sure Mr. Lewis would not hesitate to outface any highbrow in his lair.

I said that I thought I knew what was the matter with Mr. Ring Lardner. He comes from out in my country, from just such another town as the one in which I spent my own boyhood, and I remember certain shy lads of my own town who always made it a point to consort only with the town toughs—and for a reason. There was in them something extremely sensitive that did not want to be hurt. Even to mention the fact that there was in them a real love of life, a quick sharp stinging hunger for beauty, would have sent a blush of shame to their cheeks. They were intent upon covering up, concealing from everyone, at any cost, the shy hungry children they were carrying about within themselves.

And I always see our Ring Lardner as such a fellow. He is

covering up, sticking to the gang, keeping out of sight. And that is all right too, if in secret and in his suburban home he is really using his talent for sympathetic understanding of life, if in secret he is being another Mark Twain and working in secret on his own Huckleberry Finn. Mark Twain wrote and was proclaimed for writing his *Innocents Abroad, Following the Equator, Roughing It,* etc., etc., and was during his lifetime most widely recognized for such secondary work. And Mark was just such another shy lad, bluffed by the highbrows—and even the glorious Mark had no more sensitive understanding of the fellow in the street, in the hooch joint, the ballpark and the city suburb than our Mr. Ring Lardner.

III

Which brings me to a man who seems to me, of all our American writers, the one who is most unafraid, Mr. Paul Rosenfeld. Here is an American writer actually unashamed at being fine and sensitive in his work. To me it seems that he has really freed himself from both the high and the low brows and has made of himself a real aristocrat among writers of prose.

To be sure, to the man in the street, accustomed to the sloppiness of hurried newspaper writing, the Rosenfeld prose is sometimes difficult. His vocabulary is immense and he cares very, very much for just the shade of meaning he is striving to convey. Miss Jean Heap recently spoke of him as "our well dressed writer of prose," and I should think Paul Rosenfeld would not too much resent the connotations of that. For after all, Rosenfeld is our man of distinction, the American, it seems to me, who is unafraid and unashamed to live for the things of the spirit as expressed in the arts. I get him as the man walking cleanly and boldly and really accepting, daring to accept, the obligations of the civilized man. To my ears that acceptance has made his prose sound clearly and sweetly across many barren fields. To me it is

often like soft bells heard ringing at evening across fields long
let go to the weeds of carelessness and the general
slam-it-throughness of so much of our American writing.

IV

Of the four American writers concerning whose handling
of our speech I have had the temerity to express my own
feeling there is left Mr. Sinclair Lewis.

The texture of the prose written by Mr. Lewis gives one
but faint joy and one cannot escape the conviction that for
some reason Lewis has himself found but little joy, either in
life among us or in his own effort to channel his reactions to
our life into prose. There can be no doubt that this man, with
his sharp journalistic nose for news of the outer surface of
our lives, has found out a lot of things about us and the way
we live in our towns and cities, but I am very sure that in the
life of every man, woman and child in the country there are
forces at work that seem to have escaped the notice of Mr.
Lewis. Ring Lardner has seen them and in his writing there is
sometimes real laughter, but one has the feeling that Lewis
never laughs at all, that he is in an odd way too serious about
something to laugh.

For after all, even in Gopher Prairie or in Indianapolis,
Indiana, boys go swimming in the creeks on summer
afternoons, shadows play at evening on factory walls, old
men dig angleworms and go fishing together, love comes to at
least a few of the men and women and, everything else
failing, the baseball club comes from a neighboring town and
Tom Robinson gets a home run. That's something. There is
an outlook on life across which even the cry of a child,
choked to death by its own mother, would be something.
Life in our American towns and cities is barren enough and
there are enough people saying that with the growth of
industrialism it has become continually more and more ugly,
but Mr. Paul Rosenfeld and Mr. Ring Lardner apparently do
not find it altogether barren and ugly. For them and for a

31

growing number of men and women in America there is something like a dawn that Mr. Lewis has apparently sensed but little, for there is so little sense of it in the texture of his prose. Reading Sinclair Lewis, one comes inevitably to the conclusion that here is a man writing who, wanting passionately to love the life about him, cannot bring himself to do so, and who wanting perhaps to see beauty descend upon our lives like a rainstorm has become blind to the minor beauties our lives hold.

And is it not just this sense of dreary spiritual death in the man's work that is making it so widely read? To one who is himself afraid to live there is, I am sure, a kind of inverted joy in seeing other men as dead. In my own feeling for the man from whose pen has come all of this prose over which there are so few lights and shades, I have come at last to sense, most of all, the man fighting terrifically and ineffectually for a thing about which he really does care. There is a kind of fighter living inside Sinclair Lewis and there is, even in this dull, unlighted prose of his, a kind of dawn coming. In the dreary ocean of this prose, islands begin to appear. In *Babbitt* there are moments when the people of whom he writes, with such amazing attention to the outer details of lives, begin to think and feel a little, and with the coming of life into his people a kind of nervous, hurried beauty and life flits, like a lantern carried by a night watchman past the window of a factory as one stands waiting and watching in a grim street on a night of December.

(1922)

HAMILTON BASSO

Thomas Wolfe: A Summing Up

You Can't Go Home Again. This is the last novel that will
carry Thomas Wolfe's name on its title page. The first thing
to be said is that his publishers do no great service to his
reputation by presenting it as a finished product of his
mature talent. "By 1936," they tell us, "Wolfe had
completed what he looked upon as his period of
apprenticeship, and was ready to embark upon a vast new
enterprise—a novel or a series of novels (he did not yet know
which) into which he wanted to pack everything he had
learned about life. Through several years he labored
strenuously at it, and as the manuscript took shape it grew
into two novels, both of which were finished and turned over
to his publishers in May, 1938." This statement is not
altogether correct. It is best to let Wolfe himself tell what
happened—what he hoped to do and how he hoped to do it.
In July, 1937, he wrote to me:

> I brought most of the manuscript of the last five or six years down
> with me; millions of words of it, and I hope to write several hundred
> thousand more this summer. Eventually I hope it will begin to take
> shape, like another monster of the deep, and I will have another

tremendous book. I believe I learn a little something about writing all the time; but I am not so sure that I will be worried so much this time by apprehensions over size and length. The very nature of a book like this is that everything can go into it. To tell such a story is to try to loot the whole treasury of human experience. . . . So I have come back here to "set a spell and think things over"—freer, I hope, from the degrading egotisms all men know in youth; here to strike out, I hope to God, a living word. To do out of the substance of my own life, my single spirit, a better and truer work than I have ever done.

The three years from 1935 to 1938 were a period during which we saw much of each other—in New York and in the mountains of North Carolina. Occasionally he would give me a batch of manuscript to read. I know, then, that in the "millions of words" Wolfe talks about, substantial portions of this novel, and the one that preceded it, were included. Most of the section called "The Locusts Have No King," for instance, stands—as far as memory can judge—just as it stood in 1936. Another section, "I Have a Thing to Tell You," was pared to the bone and published in these pages about the same time. And the part of the book revolving about the famous novelist Lloyd McHarg—or a sizable portion of it—was also in manuscript before 1937. It is not accurate, consequently, to say that Wolfe's last two books marked a "new enterprise" or that they were finished before he died. As for the critics, those who found no "advancement" in "The Web and the Rock," will likewise probably find no advancement here. But let them hold their horses! Let them remember that this book not only contains the last writing Wolfe did—the section called "The House That Jack Built," for example, which was written in the spring and summer of 1937, just about a year before he died—but also many pages that were written as early as 1934. This is one time when no generalizations are permissible.

Wolfe disliked the critics as much as any creative writer. The charge that he wrote autobiographical novels particularly annoyed him. This is worth mentioning only because the

critics were partially responsible for the rebirth of Eugene
Gant as George Webber: and this in an interesting way.

Wolfe's anger with the critics frequently took the form of
torrential outbursts in which he argued that all good fiction is
basically autobiographical. It also kept cropping up in his
letters. In one of them, partially devoted to a statement of
his belief that most writers were surveyors rather than
explorers, he wrote:

> In another way as well, our love of neat definitions in convenient
> forms, our fear of essential exploration, may be the natural response of
> people who have to house themselves, wall themselves, give their lives
> some precise and formal definition. . . . Anyway, all of these things
> have seemed to me to be worth thinking of, and I know that we still
> have to fight to do our work the way we want to do it—not only against
> the accepted varieties of surveyordom, that is book publishers, most of
> the critics, popular magazines, etc.—but against even deadlier and more
> barren forms; deadlier because they set up as friends of exploration
> when they are really betrayers and enemies; I mean little magazinedom,
> hound and horners, young precious boys, esthetic Marxians and all the
> rest of it.

Nevertheless, the charges leveled at him—"autobiographical
novels," "lack of objectivity," etc.,—were still a source of
annoyance. The neat definitions buzzed in his mind like
mosquitoes. Then, about this time, he changed
publishers—taking along with him several crates of
manuscript; "millions of words." A large part of this
manuscript, as has been said, went into these last two
novels—but the hero of the manuscript was the same hero as
that of *Look Homeward, Angel* and *Of Time and the River.*
His name was Eugene Gant.

When he changed publishers, Wolfe found himself faced
with this major problem: How to use his unpublished parts of
Eugene Gant's life in a new novel or group of novels. The
hereo's name, of course, had to be changed. The demands of
publishing called for that. More than a mere rechristening,
however, was required. The life of George Webber had to be
brought to the point where his early years would flow

naturally into the later years of Eugene Gant. And, in writing about Webber, Wolfe believed that he could prove that he could create a non-autobiographical character—and also prove that it was within his power to write "objectively."

The whole unhappy effort was doomed from the start. If only for credibility's sake, the new hero had to be a man exactly like Eugene Gant. How else could the books have any pattern: any meaning whatsoever? This, then, is why the early pages of *The Web and the Rock* read like a loose rewriting of *Look Homeward, Angel.* How could it be otherwise? Webber had to be grafted on to Gant. A trunk had to be provided for the branches and foliage already at hand. Wolfe unquestionably believed what he wrote in the preface to *The Web and the Rock*—that it was the most objective novel he had ever written. It was. But only to the extent that he was obliged to reexamine and rework some of his basic material. Gant became Webber but Gant remained. And Gant, of course, was Thomas Wolfe.

With the publication of this novel it is possible to discern the general outlines of the job Wolfe set for himself. His plan was to write a vast cycle of novels through which the life of Eugene Gant was to run as a kind of blood-stream. They were to go back to the Civil War (somewhere among his unpublished manuscripts there must be a long short story called "Chickamauga") and would project into the future as far as Eugene Gant, in the person of Thomas Wolfe, managed to live. Speculation as to how far he would have been able to carry out this plan, and how successfully, is purposeless. It would be equally purposeless for me to try to weigh this particular book. Even if I had not already disqualified myself, I would be reluctant to say more than I used to say after reading one of his manuscripts. "When it's fine it's fine. You know what you're after better than anyone else." I still feel the same way—that he was after something, that it was something most important to be after, and that, considering the number of times he gets hold of it, the flaws in his writing do not particularly matter. I soon learned that he would never be a terse writer because he was not the least bit interested in becoming one. So what of it? It also became obvious that he would never bring the tremendous engine of his creative ability under full control and that he would be forever loose and sprawling and sometimes windy enough to blow your hat off. So what of that? The fact remains that when he gets hold, when he digs through to what he is after, he is magnificent in a way few American writers ever have been—making his detractors seem puny and feeble by comparison. This book is full of such magnificence.

The last word I had from Wolfe was a postcard mailed from Yellowstone Park about two months before he died. It was a picture of Old Faithful and on the back he had scrawled in pencil: "Portrait of the author at the two-million-word point." It seems to me that that geyser is a pretty good picture of him. It looks vaguely like the way he used to look walking down First Avenue about two o'clock on a blowy morning and, like it, he gushed boiling and furious from his American earth. The landscape is lonelier without him.

(1940)

KAY BOYLE

The Unvanquished

There are two Faulkners—at least to me there are two: the
one who stayed down South and the one who went to war in
France and mixed with foreigners and aviators; that is, the
Faulkner of the Sartoris saga (and the countless other
savagely and tenderly chronicled documents of the South)
and the Faulkner who wrote "Turn About," for instance, and
"All the Dead Pilots" and "Pylon" with no perceptible
cooling of that hot devotion to man's courage although the
speech, the history, the conflict were no longer his strict
heritage. I believe these two separate Faulkners (separated
more by a native shyness of the foreigner than any variance
in ideology or technique) possess between them the strength
and the vulnerability which belong only to the greatest
artists: the incalculable emotional wealth, the racy comic
sense, the fury to reproduce exactly not the recognizable
picture but the unmistakable experience, the thirst for
articulation as well as the curiosity and the vocabulary—that
rarity—to quench it. The weaknesses there are, the errors, the
occasionally strained effects, are accomplished by the same
fearless, gifted hand.

It is not difficult to reconcile the two Faulkners; perhaps as simple as recognizing that a man is a good host or a good guest, but rarely both. On his own ground Faulkner is explicit, easy, sure; on someone else's he is a little awed, a little awkward, provincially aware of the chances he is taking. But I believe it is in the willingness to take these risks that Faulkner's whole future lies. That *The Unvanquished* happens to be one more chapter in the Sartoris saga is no valid description of it, nor that it is a book about the Civil War—a Civil War in which the issue of black and white is lost in the wider issue not of justice and tyranny, subjection and freedom, or even sin and virtue, but merely of life and death. For one who loves Faulkner's work and has followed it closely and impatiently, the difficulty lies in isolating this book or any book from the others and trying to say this or that of it: his genius is not this book or perhaps any given book but resides in that entire determined collection of volumes which reveal him to be the most absorbing writer of our time.

On the face of it, this book is the story of an old lady whose home has been razed by Yankees and who sets out across the country, first driving two mules and then, when these are confiscated, two horses, wearing a borrowed hat on her head and holding over it a borrowed parasol. It is told in her grandson's words, at the outset a boy of twelve who goes with her on that imperiously reckless adventure which leads toward Jordan, toward her career of racketeering and, like any Chicago gangster's, toward atrocious death; a boy who in the twelve years covered by the story matures first in emotion, then in conviction, and finally in act. "Ringo and I had been born in the same month," he says of the Negro boy who is their sole companion of the drive toward retribution, "and had both been fed at the same breast and had slept together and eaten together for so long that Ringo called Granny 'Granny' just like I did, until maybe he wasn't a nigger any more or maybe I wasn't a white boy any more, the two of us neither, not even people any longer. . . ." And toward the end of the book when they are both twenty-four, he says of Ringo in a man's language then: "He was sitting quietly in a chair beside the cold stove, spent-looking too who had ridden forty miles (at one time, either in Jefferson or when he was alone at last on the road somewhere, he had cried; dust was now caked and dried in the tear-channels on his face) and would ride forty more yet would not eat, looking up at me a little red-eyed with weariness (or maybe it was more than just weariness and so I would never catch up with him). . . ." This process of development, subtly, heedfully, skillfully accomplished through the seemingly inevitable metamorphosis of speech makes the book a record not only of an individual's but a nation's, possibly a civilization's progression from violence to a passive and still undefinable bewilderment.

Elsewhere, the movement of that other group, the march of the liberated Negroes toward Jordan, starts like a whisper in the book, becomes "a kind of panting murmur" as they pass in the night, and swells to "women and children singing and chanting and trying to get to that unfinished bridge or even down into the water itself, and the cavalry beating them back with sword scabbards. . . . They just pass here without food or anything, exactly as they rose up from whatever they were doing when the spirit or the voice . . . told them to go. . . . Going to cross Jordan. . . ."

It is, then, the sentimental and glamorous story of one old lady who set out to find and ask a Yankee Colonel to return to her a chest of family silver tied with hemp rope, two darkies, Loosh and Philadelphy, and the two confiscated mules, "Old Hundred" and "Tinney"; and like a single and undaunted fife still playing, it is as well the essence of that war, a thing as intrinsically and nationally and gallantly the South's as the revolution is France's and the rebellion Ireland's: become now a legend, almost a fable of tattered banners, makeshift uniforms, incredible courage and inhuman ferocity. It has those weaknesses which can be found throughout Faulkner's work: the full-length portraits which abruptly become caricatures not likenesses of the living, the "ladies" without face or substance, the repetitions, the maudlin lapses, the shameless voice of the evangelist declaiming in solemn, flowery passages. But it has that fabulous, that wondrous, fluxing power which nothing Faulkner touches is ever without. The word for it may be glamor or may be sentiment, but both these words are mutable and I have used them here without contempt, applying them in their best sense as attributes to fact. They can confuse, they can disguise, but they can as well bring to the familiar a heightened, an isolated, and a therefore truer legibility. They were elements in that electric atmosphere and mystic climate in which Poe's men and women lived and have survived and they are a vital part of Faulkner's quicker, more comprehensive world. Faulkner and Poe, set far enough apart in time, are strangely kin: unique in our history in their immunity to literary fashion, alike in their fanatical obsession with the unutterable depths of mankind's vice and even more with his divinity.

If writing remain one of the Arts—with a capital A and be damned to the current mode of splitting it two ways in a poem or a fresco on a wall—if its sensitive execution still demand the heart and the endurance which have kept artists lying prone on scaffoldings painting year in, year out, and if its success depend on its acceptance as convincing tragedy or comedy, then it can quite simply be said of Faulkner that he is the rare, the curious, the almost ludicrously authentic thing. In this book, as in his others, he writes with that "fierce desire of perfection" which contemporaries said Michelangelo evidenced when "flinging himself on the material of marble," vehemently seeking expression for "the human elements of fervor and tenderness."

(1938)

ANATOLE BROYARD

Portnoy's Complaint

Early in *Portnoy's Complaint,* the hero discovers that he has an undescended testicle. The image sticks in the mind, because one feels that, as a writer, Philip Roth has had a similar problem. *Goodbye, Columbus,* which made his reputation, is a talented book by a young man whose voice is still changing. *Letting Go* impresses one as the work of a promising but temporarily impotent imagination. *When She Was Good* is absolutely without vital juices—one of those unreadable novels that good writers, through some inexplicable alchemy, occasionally produce.

Now that the testicle has begun to descend, in *Portnoy's Complaint,* we can see that it is not an unmixed blessing. For the first half, the book is a sort of *Moby Dick* of masturbation; in the second part, Portnoy masturbates with girls, a change only in the *dramatic personae.*

The book is a kind of *Catch-22* of sexuality, and much funnier. More Jewish even than *A Mother's Kisses* and *To an Early Grave,* it is also part of a growing rebellion against the old highbrow or "orthodox" Jewish novel of ideas. In fact, it appears that the orthodox novel is already so done in that

Herzog—the ultimate halvah of the Jewish intellectual—may go down in literary history as the last great convulsion of this kind of writing.

Like Einstein, Freud and Salk, Herzog was a prodigy of humaneness, the quality that has always been the pride and strength of the Jew. But like a statue in a public park, the Jew in literature is a prey to the climate. The climate now is sexy: Portnoy, then, is a sexual prodigy, a real (matzoh) ballsy guy. Like the homosexual and Negro, the Jew seems finally to have emancipated himself. After centuries of sublimation, he's exposing himself in Brentano's window. He has discovered his id, and if you think the Jewish super-ego was formidable, just wait.

Portnoy's problem is that he has a mother. As any casual reader of contemporary fiction knows, only Jewish writers have mothers. It may even be the same one. At any rate, she fills Portnoy with doubts about himself; to counteract these doubts, he masturbates continually, as if to say "I feel: therefore I am." When he is old enough to attempt girls, he can only invest this one part of himself in them. They are merely images or engines for his pleasure or reassurance.

Although there may have been others, we are told only about the Gentile girls, those who are not kosher, but Pure Food and Drug Act products. Portnoy tries to circumvent his history by climbing out of his mother's lap into Kay Campbell's or Sarah Abbott Maulsby's. His *shikse* mistresses divide into two types: those in whose mouth neither butter nor Portnoy will melt, and The Monkey, an ex-model who has been so jewed down in her personality by the author that she is *all* sex. But—poor Portnoy!—he can no more forgive The Monkey's 1969 ways of exciting him than the others' failures.

Some of Portnoy's sexual ups and downs are amusing enough to guarantee them a place in our folklore. Bubbles Gerardi, a Neanderthal nymphomaniac, almost turns what was to be his deflowering into an uprooting. Kay Campbell, a big butter churn of a girl, takes him home for Thanksgiving,

43

and there, in the Midwest, he is introduced to the ineffable element in American life, and comes to understand the metaphysics, you might say, of complacency. Sarah Abbot Maulsby, the pilgrim, is Portnoy's wet dream of conspicuous consumption, but when he actually gets her into his bed, he finds it a pretty cut-and-dried business. The Monkey, who lasts longer than the others, is an oxymoron: a sexy *shikse*. She pays for it by being an ordinary moron too, as she leads Portnoy down the garden path of his pathology.

There are two Jewish girls in the book, and these are notoriously less successful creations, either because they're too close to home, or because Jewish girls are inherently less absurd, when you turn them upside down, than *shikses*. Portnoy meets these soul sisters when he abandons the marriage-bent Monkey in Greece and flees to Israel.

Yes, unfortunately, that's the symbol Roth has chosen to impose on Portnoy's search for self-through-sex. In an ending that is not an epiphany, but a punch line, Portnoy is impotent in Israel. He can't rise to Jewish girls. *Nu,* what else is new?

Though the novel is a triumph for Roth—he has thrown his *yarmulke* in the air and *let go* as he had promised in his second book—it may be something less for readers who feel they've been here before, who've been told these stories, with slight variations for better or worse, in midtown bars. Others may hear in *Portnoy's Complaint* the boastful whine of a patient raking over the ashes of his analysis. And, in fact, this is the scheme of the book.

The device is very congenial to Roth, and he moves easily in it. There's a feeling of spontaneous combustion through all but the end of the book; you can tell that the author is riding a hot streak. His ear is just about perfect and his invention hardly ever seems—as it all too often does in the new Jewish novel—merely manic.

Talking to someone—even though the analyst is a rather unconvincing presence—allows Roth to achieve all the me-to-you immediacy, all the rhetorical effects, of direct address. But it is limiting too, because it narrows the possibilities to only those things Portnoy would *say*. The rhetoric is all oral. And it inevitably tends toward Jewish writing of the familiar sort, depending on exclamations, hyperboles and italics, and eliminating, except for a few short passages, any other kind of modulation.

Though the satire in *Portnoy's Complaint* is generally first-rate, the book hardly ever rises to irony. Irony requires dimension, the possibility of grandeur, and what we have here is a series of caricatures. Father, mother, sister, mistresses—even Portnoy himself—each has one act, one *shtik*. Mother is a statue of illiberty; father a constipated *nebbish;* sister a fat, graceless non-*shikse;* each of the mistresses merely one of the main currents in American thought. And Portnoy is not so much a human being as a monomaniacal hangup.

Everything is as oversimplified as a comic strip. This is not the tickle of catastrophe or Santayana's "golden laughter"—it's closer to the brassy stand-up comic kind. And the comparison is not flattering, because the Jewish comic has so far anticipated the Jewish writer than when he turns out a funny novel, much of it seems dated. We feel a sense of *déja-vu,* for Sid Caesar, Lenny Bruce, Mort Sahl, Nichols and May—to name just a few—were working Portnoy's territory more than ten years ago. This is especially true of the family scenes; in the sexual passages, Roth has the advantage over the comics in being less censored than they are—or were.

In spite of these reservations, *Portnoy* is sure to be regarded as a kind of literary Second Coming. Halfway between Oy! and Wow! it proves that the Jew is just as good a jerk, just as magnificently and mysteriously irrational, as any *goy*. In fact, it may well earn immortality on even another ground: that it is the first novel to be written by a Jew who was voted one of the hundred best-dressed men in the world.

Grateful readers, when they can stop laughing, will cry

Sholom! But there may also be a few cranks here and there who will say to Roth, like the analyst in the last line of the book, "Now vee may perhaps to begin."

(1969)

ROBERT BRUSTEIN

Catch-22

"The man who declares that survival at all costs is the end of existence is morally dead, because he's prepared to sacrifice all other values which give life its meaning."

[Sidney Hook]

". . . It's better to die on one's feet than live on one's knees," Nately retorted with triumphant and loftly conviction. "I guess you've heard that saying before."

"Yes, I certainly have," mused the treacherous old man, smiling again. "But I'm afraid you have it backward. It is better to live on one's feet than die on one's knees. That is the way the saying goes."

[Catch-22]

Like all superlative works of comedy—and I am ready to argue that this is one of the most bitterly funny works in the language—*Catch-22* is based on an unconventional but utterly convincing internal logic. In the very opening pages, when we come upon a number of Air Force officers malingering in a hospital—one censoring all the modifiers out of enlisted men's letters and signing the censor's name "Washington Irving," another pursuing tedious conversations with boring

Texans in order to increase his life span by making time pass slowly, still another storing horse chestnuts in his cheeks to give himself a look of innocence—it seems obvious that an inordinate number of Joseph Heller's characters are, by all conventional standards, mad. It is a triumph of Mr. Heller's skill that he is so quickly able to persuade us (1) that the most lunatic are the most logical, and (2) that it is our conventional standards which lack any logical consistency. The sanest looney of them all is the apparently harebrained central character, an American bombardier of Syrian extraction named Captain John Yossarian, who is based on a mythical Italian island (Pianosa) during World War II. For while many of his fellow officers seem indifferent to their own survival, and most of his superior officers are overtly hostile to his, Yossarian is animated solely by a desperate determination to stay alive:

It was a vile and muddy war, and Yossarian could have lived without it—lived forever, perhaps. Only a fraction of his countrymen would give up their lives to win it, and it was not his ambition to be among them. . . . That men would die was a matter of necessity; *which* men would die, though, was a matter of circumstance, and Yossarian was willing to be the victim of anything but circumstance.

The single narrative thread in this crazy patchwork of anecdotes, episodes, and character portraits traces Yossarian's herculean efforts—through caution, cowardice, defiance, subterfuge, strategem, and subversion, through feigning illness, goofing off, and poisoning the company's food with laundry soap—to avoid being victimized by circumstance, a force represented in the book as Catch-22. For Catch-22 is the unwritten loophole in every written law which empowers the authorities to revoke your rights whenever it suits their cruel whims; it is, in short, the principle of absolute evil in a malevolent, mechanical, and incompetent world. Because of Catch-22, justice is mocked, the innocent are victimized, and Yossarian's squadron is forced to fly more than double the number of missions prescribed by Air Force code. Dogged by Catch-22, Yossarian becomes the anguished witness to the ghoulish slaughter of his crew members and the destruction of all his closest friends, until finally his fear of death becomes so intense that he refuses to wear a uniform, after his own has been besplattered with the guts of his dying gunner, and receives a medal standing naked in formation. From this point on, Yossarian's logic becomes so pure that everyone thinks him mad, for it is the logic of sheer survival, dedicated to keeping him alive in a world noisily clamoring for his annihilation.

According to this logic, Yossarian is surrounded on all sides by hostile forces: his enemies are distinguished less by their nationality than by their ability to get him killed. Thus, Yossarian feels a blind, electric rage against the Germans whenever they hurl flak at his easily penetrated plane; but he feels an equally profound hatred for those of his own countrymen who exercise an arbitrary power over his life and well-being. Heller's huge cast of characters, therefore, is dominated by a large number of comic malignities, *genus Americanus,* drawn with a grotesqueness so audacious that they somehow transcend caricature entirely and become vividly authentic. These include: Colonel Cathcart, Yossarian's commanding officer, whose consuming ambition to get his picture in the *Saturday Evening Post* motivates him to volunteer his command for every dangerous command, and to initiate prayers during briefing sessions ("I don't want any of this Kingdom of God or Valley of Death stuff. That's all too negative. . . . Couldn't we pray for a tighter bomb pattern?"), an idea he abandons only when he learns enlisted men pray to the same God; General Peckem, head of Special Services, whose strategic objective is to replace General Dreedle, the wing commander, capturing every bomber group in the US Air Force ("If dropping bombs on the enemy isn't a special service, I wonder what in the world is"); Captain Black, the squadron intelligence officer, who inaugurates the Glorious Loyalty Oath Crusade in order to discomfort a rival, forcing all officers (except the rival, who is thereupon declared a Communist) to sign a new oath whenever they get their flak suits, their pay checks, or their haircuts; Lieutenant Scheisskopf, paragon of the parade ground, whose admiration for efficient formations makes him scheme to screw nickel-alloy swivels into every cadet's back for perfect ninety degree turns; and cadres of sadistic officers, club-happy MPs, and muddleheaded agents of the CID, two of whom, popping in and out of rooms like farcical private eyes, look for Washington Irving throughout the action, finally pinning the rap on the innocent chaplain.

These are Yossarian's antagonists, all of them reduced to a single exaggerated humor, and all identified by their totally mechanical attitude towards human life. Heller has a profound hatred for this kind of military mind, further anatomized in a wacky scene before the Action Board which displays his (and their) animosity in a manner both hilarious and scarifying. But Heller, at war with much larger forces than the army, has provided his book with much wider implications than a war novel. For the author (apparently sharing the Italian belief that vengeance is a dish which tastes best cold) has been nourishing his grudges for so long that they have expanded to include the post-war American world. Through the agency of grotesque comedy, Heller has found a way to confront the humbug, hypocrisy, cruelty, and sheer stupidity of our mass society—qualities which have made the few other Americans who care almost speechless with baffled rage—and through some miracle of prestidigitation, Pianosa has become a satirical microcosm for many of the macrocosmic idiocies of our time. Thus, the author flourishes his Juvenalian scourge at government-subsidized agriculture (and farmers, one of whom "spent every penny he didn't earn on new land to increase the amount of alfalfa he did not grow"); at the exploitation of American Indians, evicted from their oil-rich land; at smug psychiatrists; at bureaucrats and patriots; at acquisitive war widows; at high-spirited American boys; and especially, and most vindictively, at war profiteers.

This last satirical flourish, aimed at the whole mystique of corporation capitalism, is embodied in the fantastic adventures of Milo Minderbinder, the company mess officer, and a paradigm of good natured Jonsonian cupidity. Anxious to put the war on a businesslike basis, Milo has formed a syndicate designed to corner the world market on all available foodstuffs, which he then sells to army messhalls at huge profits. Heady with success (his deals have made him Mayor of every town in Sicily, Vice-Shah of Oran, Caliph of Baghdad, Imam of Damascus, and the Sheik of Araby), Milo soon expands his activities, forming a private army which he hires out to the highest bidder. The climax of Milo's career comes when he fulfills a contract with the Germans to bomb and strafe his own outfit, directing his planes from the Pianosa control tower and justifying the action with the stirring war cry: "What's good for the syndicate is good for the country." Milo has almost succeeded in his ambition to pre-empt the field of war for private enterprise when he makes a fatal mistake: he has cornered the entire Egyptian cotton market and is unable to unload it anywhere. Having failed to pass it off to his own messhall in the form of chocolate-covered cotton, Milo is finally persuaded by Yossarian to bribe the American government to take it off his hands: "If you run into trouble, just tell everybody that the security of the country requires a strong domestic Egyptian cotton speculating industry." The Minderbinder sections—in showing the basic incompatibility of idealism and economics by satirizing the patriotic cant which usually accompanies American greed—illustrate the procedure of the entire book: the ruthless ridicule of hypocrisy through a technique of farce-fantasy, beneath which the demon of satire lurks, prodding fat behinds with a red-hot pitchfork.

It should be abundantly clear, then, that *Catch-22*, despite some of the most outrageous sequences since *A Night at the Opera*, is an intensely serious work. Heller has certain technical similarities to the Marx Brothers, Max Schulman, Kingsley Amis, Al Capp, and S. J. Perelman, but his mordant intelligence, closer to that of Nathanael West, penetrates the surface of the merely funny to expose a world of ruthless self-advancement, gruesome cruelty, and flagrant disregard for human life—a world, in short, very much like our own as seen through a magnifying glass, distorted for more perfect accuracy. Considering his indifference to surface reality, it is absurd to judge Heller by standards of psychological realism (or, for that matter, by conventional artistic standards at all, since his book is as formless as any picaresque epic). He is concerned entirely with that thin boundary of the surreal, the borderline between hilarity and horror, which, much like the apparent formlessness of the unconscious, has its own special integrity and coherence. Thus, Heller will never use comedy for its own sake; each joke has a wider significance in the intricate pattern, so that laughter becomes a prologue for some grotesque revelation. This gives the reader an effect of surrealistic dislocation, intensified by a wierd, rather flat, impersonal style, full of complicated reversals, swift transitions, abrupt shifts in chronological time, and manipulated identities (e.g. if a private named Major Major Major is promoted to Major by a faulty IBM machine, or if a malingerer, sitting out a doomed mission, is declared dead through a bureaucratic error, then this remains their permanent fate), as if all mankind was determined by a mad and merciless mechanism.

Thus, Heller often manages to heighten the macabre obscenity of total war much more effectively through its gruesome comic aspects than if he had written realistic descriptions. And thus, the most delicate pressure is enough to send us over the line from farce into phantasmagoria. In the climactic chapter, in fact, the book leaves comedy altogether and becomes an eerie nighmare of terror. Here Yossarian, walking through the streets of Rome as though through an Inferno, observes soldiers molesting drunken women, fathers beating ragged children, policemen clubbing innocent bystanders until the whole world seems swallowed up in the maw of evil:

The night was filled with horrors, and he thought he knew how Christ must have felt as he walked through the world, like a psychiatrist

52

through a ward of nuts, like a victim through a prison of thieves. . . . Mobs . . . mobs of policemen. . . . Mobs with clubs were in control everywhere.

Here, as the book leaves the war behind, it is finally apparent that Heller's comedy is his artistic response to his vision of transcendent evil, as if the escape route of laughter were the only recourse from a malignant world.

It is this world, which cannot be divided into boundaries or ideologies, that Yossarian has determined to resist. And so when his fear and disgust have reached the breaking point, he simply refuses to fly another mission. Asked by a superior what would happen if everybody felt the same way, Yossarian exercises his definitive logic, and answers, "Then I'd be a damned fool to feel any other way." Having concluded a separate peace, Yossarian maintains it in the face of derision, ostracism, psychological pressure, and the threat of court martial. When he is finally permitted to go home if he will only agree to a shabby deal whitewashing Colonel Cathcart, however, he finds himself impaled on two impossible alternatives. But his unique logic, helped along by the precedent of an even more logical friend, makes him conclude that desertion is the better part of valor; and so (after an inspirational sequence which is the weakest thing in the book) he takes off for neutral Sweden—the only place left in the world, outside of England, where "mobs with clubs" are not in control.

Yossarian's expedient is not very flattering to our national ideals, being defeatist, selfish, cowardly, and unheroic. On the other hand, it is one of those sublime expressions of anarchic individualism without which all national ideals are pretty hollow anyway. Since the mass State, whether totalitarian or democratic, has grown increasingly hostile to Falstaffian irresponsibility, Yossarian's anti-heroism is, in fact, a kind of inverted heroism which we would do well to ponder. For, contrary to the armchair pronouncements of patriotic ideologues, Yossarian's obsessive concern for survival makes him not only *not* morally dead, but one of the most morally vibrant figures in recent literature—and a giant of the will beside those weary, wise and wistful prodigals in contemporary novels who always accommodate sadly to American life. I believe that Joseph Heller is one of the most extraordinary talents now among us. He has Mailer's combustible radicalism without his passion for violence and self-glorification; he has Bellow's gusto with his compulsion to affirm the unaffirmable; and he has Salinger's wit without his coquettish self-consciousness. Finding his absolutes in the freedom to *be,* in a world dominated by cruelty, carnage, inhumanity, and a rage to destroy itself, Heller has come upon a new morality of refusal. Perhaps—now that Catch-22 has found its most deadly nuclear form—we have reached the point where even the logic of survival is unworkable. But at least we can still contemplate the influence of its liberating honesty on a free, rebellious spirit in this explosive, bitter, subversive, brilliant book.

(1961)

KENNETH BURKE

Thurber Perfects Mind Cure

That skillful literary man, St. Augustine, has warned that one should never smite an opponent in bad grammar. Applying a loose interpretation, we could translate his wise teaching thus: If a man would carry a discussion through points A, B, C and D, don't let him think he has got anywhere, in the way of cogency, simply by lining up a good argument. For should he have a lisp, or should someone in his audience periodically sneeze in a notable way, or should there be an irrelevant voice echoing from the corridors, our hero is all Achilles' heel. Especially when there is a Thurber about.

In fact, if he should make a statement that requires as many as three sentences, and there is a Thurber about, he is as vulnerable. For Thurber may choose to hear only the first sentence, proceeding joyously and outrageously to build upon it. We generally think of funny men as irrational. But they are as rational as the constructor of a Mother Goose rhyme (who gets to his crooked house via a crooked man, crooked smile, crooked sixpence, crooked stile, crooked cat and crooked mouse). And one thing they learn early is that, if a thought requires three sentences for self-protective presentation, they would be disloyal to their method in hearing out the three. Where three parts are needed, the professional funny man just *knows* that he should stop at part one. His one Marquis of Queensberry rule is: Belts are to hit below.

A Thurber, having singled out part one, will next proceed, with perverse rational efficiency, to ponder this broken part. He will invent "case histories" with which to try it out—and of course, they won't fit.

But a mere bad fit is not enough. The funny man will also seek a situation such that his readers *want* a bad fit. If they are good Catholics, for instance, he knows it will be hard to make them meet him halfway should he decide to play havoc with an encyclical. He will lay off such dynamite, leaving it for the news itself to provide the outrageous incongruities, as when, reporting a Papal blast on communism at the time of Mussolini's triumph in Africa, the dispatch proceeded: "On the subject of Ethiopia, His Holiness was less explicit." On the other hand, readers of *The New Yorker*, in which all but two of the articles in *Let Your Mind Alone!* appeared, are likely to be less problematical when leftward-looking politics is the subject—so we get "What Are the Leftists Saying?" I thought it tearfully lame; but for all I know it may be judged by typical *New Yorker* readers the most devastating bit of fun since the discovery of the banana peel.

The first ten pieces, which give this volume its title, are a very amusing burlesque of psychoanalysis. The field offers a good opportunity for Thurber's phenomenal gifts. The study of the mind has brought to the fore many paradoxes. A man may *think* he is doing one thing when he is *actually* doing another. This state of affairs outrages common sense—the thought of it makes one uneasy—hence we are glad to meet that man halfway who will expend his jocular enterprise to vindicate the judgments of common sense.

There are pages that make one laugh very hard. One is glad that Thurber does his part to keep the leftward-lookers on their toes. I am even willing to concede him his constitutional right, as funny man, to start too soon, to remain dumb on purpose, dying that others may live—though he tends somewhat to flatter stupidity, making it a kind of accomplishment within reach of all, like getting drunk, as in his soothing challenges of this sort: "I know very little about electricity and I don't want to have it explained to me" (the medicinal effect of such trivializing bravado being necessary, since there are so many things now to know very little about, and we might feel like worms if we didn't have people of Thurber's authority to help mend our humiliation).

His skill at turning little domestic rows into transmogrifications of themselves is picturesque. In such scenes, I believe, the perception of his draughtsmanship is carried over. You see the people in watching the drama. Tight shoes, he says, make one walk "with the gait of a man who is stalking a bird across wet cement." And he hates women "because they throw baseballs ... with the wrong foot advanced." There's something I had been working on since the eighth grade, and never understood until Thurber brought it clearly into consciousness by his combined skill as draughtsman and verbalizer. (Incidentally, I here select examples that I think are good—but I might illustrate his own method by adding that, were I to employ it here, I should pick out some of the weakest quips in the book and hold them up for rapt admiration.)

His drawings are good *always* for the perception his writing has *sometimes*. But I do wish he'd go after bigger game. He shoots too many cockroaches. To get such heightened value, I'd even be willing to hand him over to the reactionaries. Let him hound the "socially conscious" more consistently, in case he finds their attitude of "uplift" too much for his antinomian perversity. He need not join the author of "Redder Than the Rose." But let him at least make an indirect contribution, in serving to keep the statements of the Left alert (though they could never be alert enough to forestall all possibility of Thurberization). I have just been reading Jacques Barzun's book on theories of racial superiority. I think fondly of what a Thurber might do by examining these documents on crooked thinking and translating them into the idiom of hilarity. But that would be asking too much (at least until his waggish remarks on cocktail parties run out—and he is so ingenious and fertile with them that I doubt whether they ever will run out). So I am willing to have him become our Lord Macaulay of fun-making, a reactionary keeper-thin of the Left. Unction must be made difficult—so let him be the deunctifyer. But as things now stand, he too is purveying a patent medicine. The trivial has its medicinal aspect—but too often he expends his talents to load the trivial with all the traffic can bear.

(1937)

NICOLA CHIAROMONTE

Sunday After the War

One could say that Henry Miller is a preacher who frequently hits on a perfect piece of narration, or that he is an extremely good story-teller who occasionally writes a lot of nonsense about Lawrence, the astrological destinies of the world and various apocalypses, including the apocalypse of Henry Miller himself. The fact is that one cannot get away from Miller so easily. I mean by simply admitting on one hand that he is a good writer while ignoring the substance of his writing, and by overlooking, on the other hand, the perfection and compactness of his best pieces because his generalizations about himself and the world are so often, and so literally, extravagant: flights into universes for which he has no essential concern.

Essentially, he is just Henry Miller, from Brooklyn, who left America in 1930 because he couldn't stand it any longer, lived in Paris for nine years, writing there the first book of his new life "as an act of desperation," and was forced to return to America from Greece in 1940 because of the war. In a revealing biographical note added to *The Cosmological Eye* he reveals how as a young man he worked "at anything and

59

everything," and started writing, although "almost afraid to think" of becoming a writer. His readers know of his astonishing way of handling the job of a personnel director for Western Union, and the things he learned there. And it is not unimportant to keep in mind, in connection with Miller's indictment of the ways of modern society, what he himself has taken care to point out: "The most important encounter of my life," he writes in the same biographical note, "was with Emma Goldman in San Diego, California. She opened up the whole world of European culture for me and gave new impetus to my life, as well as direction. I was violently interested in the IWW movement at the time it was in swing, and remember with great reverence and affection such people as Jim Larkin, Elizabeth Gurley Flynn, Giovannitti and Carlo Tresca." But the real autobiography of Henry Miller has to be sought in his books.

It is easy to point out, in this last collection of pieces from Miller's work, the story, "Return to Brooklyn," as a masterpiece. It is the plain, admirably firm and even tale of the return of Henry Miller (not of any imaginary character, and not of the artificial "I" which helps to dodge so many questions and facts, just Henry Miller, the *real* character that Henry Miller has been describing for ten years) to his mother, father and sister, to his home in Brooklyn, after ten years of exile. Céline has written some forceful pages on the family, but Céline is jittery and mean; he hates the family because it is the thing most hostile to his moods. His revolt has no dignity. In Miller there is neither hate nor revolt, rather a most controlled pity and a very human modesty. To him, the family is simply the desolate core of the inertia of which our society is dying.

The description is hopeless and pitiless, yet with no overtones of despair or disgust. Even in the details about the miserable disease of which the father is dying, there is no crudity, but rather the compassionate detachment of the monk (and a peculiar kind of monk Miller certainly is) who cannot think of the sick he is tending otherwise than as samples of human misery. The horror is not in physical disease or death. The horror is in the existence of beings drained of all life, neither by fate nor time, but by the blind machine which has taken the place of human society. One has only to think of what Céline would have done with the same material, or for that matter, of the truculence in which Miller used to indulge in his early work, to realize how near he has come to a real harmony.

To stop here would be merely to praise Miller from a distance, and avoid his personality, a philistine attitude and one which would not do justice to the writer. The originality and forcefulness of "Return to Brooklyn" do not consist in the realistic description of a milieu, but in the honest account of a relationship. The main character of the story is neither Henry Miller nor his family, but their relationship, their presence together as individuals on equal terms, and the questions that this co-presence raises. In other words, the real subject of the story, what creates its suspense and dramatic quality, is a moral struggle, the struggle of Henry Miller, the character, against the torpor of sentimental ties, against his own frailty and helplessness, and more especially against the smoldering fire of rage and disgust, to attain whatever clarity and justice it is possible for him to attain toward that environment and those human beings. From this struggle, Henry Miller comes out the winner, not perhaps in the sense that he thinks as a man who has discovered essential truths, but as one who has succeeded in mastering his inner chaos and in not allowing the external clutter to overcome him.

It is in this sense, I think, that Miller was right when he wrote of himself: "I am at bottom a metaphysical writer, and my use of drama and incident is only a device to posit something more profound." A device, I would add, to elucidate as far as he can what is actually going on around him from the point of view of the unattached individual with no special interests to defend or hide, except the personal whims and twists of which he is a victim like anybody else.

I don't know any other writer who has succeeded in

completely humanizing the writer as a character, stripping him of any special prestige, making of him a true Everyman who wins his laurels, if any, only in actual competition with other individuals for the possession of human qualities and for the enjoyment of whatever there is to be enjoyed in life. The exhilarating quality of Miller's best things come precisely from the fact that he has succeeded in making of writing a natural way of existing, and also in making of the reader a companion in the material and moral odyssey, the dejection, the hunger, the shame, and the very real pitfalls which have to be experienced by an individual in order to have that kind of existence. Before preaching about deliverance from what he calls the dumb sleep of the present world, and one would add, more than preaching about deliverance, Miller has shown the actual process of deliverance of a perfectly ordinary human being from the gutter of Broadway and the offices of Western Union to the streets of Paris, from the blind rage and despair of the cornered individual to the conquest of that tense detachment which is the best quality of Henry Miller, the character and story-teller. Writing, for him, is the actual process of purification from confusion and insincerity, by no means an end in itself, as he explains very clearly in some pages of this last book:

The little phrase—*Why don't you try to write?*—involved me, as it had from the very beginning, in a hopeless bog of confusion. I wanted to enchant but not to enslave; I wanted a greater, richer life, but not at the expense of others. . . . I had no respect for writing *per se* . . . By a chain of circumstances having nothing to do with reason or intelligence I had become like the others—a drudge. . . . I gave nothing to the world in fulfilling the function of breadwinner; the world exacted its tribute of me, that was all. The world would only begin to get something of value from me the moment I stopped being a serious member of society and became—*myself.* . . . What I secretly longed for was to disentangle myself of all those lives which had woven themselves into the pattern of my own life. . . . To shake myself free of these accumulating experiences which were mine only by force of inertia required a violent effort.

It is in the tenacity and consistency of such an effort that the seriousness and uniqueness of Miller's personality lie, no matter how often Miller himself falls victim to what he calls the "vice" of uncontrolled imagination, metaphysical, psychoanalytical or simply erratic, and also no matter how often he boasts of having attained perfection.

I must confess that when I first read *Tropic of Cancer,* as much as I admired his talent as a narrator, and realized that here was somebody arriving from "the end of the night" and who had, as such, the right to be respected, I was mystified by the atmosphere of elusive egotism which accompanied him, and would have agreed with what George Orwell was later going to write: that Miller was seeking a refuge from the murderous nonsense of the present world "inside the whale," in an attitude of total indifference and frantic self-preservation. Still, I was not convinced. I felt there was in Miller's work an additional quality which I was unable to grasp. It was under the impact of the insistence and consistency of his successive works that I realized there was more than good story-telling in him. His tales of desperate wanderings through Paris, of New York tailor shops, of true trivialities and obscenities, of crazy bohemians and nasty tricks, not only gave one the immediate feeling of the casualness, the lack of logic, the utter imperviousness, the humor of real life; they also compelled one to enjoy it with a sense of liberation, the liberation from any special sentiment, from any moral or intellectual prejudice. And most important of all, it was a keen pleasure to know that such a man existed in such a world as the world of today.

As for Miller's aloofness, I would agree that he prefers to play with astrological symbols rather than with political ideas, and to praise Bahai rather than Marx. I would not deny that he often shows more than a little affectation in this sense. But on the other hand, it is so clear that everything he conceives or feels is conceived and felt against the world of today, that I would hesitate to insist on the theme of indifference, for fear of having to accuse him of the very opposite, too emotional a concern with some of the most obvious aspects of the present evils. In his beautiful book on Greece, every discovery, every pleasure, and laugh, and moment of pure oblivion is felt against the background of impending catastrophe. Greece would not be so beautiful and pacifying were not the world outside of Greece so ugly and inhuman. Miller's egotism, in so far as it is insistence on self-possession, seems to me perfectly valuable, and it certainly is one of the inescapable themes of modern literature. As for his vaunted bliss, it is not without meaning if considered against the background of pointless sadness which one finds everywhere today, among all kinds of people, and which Miller calls "Hamletism."

In any case, I think that Henry Miller means it when he writes:

> I am here on earth to work out my private destiny. My destiny is linked with that of every other living creature. . . . I refuse to jeopardize my destiny by regarding life within the narrow rules which are now laid down to circumscribe it. I dissent from the current view of things as regards murder, as regards religion, as regards society, as regards our well-being. I will try to live my life in accordance with the vision I have of things eternal.

(1944)

PADRAIC COLUM

Joyce: From a Work in Progress

In his late thirties James Joyce recast the most used of literary mediums, the novel; he recast it with *Ulysses*. He is now recasting the novel more radically, and he is recasting language as the medium of writers who know that what they write should tend toward poetry.

In his late forties, then, he is engaged in the most heroic effort that is being made by any writer of our epoch. His *Work in Progress* represents that effort. It is not completed, but already it has had effect: language, writers have been shown, is evocative as well as descriptive. And narrative can be made to tell us about other than diurnal happenings. As narrative, *Work in Progress* is more like a piece of mythology than it is like a novel; it seems to me to have a likeness to that curious fragment of Central American mythology that we call the Popul Vuh. *Haveth Childers Everywhere* is the third fragment from *Work in Progress* to appear in book form: already there have been published *Anna Livia Plurabelle* and *Tales Told of Shem and Shaun*.

Haveth Childers Everywhere is to be compared with *Anna Livia Plurabelle*. The latter is about a river and about river civilizations; specifically, it is about the River Liffey. The former is about a city, about Dublin. And as the book about the river had the rhythm of flowing water, the ripple, the sweep, the still spread of the river, this third fragment has in its rhythm the blare of the city. The river was incarnated in a woman, Anna Livia; the city is incarnated in a man, H. C. E.

Considered as a man, H. C. E. is the boss man—in every situation—he is Adam, he is Abraham, he is the Duke of Wellington, he is Daniel O'Connell. In his origin he is Norse, for Dublin was founded by Vikings and Norse merchants. It was made a municipality in the interests of Bristol merchants. And so H. C. E. has the belligerency of an intruder. As he appears before us in the present fragment, he is Everyman, for he is answering to the charge that is brought against all of us—call it Original Sin or the Fall of Man. Something has happened in a garden, in the city park, and he is protesting his detachment from it. And in the course of his defense he brags of all that he has accomplished—all that Dublin has done.

James Joyce has no interest in what we call history. Long ago, in an essay which he wrote in his twenties, an essay on James Clarence Mangan that was published in his college magazine, he denied the validity of history. As he is a man whose opinions on intellectual things have never changed since he first had such opinions, it is worth while quoting from his youthful essay:

> Poetry . . . as it is often found at war with its age, so it makes no account of history, which is fabled by the daughters of memory, but sets store by every time less than the pulsation of an artery, the time in which its intuitions start forth, holding it equal in its period and value to six thousand years. No doubt they are only men of letters who insist on the succession of the ages, and history or the denial of reality, for they are two names for the one thing, may be said to be that which deceives the whole world.

But what has gone before lives. It lives in hereditary character, in typical personalities in the mind of the populace, in patterns formed in the popular mind through invasion, or expansion, or startling occurrences. In other words, history is not a denial of reality when it is known as mythology. It is mythology of this kind that we have in *Work in Progress*. In *Anna Livia Plurabelle*, James Joyce introduced hundreds of river names as verbs and nouns and adjectives. In this fragment, which is about the metropolis, he introduces hundreds of words derived from names in other cities to describe scenes and events—"madridden mustangs and buckarestive bronchos" appear in the last passage of *Haveth Childers Everywhere*, passages that describe the city's transportation.

A rhythm which has a scriptural powerfulness bears everything along. H. C. E., who is a blusterer as well as a builder, a comic as well as an heroic character, addresses the Four who are the Justiciars before whom he is brought—they are any of the quaternities we have thought of—the Four Elements, the Four Evangelists, the Four Provinces of Ireland. He begins:

> Amtsadam, sir, to you! Eternest cittas, heil! Here we are again. I am bubub brought up under a camel act of dynasties long out of print, the first of Shitric Shilkanbeard (or is it Owallagh Mac Auscullpth the Thord)... . On my verawife I never was nor can afford to be guilty of crim crig con, of malfeasance trespass against parson with the person of a youthful gigirl friend chirped Apples, acted by Miss Dashe, in Kissilov's Slutgarten or Gigillotte's Hill... .

A reader who is not prepared for this development in Joyce's writing will protest that these are meaningless successions of words. I can get, such a reader may say, a sense of rhythm, I can feel that somebody is talking loudly and compellingly. But what it is about I do not know. Well, the first word suggests a city; it also suggests the first man. The second sentence is a slogan—a slogan for all cities. The comic H. C. E. has begun to stutter with his "bubub brought up." The law has had its origin with the Norse Kings of Dublin whose names have become degraded in the populace-mind—Sitric Silkenbeard is one of the two. A "gigirl" is much more youthful than any youthful girl could be—we get a combination of something giggling and girlish. "Kissilov's Garden" is a park in some continental city—in Bucharest or Budapest; "Gigillotte's Hill" is a park in some German city. But why, it will be asked, has James Joyce found it necessary to use this arcane language?

Briefly, because *Work in Progress* deals with the night life of humanity, that dream life which is the one-third of our mortal career. The language of the day cannot be the language of the night; another language has to be found to render this state. And, as any of us know who have caught ourselves in the stage between sleeping and waking, a number of memories and notions are imposed, one on the other, in our unwakeful condition.

Joyce finds his language in words in which a number of meanings are telescoped. We have all noted such words. Chesterton noted that Francis Thompson, when he used the phrase "pontifical death," had telescoped several meanings in the adjective: death as a priest, a viceregent, a bridge builder—all resumed in a word which carries a suggestion of majesty. But it is not the poets alone who discover words that have manifold meaning: the multitude discovers them. The boys and girls who use the word "wristwatchdog" for that small edition of a lap dog, use such a manifold: the word suggests a miniature, something that belongs to the arm, something that barks. The other day I noted that a local newspaper spoke of "our fire laddies," telescoping in the phrase "fire" and "ladders" with the young men of the brigade. James Joyce has his words change as the situation changes. Thus, the Phoenix Park in Dublin becomes the Fiendish Park when H. C. E. offended or was framed up in it, and the Pynix Park when Athens, as one of the world's metropolises, was to give a name to H. C. E.'s city. I need not point out that in the epics and mythologies there are frequent changes in names: rivers are known to men and gods under different names; the gods have different names in their different aspects. "The young Englanders walk it every day," a wayfarer in Switzerland said to me when I asked how far a certain town was. I thought it right that the word for an Englishman walking in Switzerland should be different from the word for an Englishman walking in England.

In the medium that Joyce is establishing, poetry and humor have fresh reaches. Take the poetry of the passage which evokes the cathedral, with its bells, music and lights:

> Her paddypalace on the crossknoll with massgo bell, sixton, clashcloshant duominous and muezzatinties to commind the fitful: doom adimdim adoom adimdim: and the orgel of the lauds to tellforths' glory: and added thereunto a shallow laver to slub out her hellfire and posied windows for her oriel house: gospelly pewmillieu christous pewmillieu: zackbutts babazounded ollguns tararulled: and she sass her nach, chillybom and forty bonnets, upon the altarstane.

And the humor of the passage describing those direful portraits—"painted by hand" as we are always informed, but looking like photographs of wax figures that we see in provincial town halls:

> We had our lewd mayers and our lardie meiresses kiotowing and smuling fullface on us out of their framous latenesses, oilclothed over for cohabitation and allpointed by Hind.

The effect that James Joyce is working for can only be realized in a complete work; he cannot achieve it by introducing such passages of poetry or humor into writing that is close to our norm. It is heroic of him and it is right on his part to make a complete departure and to put all his discoveries in an integral work. But to a man engaged in such heroic effort one might counsel prudence. It is not prudent on his part to bring into his work some private piece of knowledge or to overelaborate some element of his meaning. I fancy I detect instances of both imprudences in *Haveth Childers Everywhere*. Take, for example, the description of the metropolitan cathedral already quoted. Besides all that refers to bells, music, color, anthem, there are references to local and national affairs. When he says "to tellforths' glory" one who knows Dublin remembers that the organ builders of the city are Telfords; one who knows Irish history remembers that a Norse chieftain put his wife sitting on the high altar of a cathedral, and so one gets the reference in "she sass her nach, chillybombom . . . upon the altarstane." But what has "forty bonnets" to do with this? One suspects that this is some private understanding of Joyce's. And when he speaks of "such gretched youngsters" we are delighted with a phrase that combines "Gretchen" with "wretched." But why is it elaborated by adding, to "I would not know to contact such gretched youngsters," the cryptic words, "in my ways from Haddem or any suisterees or heiresses of theirn, claiming by, through or under them." One has to work hard to get even thirty percent of understanding of *Work in Progress.* But even less than thirty percent gives one humor, poetry, a sense of mythological character, that one cannot get in any other writing of the present day.

(1930)

HILARY CORKE

The Wapshot Scandal

The hardened review-reader knows what to expect from a notice that begins with praises; he will be quite aware of the giant BUT lurking in the wings. It can only be ominous therefore, that I start by observing that John Cheever is an intelligent, original and in many respects brilliant man; that he is one of the best living short-story writers in the language; that he has a remarkably acute nose for the significantly fascinating relation or situation, and a remarkably acute ear for the thing said, as such and such a person says it. He is possessed in fact, of almost all the talents.

So it is that *The Wapshot Scandal*, like its predecessor *The Wapshot Chronicle*, is full of plums. The characters (inhabitants of the small New England port of St. Botolphs) are much the same as those in the Chronicle, apart from those who died there and were committed to the sepulchre with full literary honors. There are the two Wapshot brothers: Moses—the handsome and pushing, quick to succeed and, as we now learn, quick to degenerate too; and Coverly—the honest and dubious, who doesn't "make good" but all the same is the better sort of apple. Cousin Honora, the embodiment of the eternal youth of old age, is still with us—until the last pages, when she too receives a fine interment. Moses' wife, Melissa, deteriorates like her husband, going down roughly the same slope of the same hill and finally running off with the grocer's boy to live in sin in Rome. Coverly's wife, Betsey, is her old complaining, disappointed—indeed pointless—self of the *Chronicle*, only more so, And so on; *The Wapshot Scandal* is not less of a "chronicle" than the other. It is frankly episodic.

So episodic, in fact, that a large number of readers will already have encountered substantial chunks of it in the pages of *The New Yorker*. If they share my tastes, moreover, they will have admired and enjoyed those chunks, and have been predisposed to admire and enjoy the whole picture as well as the magnified details. BUT. I find the whole fatally flawed, and by some cause that it is not very easy at first to identify. It is, I think, that Mr. Cheever is what, if one were counsel for his defense, and trying to stretch a point as far as it would go without parting in the middle, one would describe as "too relaxed"; and what the prosecutor would term "sloppy."

There is a lack of grip, even of the will to grip, and it seems to adversely affect the Wapshot books in two main ways: it leads to unredeemable carelessnesses and loosenesses of construction—and, on the emotional or even (it may be) moral side, to bouts of arrant sentimentality.

Take the constructional side first. *The Wapshot Scandal* can hardly claim the proud title of novel. Whole episodes seem simply glued in in order to swell the bulk—as if they were short stories (and good short stories too), pressed into service by altering the name of some minor figure in them into "Wapshot" and leaving it at that. There is, for instance, a long section on the Roman holiday of a rocket physicist, a Dr. Cameron, and another recounting his hearing before a Congressional security committee. Neither has more than the most formal connection with the main body of the book. The second (but not the first) is also couched in a fanciful satirical vein that is quite out of key with most of the remainder. Worse still, these two interpolated pieces don't even tie up with each other: for instance, in the first Cameron's character is described in terms of "cleanliness," "decency," "a good man"—whereas in the second he appears as a fiend in human shape who has destroyed his small son's reason by continual beatings. (And this, as it appears in context, is unmistakably a careless, not an ironic, discrepancy).

One begins to speculate on whether Mr. Cheever writes a lot of short stories and then sews them together; or whether he takes care to write the sort of novel from which a number of complete short stories can be painlessly extracted. I don't mean to sound pedantically narrow here; there is an honorable place for the novel-of-episodes, even though that form, in order to make its short-term gains of apparant breadth of canvas and quick effects, is obliged to surrender the novel's fundamental dynamic (which is that we are carried on, not transported for short distances and then set down to await the next vehicle). But there is not a place for the novel of contradictory episodes: particularly if it is written in such a way as to promise an over-all unity, and if the cracks are so carefully pasted over with decorative tinsel. *The Wapshot Scandal* (and after a careful reading, I remain completely in the dark as to what incident may be referred to in the title) would have been much better issued as a volume of short stories.

Furthermore: this looseness is not confined to construction. It runs right through, down to the small details. For instance, in an incident which has neither antecedent nor after-history, Coverly Wapshot puts the vocabulary of Keats through a computer:

The vocabulary was eight thousand five hundred and three and the words in the order of their frequency were: "Silence blendeth grief's awakened fall / The golden realms of death take all . . ."

"My God," Coverly said. "It rhymes. It's poetry."

73

And he goes on to philosphize about this. But one doesn't have to be anything of a statistician, one needs no more than an elementary sense of the way the word, and its languages, are put together, to be sure that a frequency count yields something of the nature of *the and of that to it*. If one is going to fool about with science, and then draw wise conclusions, one has to make one's science, if not accurate, then at least conceivable. Or, if one is going to be frankly fantastic, one must not embed one's fantasy in a wholly realistic context.

Irrelevancies. Contradictions. Unrealities. Hiatuses, if we are to consider the *Scandal* as a follow-on from the *Chronicle* (what for instance of Cousin Justina, and how did Moses and Melissa get themselves where the beginning of the second book finds them?) And repetitions. Mr. Cheever has a number of tricks that he happily repeats, even applying the same psychological quirk to quite different characters (for instance, pages 50-52 give an account of how Melissa used to pretend that things that had happened hadn't; and page 69 details exactly the same peculiarity in Coverly). Goodness knows how many of the male characters (in both books) lie on the beds bursting with desire while listening to the maddening, deliberate ablutions of their women in the bathroom. Betsey's disastrous attempt to give a party (none of the guests come) is a re-write of a similar occasion in the *Chronicle*. On the tiniest scale (contradictions again), the St. Botolphs watch-repairer is called Spofford on page 15 and Sturgis on page 31; and one could fill half a page with discrepancies of that sort. All these leap out in glaring contrast to the loving and exact care that Mr. Cheever brings to his characters, their speech, his descriptions, and the always sensitive and often dazzling texture of his writing.

Mr. Cheever has plenty of feeling and isn't frightened to show it, and I for one am prepared to cheer him all the way for that: if it is a fault, it is a fault on the right side. But sentimentality, I take it, means feeling that is out of control, feeling that no longer troubles to relate properly to its object or cause but detaches itself from reality and begins to feed on itself and to exist solely for its own sake. It leads Mr. Cheever at times into scenes that might have made Dickens, at his absurdest, pause and blush: such as when Coverly, on Christmas Eve, goes to rescue Moses from the whore-house in which he is busily degenerating—

Then Coverly opened the door. "Come home, Moses," he said. "Come home, brother. It's Christmas Eve." [End of paragraph, end of scene.]

So too, in the *Chronicle*, we have the set scene of the "burning of the great house," a purely sentimental cliché-event that goes straight back through *Rebecca*, to *Jane Eyre*, to take it no further.

But it is not merely individual scenes: the whole atmosphere is just one shade of baby-pink warmer than life. The general purpose of these books is presumably to draw a picture of a certain form of society, a certain way of life—the *modus vivendi* of a small and ancient Massachusetts port which is earthy, eccentric, individualistic, innocent, passionate, rich, as contrasted with the smooth, impoverished, sophisticated uniformity of the city. Fine: but the vision gets over-simple, over-stressed, over-ripe—and, finally and disastrously, self-indulgent. It sets out to be social history but, the fatal specter of the Great American Novel hovering somewhere near, becomes an anatomy not of a life as it is, or recently was, but of a dream-life as a basically conventional and sentimental literary sense would have it be.

To put it another way, Mr. Cheever unluckily falls in love with his theme, and falls in love with it in a hopelessly uncritical way. He falls in love with his characters too. And again that's a fault on the right side, but he goes too far: he tends to introduce them with haloes of lovableness about their brows. It is as if he were saying "Look! this man is great, he's adorable, he's splendid, you just take my word for that, I know." Well, as a matter of fact he is dead right: Leander Wapshot, of the *Chronicle*, is lovable and all the rest,

75

there's no denying it. Only one feels that Mr. Cheever ought to conceal his confidence, his love-affair, more discreetly.

The trouble about sentimentality is that it debases the coinage. The whole tone of Mr. Cheever's mind is attractive: intelligent, sympathetic, exploring, sweet, clean. But in the end, feeling flows too readily, taps are dripping all over the place. Emotion gives way to acrobatics and the crises become unreal, unurgent, because we are so certain that all will happily be resolved in a page or two. Even such an incident as poor old Cousin Honora's determination to hang herself in her attic is all great fun and even Mr. Cheever can't be bothered to consider the tragic implications of it. All tends to the facile, the quick trick, and often to archness—"And now we come to the unsavory or homosexual part of our tale and any disinterested reader is encouraged to skip." Don't worry, reader, nothing naughty happens, it's all a false alarm. Just relax. You are safe with John Cheever. I seem to descry the hooves and horns of the deliberately contrived best-seller. "I think the whole book is marvelous," says Malcolm Cowley, and thousands and thousands of readers are going to feel the same way.

(1964)

MALCOLM COWLEY

1919

John Dos Passos is in reality two novelists. One of them is a late-Romantic, an individualist, as esthete moving about the world in a portable ivory tower; the other is a collectivist, a radical historian of the class struggle. These two authors have collaborated in all his books, but the first had the larger share in *Three Soldiers* and *Manhattan Transfer*. The second, in his more convincing fashion, has written most of *The 42nd Parallel* and almost all of *1919*. The difference between the late-Romantic and the radical Dos Passos is important not only in his own career: it also helps to explain the recent course of American fiction.

The late-Romantic tendency in his novels goes back to his years in college. After graduating from a good preparatory school, Dos Passos entered Harvard in 1912, at the beginning of a period which was later known as that of the Harvard esthetes. I have described this period elsewhere, in reviewing the poems of E. E. Cummings, but I did not discuss the ideas which underlay its picturesque manifestations, its mixture of incense, patchouli, and gin, its erudition displayed before barroom mirrors, its dreams in the Cambridge subway of laurel-crowned Thessalian dancers. The esthetes themselves were not philosphers; they did not seek to define their attitude; but most of them would have subscribed to the following propositions:

That the cultivation and expression of his own sensibility are the only justifiable ends for a poet.

That originality is his principal virtue.

That society is hostile, stupid and unmanageable: it is the world of the philistines, from which it is the poet's duty and privilege to remain aloof.

That the poet is always misunderstood by the world. He should, in fact, deliberately make himself misunderstandable, for the greater glory of art.

That he triumphs over the world, at moments, by mystically including it within himself: these are his moments of *ecstasy,* to be provoked by any means in his power—alcohol, drugs, madness or saintliness, venery, suicide.

That art, the undying expression of such moments, exists apart from the world; it is the poet's revenge on society.

That the past has more dignity than the present.

There are a dozen other propositions which might be added to this unwritten manifesto, but the ideas I have listed were those most generally held, and they are sufficient to explain the intellectual atmosphere of the young men who read *The Hill of Dreams,* and argued about St. Thomas in Boston bars, and contributed to *The Harvard Monthly.* The attitude was not confined to one college and one magazine. It was often embodied in *The Dial,* which for some years was almost a postgraduate edition of *The Monthly;* it existed in earlier publications like *The Yellow Book* and *La Revue Blanche;* it has a history, in fact, almost as long as that of the upper middle class under capitalism. For the last half-century it has furnished the intellectual background of poems and essays without number. It would seem to preclude, in its adherents, the objectivity that is generally associated with good fiction; yet the esthetes themselves sometimes wrote novels, as did their predecessors all over the world. Such novels, in fact, are still being published, and favorably criticized: "Mr. Zed has written the absorbing story of a talented musician tortured by the petty atmosphere of the society in which he is forced to live. His wife, whom the author portryas with witty malice, prevents him from breaking away. After an unhappy love affair and the failure of his artistic hopes, he commits suicide. . . ."

Such is the plot forever embroidered in the type of fiction that ought to be known as the Art Novel. There are two essential characters, two antagonists, the Poet and the World. The Poet—who may also be a painter, a violinist, an inventor, an architect or a Centaur—is generally to be identified with the author of the novel, or at least with the novelist's ideal picture of himself. He tries to assert his individuality in despite of the World, which is stupid, unmanageable and usually victorious. Sometimes the Poet triumphs, but the art novelists seem to realize, as a class, that the sort of hero they describe is likely to be defeated in the sort of society which he must face. This society is rarely presented in accurate terms. So little is it endowed with reality, so great is the author's solicitude for the Poet, that we are surprised to see him vanquished by such a shadowy opponent. It is as if we were watching motion pictures in the dark house of his mind. There are dream pictures, nightmare pictures; at last the walls crash in and the Poet disappears without ever knowing what it was all about; he dies by his own hand, leaving behind him the memory of his ecstatic moments and the bitter story of his failure, now published as a revenge on the world of the philistines.

The art novel has many variations. Often the World is embodied in the Poet's wife, whose social ambitions are the immediate cause of his defeat. Or the wife may be painted in attractive colors: she is married to a mediocre Poet who finally and reluctantly accepts her guidance, abandons his vain struggle for self-expression, and finds that mediocrity has its own consolations, its country clubs and business triumphs—this is the form in which the art novel is offered to readers of *The Saturday Evening Post.* Or again the Poet may be a woman who fights for the same ambitions, under the same difficulties, as her male prototypes. The scene of the struggle may be a town on the Minnesota prairies, an English rectory, an apartment on Washington Square or Beacon Hill; but always the characters are the same; the Poet and the World continue their fatal conflict; the Poet has all our sympathies. And the novelists who use this plot for the thousandth time are precisely those who believe that originality is a writer's chief virtue.

Many are unconscious of this dilemma. The story rises so immediately out of their lives, bursts upon them with such freshness, that they never recognize it as a familiar tale. Others deliberately face the problem and try to compensate for the staleness of the plot by the originality of their treatment. They experiment with new methods of story-telling—one of which, the stream of consciousness, seems peculiarly fitted to novels of this type. Perhaps they invest their characters with new significance, and rob them of any real significance, by making them symbolic. They adopt new manners, poetic, mystical, learned, witty, allusive or obfuscatory; and often, in token of their original talent, they invent new words and new ways of punctuating simple declarative sentences. Not all their ingenuity is wasted. Sometimes they make valuable discoveries; a few of the art novels, like *The Hill of Dreams,* are among the minor masterpieces of late-Romantic literature; and a very few, like *A Portrait of the Artist as a Young Man,* are masterpieces pure and simple.

Dos Passos' early books are neither masterpieces nor are they pure examples of the art novel. The world was always real to him, painfully real; it was never veiled with mysticism and his characters were rarely symbolic. Yet consider the plot of a novel like *Three Soldiers.* A talented young musician, during World War I, finds that his sensibilities are being outraged, his aspirations crushed, by society as embodied in the American army. He deserts after the Armistice and begins to write a great orchestral poem. When the military police come to arrest him, the sheets of music flutter one by one into the spring breeze; and we are made to feel that the destruction of this symphony, this ecstatic song choked off and dispersed on the wind, is the real tragedy of the War. Some years later, in writing *Manhattan Transfer,* Dos Passos seemed to be undertaking a novel of a different type, one which tried to render the color and movement of a whole city; but the book, as it proceeds, becomes the story of Jimmy Herts (the Poet) and Ellen Thatcher (the Poet's wife), and the Poet is once again frustrated by the World: he leaves a Greenwich Village party after a last drink of gin and walks out alone, bareheaded, into the dawn. It is obvious, however, that a new conflict has been superimposed on the old one: the social ideas of the novelist are now at war with his personal emotions, which remain those of *The Dial* and *The Harvard Monthly.* Even in *1919,* this second conflict persists, but less acutely; the emotional values themselves are changing, to accord with the ideas; and the book as a whole belongs to a new category.

1919 is distinguished, first of all, by the very size of the project its author has undertaken. A long book in itself, containing 473 pages, it is merely the second chapter, as it were, of a novel which will compare in length with *Ulysses,* perhaps even with *Remembrance of Things Past.* Like the latter, it is a historical novel dealing with the yesterday that still exists in the author's memory. It might almost be called a news novel, since it uses newspaper headlines to suggest the flow of events, and tells the story of its characters in reportorial fashion. But its chief distinction lies in the author's emphasis. He is not recounting the tragedy of bewildered John Smith, the rise of ambitious Mary Jones, the efforts of sensitive Richard Robinson to maintain his ideals against the blundering malice of society. Such episodes recur in this novel, but they are seen in perspective. The real hero of *The 42nd Parallel* and *1919* is society itself, American society as embodied in forty or fifty representative characters who drift along with it, struggle to change its course, or merely to find a secure footing—perhaps they build a raft of wreckage, grow fat on the refuse floating about them; perhaps they go under in some obscure eddy—while always the current sweeps them onward toward new social horizons. In this sense, Dos Passos has written the first American collective novel.

The principal characters are brought forward one at a time; the story of each is told in bare, straightforward prose. Thus, J. Ward Moorehouse, born in Wilmington, Delaware, begins his business career in a real-estate office. He writes songs, marries and divorces a rich woman, works for a newspaper in Pittsburgh—at the end of fifty-seven pages he is a successful public-relations counselor embarked on a campaign to reconcile labor and capital at the expense of labor. Joe and Janey Williams are the children of a tugboat captain from Washington, D. C.: Janey studies shorthand; Joe plays baseball, enlists in the navy, deserts after a brawl and becomes a merchant seaman. Eleanor Stoddard is a poor Chicago girl who works at Marshall Field's; she learns how to speak French to her customers and order waiters about "with a crisp little refined moneyed voice." All these characters, first introduced in *The 42nd Parallel*, reappear in *1919*, where they are joined by others: Richard Ellsworth Savage, a Kent School boy who goes to Harvard and writes poetry; Daughter, a warm-hearted flapper from Dallas, Texas; Ben Compton, a spectacled Jew from Brooklyn who becomes a Wobbly. Gradually their careers draw closer together, till finally all of them are caught up in the War.

"This whole goddam war's a gold brick," says Joe Williams. "It ain't on the level, it's crooked from A to Z. No matter how it comes out, fellows like us get the s——y end of the stick, see? Well, what I say is all bets is off . . . every man go to hell in his own way . . . and three strikes is out, see?" Three strikes is out for Joe, when his skull is cracked in a saloon brawl at St. Nazaire, on Armistice night. Daughter is killed in an airplane accident; she provoked it herself in a fit of hysteria after being jilted by Dick Savage—who for his part survives as the shell of a man, all the best of him having died when he decided to join the army and make a career for himself and let his pacifist sentiments go hang. Benny Compton gets ten years in Atlanta prison as a conscientious objector. Everybody in the novel suffers from the War and finds his own way of going to hell—everybody except the people without bowels, the empty people like Eleanor Stoddard and J. Ward Moorehouse, who stuff themselves with the proper sentiments and make the right contacts.

The great events that preceded and followed the Armistice are reflected in the lives of all these people; but Dos Passos has other methods, too, for rendering the sweep of history. In particular he has three technical devices which he uses both to broaden the scope of the novel and to give it a formal unity. The first of these consists of what he calls "Newsreels," a combination of newspaper headlines, stock-market reports, official communiqués and words from popular songs. The Newsreels effectively perform their function in the book, that of giving dates and atmospheres, but in themselves, judged as writing, they are not successful. The second device is a series of nine biographies interspersed through the text. Here are the lives, briefly told, of three middle-class rebels, Jack Reed, Randolph Bourne and Paxton Hibben; of three men of power, Roosevelt, Wilson and J. P. Morgan; and of three proletarian heroes. All these are successful both in themselves and in relation to the novel as a whole; and the passage dealing with the Wobbly martyr, Wesley Everest, is as powerful as anything Dos Passos has ever written.

The "Camera Eye," which is the third device, introduces more complicated standards of judgment. It consists in the memories of another character, presumably the author, who has adventures similar to those of his characters, but describes them in a different style, one which suggests Dos Passos' earlier books. The Camera Eye gives us photographs rich in emotional detail:

...Ponte Decimo   in Ponte Decimo ambulances were parked in a
moonlit square of bleak stone workingpeople's houses   hoarfrost
covered everything   in the little bar the Successful Story Writer taught
us to drink cognac and maraschino half and half

    havanuzzerone

    it turned out he was not writing what he felt he wanted to be
writing   What can you tell them at home about the war?   it turned
out he was not wanting what he wrote he wanted to be feeling cognac
and maraschino   was no longer young   (It made us damn sore we
greedy for what we felt we wanted tell 'em all they lied see new towns
go to Genoa)   havanuzzerone?   it turned out that he wished he was a
naked brown shepherd boy sitting on a hillside playing a flute in the
sunlight.

Exactly the same episode, so it happens, is described in
Dos Passos' other manner, his prose manner, during the
course of a chapter dealing with Dick Savage:

> That night they parked the convoy in the main square of a
> godforsaken little burg on the outskirts of Genoa. They went with
> Sheldrake to have a drink in a bar and found themselves drinking with
> the Saturday Evening Post correspondent, who soon began to get tight
> and to say how he envied them their good looks and their sanguine
> youth and idealism. Steve picked him up about everything and argued
> bitterly that youth was the lousiest time in your life, and that he ought
> to be goddam glad he was forty years old and able to write about the
> war instead of fighting in it.

The relative merit of these two passages, as writing, is not
an important question. The first is a good enough piece of
impressionism, with undertones of E. E. Cummings and
Gertrude Stein. The style of the second passage, except for a
certain conversational quality, is almost colorless; it happens
to be the most effective way of recording a particular series
of words and actions; it aspires to no other virtue. The first
passage might add something to a book in which, the plot
being hackneyed or inconsequential, the emphasis had to be
placed on the writing, but *1919* is not a novel of that sort.
Again, the Camera Eye may justify itself in the next volume
of this trilogy—or tetralogy—by assuming a closer relation to

the story and binding together the different groups of characters; but in that case, I hope the style of it will change. So far it has been an element of disunity, a survival of the art novel in the midst of a different type of writing, and one in which Dos Passos excels.

He is, indeed, one of the few writers in whose case an equation can accurately and easily be drawn between social beliefs and artistic accomplishments. When he writes individualistically, with backward glances toward Imagism, Vorticism and the Insurrection of the Word, his prose is sentimental and without real distinction. When he writes as a social rebel, he writes not flawlessly by any means, but with conviction, power and a sense of depth, of striking through surfaces to the real forces beneath them. This last book, in which his political ideas have given shape to his emotions, and only the Camera Eye remains as a vestige of his earlier attitude, is not only the best of all his novels; it is, I believe, a landmark in American fiction.

(1932)

MALCOLM COWLEY

Tender is the Night

Tender Is the Night is a good novel that puzzles you and ends by making you a little angry because it isn't a great novel also. It doesn't give the feeling of being complete in itself.

The theme of it is stated in a conversation among the three principal characters. "What did this to him?" Rosemary asks. They are talking about Abe North, an American composer who became prominent shortly after World War I. He was shy and very talented; often he came to stay with Dick and Nicole Diver in their villa near the Cap d'Antibes and they scarcely knew he was there—"sometimes he'd be in the library with a muted piano, making love to it by the hour." But for years now he hadn't been working; his eyes had a hurt look; he got drunk every day as if trying to escape from nobody knew what. And Rosemary wondered, "Why does he have to drink?"

Nicole shook her head right and left, disclaiming responsibility for the matter: "So many smart men go to pieces nowadays."

"And when haven't they?" Dick asked. "Smart men play close to the line because they have to—some of them can't stand it, so they quit."

"It must lie deeper than that. . . . Artists like—well, like Fernand don't seem to have to wallow in alcohol. Why is it just Americans who dissipate?"

There were so many answers to this question that Dick decided to leave it in the air, to buzz victoriously in Nicole's ears.

The question remains victoriously buzzing in the reader's ears long after the story has ended. Fitzgerald tries to answer it, but obliquely. He tells us why Dr. Richard Diver went to pieces—because he married a rich woman and became so dependent on her money that his own work seemed unimportant and he no longer had a purpose in living; that is the principal reason, although he is also shaken by his love for Rosemary and by Nicole's recurrent fits of insanity, during one of which she came near killing not only her husband and herself but also their two children. Dick's case seems clear enough—but what about Abe North, whose wife was poor and sane and devoted? What about the other nice people who ended as lunatics or drunkards? Fitzgerald is continually suggesting and reiterating these questions that he leaves in the air.

The Divers and their friends are, in reality, the characters he has always written about, and written well. They are the richer members of his own generation, the young women who learned to smoke and pet in 1917 and the Yale and Princeton men who attended their coming-out parties in new uniforms.

In his early books, especially in *This Side of Paradise,* he celebrated the youth of these people in a tone of unmixed pride—"Here we are," he seemed to be saying, "the children of the conquerors, the free and beautiful and very wicked youngsters who are setting the standards for a nation." Later, when he described their business careers and their life in great country houses on the north shore of Long Island, his admiration began to be mixed with irony and disillusionment. In the present novel, which chronicles their years of exile, the admiration has almost completely vanished; the prevailing tone is one of disillusionment mixed with nostalgia. "We had good times together," Fitzgerald seems to say, "but that was a long time ago." Dick Diver is now an unsuccessful drunken country doctor, divorced and living somewhere in central New York State. Rosemary is an empty and selfish movie star; Abe North is dead, killed brawling in a speakeasy—all the kind and sensitive people of their circle have gone to pieces, and there remain only the "wooden and onanistic" women like Nicole's sister, only the *arrivistes* like Albert McKisco and the cultivated savages like Tommy Barban. A whole class has flourished and decayed and suddenly broken into fragments.

Here is a magnificent subject for a novel. The trouble is that Fitzgerald has never completely decided what kind of novel he wanted to write—whether it should center round a single hero or deal with a whole group. Both types of approach are present, the individual and the collective, and they interfere with each other. We are conscious of a divided purpose that perhaps goes back to a division in the author himself.

Fitzgerald has always been the poet of the American upper bourgeoisie; he has been the only writer able to invest their lives with glamor. Yet he has never been sure that he owed his loyalty to the class about which he was writing. It is as if he had a double personality. Part of him is a guest at the ball given by the people in the big house; part of him has been a little boy peeping in through the window and being thrilled by the music and the beautifully dressed women—a romantic but hard-headed little boy who stops every once in a while to wonder how much it all cost and where the money came from. (Fitzgerald says, "There is a streak of vulgarity in me that I try to cultivate.") In his early books, this divided personality was wholly an advantage: it enabled him to portray American society from the inside, and yet at the same time to surround it with an atmosphere of magic and romance that exists only in the eyes of people watching at the carriage entrance as the guests arrive in limousines. Since those days, however, the division has been emphasized and has become a liability. The little boy outside the window has grown mature and cold-eyed: from an enraptured spectator he has developed into a social historian. At the same time, part of Fitzgerald remains inside, among the dancers. And now that the ball is ending in tragedy, he doesn't know how to describe it—whether as a guest, a participant, in which case he will be writing a purely psychological novel; or whether from the detached point of view of a social historian.

There is another reason, too, for the technical faults of *Tender Is the Night*. Fitzgerald has been working on it at intervals for the last nine years, ever since he published *The Great Gatsby* in 1925. During these years his attitude has inevitably changed, as has that of every other sensitive writer. Yet no matter how much he revised his early chapters, he could not make them wholly agree with those written later—for once a chapter has assumed what seems to be a final shape, it undergoes a process of crystallization; it can no longer be remolded. The result is that several of his characters are self-contradictory: they don't merely change as living creatures change; they transform themselves into different people.

If I didn't like the book so much, I shouldn't have spoken at such length about its shortcomings. It has virtues that deserve more space than I can give them here. Especially it has a richness of meaning and emotion—one feels that every scene is selected among many possible scenes and that every event has pressure behind it. There is nothing false or borrowed in the book: everything is observed at first hand. Some of the minor figures—especially Gausse, the hotel keeper who was once a busboy in London, and Lady Caroline Sibley-Biers, who carries her English bad manners to the point of viciousness—are more vivid than Rosemary or Dick; and the encounter between Gausse and Lady Caroline is one of those enormous episodes in which two social castes are depicted melodramatically, farcically, and yet convincingly in a brief conversation and one gesture.

Fitzgerald says that this book is his farewell to the

members of his own generation; I hope he changes his mind. He has in him at least one great novel about them, and it is a novel that I want to read.

(1934)

MALCOLM COWLEY

Man's Fate

Man's Fate is a novel about the Chinese revolution written by a soldier of fortune who risked his life in the revolutionary cause, and yet it is not in essence a revolutionary or even a political novel. Brutal, tender, illuminating, it ends by casting more light on our own bourgeois society than on the Chinese Communists who died to change it.

This doesn't mean that it shows political events in false perspective. Malraux is writing about two days that helped to decide the history of China. On March 21, 1927, the Communists of Shanghai declared a general strike and, acting in alliance with Chiang Kai-shek, seized control of the largest city on the Asiatic mainland. Many people then believed that all China would go Communist quickly and without much bloodshed. Chiang Kai-shek had Russian officers training his troops and Russian political advisers; the great formless mass of peasants and coolies was leavened with Communist ideas. But three weeks later, on April 11, Chiang betrayed his Communist allies, dissolved their labor unions, captured their local posts and executed all his prisoners after torturing most of them; the Communist leaders were boiled in vats of oil or thrust living into the fireboxes of locomotives. The streets of the big cities ran with blood, but the revolution continued to live in the countryside, where the peasants were beginning to organize their own soviets. Malraux not only participated in these events: he has since reflected on their political meaning and has learned to estimate the part that was played in them by personal ambitions, by foreign money, by class antagonisms. Everything he says about the Chinese revolution seems keen and convincing.

But the revolution, instead of being his principal theme, is the setting and the pretext for a novel that is, in reality, a drama of individual lives. It is true that these lives are bound together by a single emotion, but this emotion is not the desire to revolt or to achieve justice. Malraux's real theme is a feeling that most men nurse, secretly, their sense of absolute loneliness and uniqueness, their acknowledgment to themselves of inadequacy in the face of life and helplessness against death—that is what he means by *la condition humaine;* this is man's lot, his destiny, his servitude. And he has chosen to depict this emotion during a revolutionary period because it is then carried, like everything else that is human, to its pitch of highest intensity.

All of his characters, though drawn from different nations and ranks of society, are obsessed by this feeling of personal solitude. All of them try to escape from it, either through dissipation or else through establishing a bond with others at the cost of no matter what sacrifice. Thus, little Ch'en, the former student in a missionary college, escapes from his loneliness by adopting terrorism as a career; he wants to found a religion of political murder and self-immolation— finally, clutching a bomb in his hand, he hurls himself under the automobile in which he thinks Chiang Kai-shek is riding. Ferral, the banker and exploiter, tries to escape from his own sterility by dominating others, and ends by despising them only a little more than he despises himself. Clappique tries to evade his personality by playing imaginary roles; he keeps repeating that "the Baron de Clappique does not exist." May finds her escape in love, and Katov finds his in an absolute devotion to the revolutionary cause. Old Gisors, the French philosopher who used to teach at the University of Peking, has two means of avoiding himself; opium and his love for Kyo, his son by a Japanese wife; after Kyo's death, he has only opium.

As for Kyo Gisors, the hero of the novel, "his life had a meaning, and he knew what it was: to give to each of these men whom famine, at this very moment, was killing like a slow plague, the sense of his own dignity." It was through his love for human dignity that Kyo became a Communist, and through dignity, too, that he met his death. On April 11, the one man who might have saved his life was Konig, the German commander of Chiang Kai-shek's secret police—and Konig, having forfeited all respect for himself during the civil war in Russia, had learned to hate every man who was not self-seeking and a coward. When Kyo refused to betray his comrades, Konig ordered him to be taken to Section A, the part of the prison reserved for those who were to be burned to death.

Man's Fate is a novel packed tight with contradictions: one feels in it the dilemma of people ill prepared by a peaceful childhood to face one of the most brutal and cataclysmic periods in human history. It is a philosophical novel in which the philosophy is expressed in terms of violent actions. It is a novel about the East that expresses the soul rather of the West. It is a novel written sympathetically about Communists by a man whose own mentality has strong traces of Fascism (perhaps this explains why it has been so popular in Italy) and a novel about proletarian heroes in which the technique is that developed by the Symbolists of the Ivory Tower. It is a good novel too, extraordinarily rich in characters and perceptions, and yet it becomes difficult to read—the emotions are so taut that one feels the need of laying down the book, lighting a cigarette, turning on the radio, doing anything to break the intolerable tension.

But if one persists, one comes at last to a scene as

tragically stirring as anything in modern literature. It is a
scene that might be compared with the terrible chapter in
The Possessed in which Kirillov is ordered to commit suicide
and finally obeys, except that Malraux is describing several
suicides and around them two hundred prisoners waiting for
the firing squad—the whole thing is magnified to the point of
intolerable melodrama, and yet is rendered true and humanly
bearable by the feeling of brotherhood existing among the
prisoners. . . . Katov, the old revolutionist, is lying wounded
in the famous Section A, which is nothing but a half-empty
space along the wall of a crowded prison yard. Beside him in
the darkness lies the dead body of Kyo, who has taken the
cyanide that all members of the Communist Central
Committee kept hidden in their square belt buckles as a final
means of escaping their tortures. Katov, too, has his cyanide
and is waiting to use it. Two new prisoners, young Chinese,
are brought into Section A; they have no poison and know
that for them there is no possible escape from being thrown
into the firebox of the locomotive whistling outside the
prison (all this, I might add, is a faithful picture of what
happened that night in Shanghai; Malraux doesn't
exaggerate). The two young men are weeping and Katov gives
them his cyanide to divide between them; it is his supreme
sacrifice.

But the scene doesn't end there; if it did, one might
conceivably forget it instead of lying awake to brood over it.
One of the young men has been wounded in the hand; he
drops both the little packages of poison; and the three of
them grope in the darkness among the pebbles and bits of
broken plaster that litter the prison yard, looking for death as
if they were looking for diamonds. This is the picture that
sticks in one's mind—this and the sense of pitiful fraternity
among the three searchers, expressed in a few words
whispered by one of the young Chinese when he suddenly
took Katov's hand, pressed it and held it. "Even if we don't
find it . . ." he said. A moment later the two boys clutched
the poison and gulped it down.

Malraux is saying that here in the prison yard, the effort to escape from man's solitude and the search for a purpose by which life is dignified both found their goal. The individual dramas and the great revolutionary drama merged into each other. Here in the darkness, Katov poured himself out in "that absolute friendship, without reticence, which death alone gives"; and here among his comrades condemned to be burned alive, Kyo felt that "he was dying, like each of these men, because he had given a meaning to his life. What would have been the value of a life for which he would not have been willing to die? It is easy to die when one does not die alone."

(1934)

MALCOLM COWLEY

Native Son

Native Son is the most impressive American novel I have read since *The Grapes of Wrath*. In some ways the two books resemble each other: both deal with the dispossessed and both grew out of the radical movement of the 1930s. There is, however, a distinction to be drawn between the motives of the two authors. Steinbeck, more privileged than the characters in his novel, wrote out of deep pity for them, and the fault he had to avoid was sentimentality. Richard Wright, a Negro, was moved by wrongs he had suffered in his own person, and what he had to fear was a blind anger that might destroy the pity in him, making him hate any character whose skin was whiter than his own. His first book, *Uncle Tom's Children,* had not completely avoided that fault. It was a collection of stories all but one of which had the same pattern: a Negro was goaded into killing one or more white men and was killed in turn, without feeling regret for himself or his victims. Some of the stories I found physically painful to read, even though I admired them. So deep was the author's sense of the indignities heaped on his race that one felt he was revenging himself by a whole series of symbolic murders. In *Native Son* the pattern is the same, but the author's sympathies have broadened and his resentment, though just as deep, is less painful and personal.

The hero, Bigger Thomas, is a Negro boy of twenty, a poolroom loafer, a bully, a liar and a petty thief. "Bigger, sometimes I wonder why I birthed you," his pious mother tells him. "Honest, you the most no-countest man I ever seen in all my life." A Chicago philanthropist tries to help the family by hiring him as chauffeur. That same night Bigger kills the philanthropist's daughter—out of fear of being discovered in her room—and stuffs her body into the furnace. This half-accidental crime leads to others. Bigger tries to cast the blame for the girl's disappearance on her lover, a Communist; he tries to collect a ransom from her parents; after the body is found he murders his Negro mistress to keep her from betraying him to the police. The next day he is captured on the snow-covered roof of a South Side tenement, while a mob howls in the street below.

In the last part of the book, which is also the best, we learn that the case of Bigger Thomas is not the author's deepest concern. Behind it is another, more complicated story he is trying hard to explain, though the words come painfully at first, and later come in a flood that almost sweeps him away. "Listen, you white folks," he seems to be saying over and over. "I want to tell you about all the Negroes in America. I want to tell you how they live and how they feel. I want you to change your minds about them before it is too late to prevent a worse disaster than any we have known. I speak for my own people, but I speak for America too." And because he does speak for and to the nation, without ceasing to be a Negro, his book has more force than any other American novel by a member of his race.

Bigger, he explains, had been trained from the beginning to be a bad citizen. He had been taught American ideals of life, in the schools, in the magazines, in the cheap movie houses, but had been denied any means of achieving them.

Everything he wanted to have or do was reserved for the whites. "I just can't get used to it," he tells one of his poolroom buddies. "I swear to God I can't .... Every time I think about it I feel like somebody's poking a red-hot iron down my throat."

At the trial, his white-haired Jewish lawyer makes a final plea to the judge for mercy. "What Bigger Thomas did early that Sunday morning in the Dalton home and what he did that Sunday night in the empty building was but a tiny aspect of what he had been doing all his life long. He was *living,* only as he knew how, and as we have forced him to live.... The hate and fear which we have inspired in him, woven by our civilization into the very structure of his consciousness, into his blood and bones, into the hourly functioning of his personality, have become the justification of his existence.... Every thought he thinks is potential murder."

This long courtroom speech, which sums up the argument of the novel, is at once its strongest and its weakest point. It is strongest when Mr. Max is making a plea for the American Negroes in general. "They are not simply twelve million people; in reality they constitute a separate nation, stunted, stripped and held captive *within* this nation." Many of them—and many white people too—are full of "balked longing for some kind of fulfillment and exultation"; and their existence is "what makes our future seem a looming image of violence." In this context, Mr. Max's talk of another civil war seems not so much a threat as an agonized warning. But his speech is weakest as a plea for the individual life of Bigger Thomas. It did not convince the judge, and I doubt that it will convince many readers.

It is not that I think Bigger "deserved" the death sentence for his two murders. Most certainly his guilt was shared by the society that condemned him. But when he killed Mary Dalton he was performing the first free action in his whole fear-tortured life; he was accepting his first moral responsibility. That is what he tried so hard to explain to his lawyer. "I ain't worried none about them women I killed. ... I killed 'em 'cause I was scared and mad. But I been scared and mad all my life and after I killed that first woman, I wasn't scared no more for a little while." And when his lawyer asks him if he ever thought he would face the electric chair, "Now I come to think of it," he answers, "it seems like something like this just had to be." If Mr. Max had managed to win a life sentence for Bigger Thomas, he would have robbed him of his only claim to human courage and dignity. But that Richard Wright makes us feel this, while setting out to prove something else—that he makes Bigger Thomas a human rather than a racial symbol—shows that he wrote an even better novel than he had planned.

(1940)

MICHAEL CRICHTON

Slaughterhouse-Five

A look at the bookstore shelves will prove it: science fiction is coming back. After a dry period in the early sixties, people are beginning to read it again, and write it. The renewed interest has carried into other fields as well, particularly television and films: "Star Trek" gathered a vociferous and cultish following; a paperback version of "Fantastic Voyage" sold more than a million copies; Stanley Kubrick's "2001" was the most expensive science fiction film ever made.

The diehard sci-fi addict will view all this with pleasure and a grim sense of vindication, for it has traditionally been true that one cannot acceptably admit to a taste for science fiction, except among scientists or teenagers. And these two groups share a strikingly low standard of literary attainment, and a correspondingly high tolerance for mangled prose.

Certainly the new ventures in films and television represent improvements over, say, Steve McQueen fighting "The Blob," or Buzz Corry of the "Spa-a-a-ace Patrol!" But this is not to say that science fiction is any better now, as literature, than it ever was. A look at the bookstore shelves will prove this, too: the vast majority of science fiction writing is abysmal. It is perhaps paradoxical that our most technologically advanced fiction should also be the most technically inadequate. Most science fiction writers cannot put together a literate sentence; only a handful can create a reasonable character; perhaps a dozen, at most, can sustain a simple plot.

There is no good explanation for the ineptitude of science fiction, as fiction. There is a commercial explanation (that the readers will put up with this stuff); there is a historical one (that science fiction has its origins in pulp fiction). And there is another: that science fiction represents, as a form, a subordination of all fictional elements to an idea—just as detective fiction represents a subordination of all elements to plot.

Only the commercial explanation, which is really no more than a simple observation of verifiable fact, holds water; the others are demonstrably wrong. For example, nearly all fictional forms have come from pulp, or its equivalent in previous generations. The majority of "classic" authors were very popular in their day. And when one surveys the great triad of pulp writing—science fiction, westerns, and detective fiction—from the early part of this century, the results are interesting. Westerns, being closest to the heart of American mythology, have been almost entirely absorbed by the ubiquitous tube. Detectives have done well in films, less well on television; in straight fiction their standards have been raised markedly, partly because "real" authors like Conrad and Graham Greene have dabbled in the form and partly because talented writers have been drawn to it—Raymond Chandler, David Cornwall, and Georges Simenon. But science fiction has remained impervious to such influences. It is still as pulpy, and as awful, as ever.

Nor can the argument that science fiction relies upon the idea over all other elements be sustained. Jules Verne and H. G. Wells between them laid out nearly all the problems, and all the gadgetry, which have since become science fiction staples. These authors are no longer widely read, not because their ideas are wrong—indeed, to an astonishing degree they are correct—but because their prancing romanticism, their treatment of ideas, has fallen out of favor.

Much of the resurgence represents a reissue of old names and old titles, from Asimov to Van Vogt, in the kind of publishing cycle that affects all fiction. But there is also new material with new origins and different sources of popularity. And all of it gives reason to believe that science fiction is about to undergo the kind of change that affected detective fiction twenty years ago.

Things have happened. Our world is changing rapidly, and as the pace of scientific development accelerates, there is a growing public tolerance for science fiction, a sense that nothing is too fantastic to be impossible. Since new developments produce new uncertainty and flux, readers look to science fiction for views of the future—sometimes, with the utmost seriousness. A number of science fiction writers are now employed as consultants to large corporations, where they are paid to predict future trends of business.

Furthermore, the drug experience has opened a new realm for writers in all fields, but perhaps for obvious reasons, it is most easily exploited by writers of fantasy and science fiction. The Hashbury hippies made a kind of bible out of Robert Heinlein's *Stranger in a Strange Land;* Leary and the Airplane grokked sister lovers and water brothers, and in time maybe others. Other science fiction writers, each as J. G. Ballard and Roger Zelazny, have joined the druggie panoply of literary heroes, which includes that old acid-head John Barth, that old juice-freak Malcolm Lowry, W. Y. Evans-Wentz, Céline, Melville, Jorges Luis Borges, P. D. Ouspensky, and Herman Hesse. Conspicuously absent are the old guard of the left wing, Huxley and Orwell; their books are found in the classroom, not the pad.

As a category, the borders of science fiction have always been poorly defined, and they are getting worse. The old distinction between science fiction and fantasy—that science fiction went from the known to the probable, and fantasy dealt with the impossible—is now wholly ignored. The new writing is heavily and unabashedly fantastical.

The breakdown is also seen in the authors themselves, who now cross the border, back and forth, with impunity. At one time this was dangerous and heretical; the only person who could consistently get away with it was Ray Bradbury. Science fiction addicts politely looked the other way when he did books such as *Dandelion Wine* and the screenplay for John Huston's "Moby Dick." It was assumed he needed the money.

Furthermore, many of the traditional science fiction preserves have been invaded by highly skilled authors, equipped to work on a very high level. Modern science stands as a vast and largely untouched reservoir of metaphor, but very recently a number of "real" authors have begun to draw upon it in various ways. One thinks immediately of Nabokov, Updike and Donleavy, and in a sloppy-effective way, Norman Mailer. (C. P. Snow, as the scientist-novelist most likely to employ the metaphors of science in the service of literature, has shown no inclination to do so, but continues to write about life in the thirteenth century.) It is inevitable that these skilled writers will destroy much of science fiction as a category, just as some of them have begun to put the sex-exploitation novel out of business by writing better novels about sex.

Invading a category is, however, much easier than leaving it. To leave the world of category fiction, with its special section in the bookstores, its special reviewers and its special readerships, is both hazardous and difficult. Witness Georges Simenon, who has had extraordinary trouble gaining acceptance in this country as anything other than a detective writer. But the transition is being attempted, with at least one notable success.

Exhibit A: Kurt Vonnegut, Jr.

When I was growing up, everybody knew damn well what Kurt Vonnegut, Jr. was. He was a science fiction writer. It said so, in the high school textbooks where his stories were reprinted. And what do you call *Player Piano* and *The Sirens of Titan* if not science fiction?

Some years ago, he began to drift, but by then there was a new category, black humor, and Vonnegut got stuck into that one. The company was a little more reputable, but the category remained. He was doing *God Bless You, Mr. Rosewater, Mother Night,* and *Cat's Cradle.* It seemed pretty blackly humorous, all right. And if he didn't have anything nasty to say about his mother, well, he'd get around to it. He was witty and he was grim, and that was enough.

However, with *Cat's Cradle* he began to get some attention. It came from varied sources: Conrad Aiken, Graham Greene, Marc Connolly and Jules Feiffer, to name a few. Greene called him one of the best living American writers. That sort of comment is guaranteed to make you an "in" writer. He was compared to Jonathan Swift.

That is not to say that he has been greated with unrestrained enthusiasm by all critics. Reviews of his latest book, *Slaughterhouse-Five,* have dragged out the old complaints: Vonnegut is too cute, Vonnegut is precious, Vonnegut is silly.

We live in an age of great seriousness. We are accustomed to getting our art in heavy, pretentious doses. Anything funny is suspect, and anything simple is doubly suspect. Here we come to the second difficulty with Kurt Vonnegut. His style is effortless, naive, almost childlike. There are no big words and no complicated sentences. It is an extraordinarily difficult style, but that fact is lost on anyone who has never tried to write that way.

A funny, simple writer is in trouble nowadays. And Vonnegut doesn't make it any easier for you. He is cheerfully, exuberantly schizophrenic.

The man who wrote a book with a stated moral, "We are what we pretend to be, so we must be careful about what we pretend to be," has described himself by saying, "Imagine me as the White Rock girl, kneeling on a boulder in a nightgown, either looking for minnows or adoring my own reflection."

The man who says "this is a hard world to be ludicrous in" admits "to have lived scenes from a woman's magazine"—and to have written those same scenes, in a woman's magazine.

"When you're dead, you're dead," he observes, but he also says, "My brand is Pall Mall. The authentic suicides ask for Pall Malls . . ." Of his writing, he has said, "I realize now that the two main themes of my novels were stated by my siblings: 'Here I am cleaning shit off of practically everything,' and 'No Pain.' " This statement is as true as anything a writer has said of his work; it is also the reason why Vonnegut is so difficult to accept.

He writes about the most excruciatingly painful things. His novels have attacked our deepest fears of automation and the bomb, our deepest political guilts, our fiercest hatreds and loves. Nobody else writes books on these subjects; they are inaccessible to normal novelistic approaches. But Vonnegut, armed with his schizophrenia, takes an absurd, distorted, wildly funny framework which is ultimately anaesthetic. In doing so, his science-fiction heritage is clear, but his purposes are very different: he is nearly always talking about the past, not the future. And as he proceeds, from his anaesthetic framework, to clean the shit off, we are able to cheer him on—at least for a while. But eventually we stop cheering, and stop laughing.

It is a classic sequence of reactions to any Vonnegut book. One begins smugly, enjoying the sharp wit of a compatriot as he carves up Common Foes. But the sharp wit does not stop, and sooner or later it is directed against the Wrong Targets. Finally it is directed against oneself. It is this switch in midstream, this change in affiliation, which is so disturbing. He becomes an offensive writer, because he will not choose sides, ascribing blame and penalty, identifying good guys and bad.

Mother Night, the clearest antecendent to *Slaughterhouse Five,* begins by giving it to the Nazis. That's all right. Then Vonnegut gives it to the Jews, then the American right wing, then the left wing, then the Negroes, then the happily marrieds—and finally manages to reduce any social or political affiliation to total absurdity, while we look on with increasing horror. It is an astonishing book, very gentle and funny and quiet and totally destructive. Nobody escapes without being shown, in a polite way what an ass he is. (And interestingly, the left-wing political activists, who generally count Vonnegut among their number, all have somehow never found time to read this particular book.)

A Vonnegut book is not cute or precious. It is literally awful, for Vonnegut is one of the few writers able to lift the lid of the garbage can, and dispassionately examine the contents. In *Slaughterhouse-Five,* the author quotes his father as saying. "You never wrote a story with a villain in it." This may be true, but Vonnegut never wrote a story with a hero in it, either. In *Slaughterhouse-Five* he also says, "Nobody was ridiculous or bad or disgusting," and it is within this framework that he writes about an event that should qualify for all those adjectives—the fire-bombing of Dresden, which Vonnegut experienced as a prisoner of war in Germany.

There is every indication that this book represents, for Vonnegut, a final statement of his thoughts about this experience. He says so explicitly, just as he says the project is doomed to failure ("There is nothing intelligent to say about a massacre"). The book also brings together characters and locales from other books—Howard W. Campbell, Jr., Eliot Rosewater, and Ilium, N.Y., giving the novel a faintly anthological flavor. The book is written in the brief segmental manner he developed in *Cat's Cradle,* organized as a collection of impressions, scattered in time and space, each told with the kind of economy one associates with poetry. It is beautifully done, fluid, smooth, and powerful.

There is also some business about a distant planet and flying saucers, but that does not make the book science fiction, any more than flippers make a cat a penguin. In the final analysis the book is hideous, ghastly, murderous—and calm. There are just people, doing what people usually do to each other.

The ultimate difficulty with Vonnegut is precisely this: that he refuses to say who is wrong. The simplest way out of such a predicament is to say that everybody is wrong but the author. Any number of writers have done it, with good success. But Vonnegut refuses. He ascribes no blame, sets no penalties. His commentary on the assassination of Robert Kennedy and Martin Luther King is the same as his comment on all other deaths: "So it goes," he says, and nothing more.

One senses that underneath it all, Vonnegut is a nice man, who doesn't really like to have to say this, but . . . his discription of one character might stand for all mankind in his view: "She had been given the opportunity to participate in civilization, and she had muffed it." And of himself, a comment by another character, the author Nazi-propagandist-pornographer-American spy Howard W. Campbell, Jr. "I speak gibberish to the civilized world, and it replies in kind."

So it goes.

(1969)

107

WILLIAM FAULKNER

The Road Back

There is a victory beyond defeat which the victorious know nothing of. A bourne, a shore of refuge beyond the lost battles, the bronze names and the lead tombs, guarded and indicated not by the triumphant and man-limbed goddess with palm and sword, but by some musing and motionless handmaiden of despair itself.

Man does not seem to be able to stand very much prosperity; least of all does a people, a nation. Defeat is good for him, for it. Victory is the rocket, the glare, the momentary apotheosis at right angles with time and so doomed: a bursting diffusion of sparks at the last, dying and dead, leaving a word perhaps, a name, a date, for the tedium of children in primary history. It is the defeat which, serving him against his belief and his desire, turns him back upon that alone which can sustain him: his fellows, his racial homogeneity; himself; the earth, the implacable soil, monument and tomb of sweat.

This is beyond the talking, the hard words, the excuses and the reasons; beyond the despair. Beyond that dreadful desire and need to justify the disaster and give it significance by clinging to it, explaining it, which is the proven best way to support the inescapable. Victory requires no explanation. It is in itself sufficient: the fine screen, the shield; immediate and final: it will be contemplated only by history. While the whole contemporary world watches the defeat and the undefeated who, because of that fact, survived.

That's where the need to talk, to explain it, comes from. That's why Remarque puts into the mouths of characters speeches which they would have been incapable of making. It's not that the speeches were not true. If the characters had heard them spoken by another, they would have been the first to say, "That is so. This is what I think, what I would have said if I had just thought of it first." But they could not have said the speeches themselves. And this method is not justified, unless a man is writing propaganda. It is a writer's privilege to put into the mouths of his characters better speech than they would have been capable of, but only for the purpose of permitting and helping the character to justify himself or what he believes himself to be, taking down his spiritual pants. But when the character must express moral ideas applicable to a race, a situation, he is better kept in that untimed and unsexed background of the choruses of Greek senators.

But perhaps this is a minor point. Perhaps it is a racial fault of the author, as the outcome of the War was due in part to a German racial fault: a belief that a mathematical calculation would be superior to the despair of cornered rats. Anyway, Remarque justifies himself: ". . . I try to console him. What I say does not convince him, but it gives me some relief. . . . It is always so with comfort."

It is a moving book. Because Remarque was moved by the writing of it. Granted that his intent is more than opportunism, it still remains to be seen if art can be made of authentic experience transferred to paper word for word, of a peculiar reaction to an actual condition, even though it be vicarious. To a writer, no matter how susceptible he be, personal experience is just what it is to the man in the street who buttonholes him because he is a writer, with the same belief, the same conviction of individual significance:"Listen. All you have to do is write it down as it happened. My life, what has happened to me. It will make a good book, but I am not a writer myself. So I will give it to you. If I were a writer myself, had the time to write it down myself. You won't have to change a word." That does not make a book. No matter how vivid it be, somewhere between the experience and the blank page and the pencil, it dies. Perhaps the words kill it.

Give Remarque the benefit of the doubt and call the book a reaction to despair. Victory has its despairs, too, since the victorious not only do not gain anything, but when the hurrah dies away at last, they do not even know what they were fighting for, what they hoped to gain, because what little percentage there was in the whole affair, the defeated got it. If Germany had been victorious, this book would not have been written. And if the United States had not got back its troops fifty-percent intact, save for the casual cases of syphilis and high metropolitan life, it would not be bought (which I hope and trust that it will be) and read. And it won't be the American Legion either that will buy the 40,000 copies, even if there are forty thousand of them that keep their dues paid up.

It moves you, as watching a child making mud pies on the day of its mother's funeral moves you. Yet at the end there is still that sense of missing significance, the feeling that, like so much that emerges from a losing side in any contest, and particularly from Germany since 1918, it was created primarily for the Western trade, to sell among the heathen like colored glass. From beyond the sentimentality, the defeat and the talking, this fact at least has emerged: America has been conquered not by the German soldiers that died in French and Flemish trenches, but by the German soldiers that died in German books.

(1931)

JOSEPH FEATHERSTONE

Katherine Anne Porter's Stories

This harvest of nearly perfect short novels and stories has been a long, careful time in the gathering. It contains three collections: *Flowering Judas* (first published in 1930 and expanded in 1935), *Pale Horse, Pale Rider* (1939), and *The Leaning Tower* (1944). Miss Porter has added four uncollected stories, one of which, "Holiday," ranks with her best.

There is not much besides this, for a lifetime's work. There is her novel, *Ship of Fools,* a slight collection of essays, and a biography of Cotton Mather still in progress. *Ship of Fools* is an extraordinary accomplishment, a kind of Pauline epistle for our times, but my guess is that Katherine Anne Porter's claim to greatness can rest on these novels and stories. Few writers in America or anywhere else have matched the purity of her English, her powers of deep poetic concentration, her intelligence, her responsiveness to the inner life of her characters, her sharp sense of the pressing forces of history, nationality, and social atmosphere.

She is a contemporary of Faulkner, and although she has always stood completely alone as a literary figure, her art suggests some reflections on the First World War generation of American writers whose restless search for values and experiments with form introduced Americans to the modern age. She, too, questioned all that she inherited. She threw off the beliefs she was raised with, the quaint, hypocritical notions about the family, the human personality, love, art. This generation was through with all that. It was setting up a new order in the world. Politics and literature were going to be wholly transformed.

For her, disillusionment with the programs of the modern age seems to have started in revolutionary Mexico, the setting for "Flowering Judas." In the dark decades that followed she concluded that newness was not in itself a virtue. (Neither, of course, was age.) A new word, a new fashion in thought, was apt to be a dodge for a writer's poverty of feeling or his inability to reason, and a new political slogan was probably, like the old slogans, a lie.

Only rare souls ever profit from the general historical experience of their times, and what we call the lessons of history are often other names for heartbreak and weariness. Katherine Anne Porter has, however, reached a kind of wisdom that a few Americans do achieve. It is the wisdom of those whose identity is a conscious reconstruction of their instincts, who have come to terms with the past they rebelled against, and who see themselves in the world with lucid impersonality. At their best, Americans like Miss Porter, or George Kennan, combine moral passion with a sense of moral complexity; their irony is profound, and its intention is never simply ironic.

She has lived much of her life outside this country, and few writers can equal her for sheer variety of characters and settings. She does city people, Texas blackland farmers, Mexicans, the American Irish, German-Americans and Germans in Germany; of all classes and generations. She never celebrates a region, although many of her stories might be called local color pieces. She gives the bitter essence of what a people's life is like, as if she were sketching an abstract stage set, and then concentrates on the dramatic revelation of character in the created setting. At the end of "The Cracked Looking Glass," a short novel of the American Irish, the reader learns the sad, specific poetry of a young girl married to an aging husband:

Here in the lamplight sat Dennis and the cats, beyond in the darkness and snow lay Winston and New York and Boston, and beyond that were far off places full of life and gayety she'd never seen nor even heard of, and beyond everything like a green field with morning sun on it lay youth and Ireland, as if they were something she had dreamed or made up in a story. . . .

She sat up and felt his sleeves carefully. "I want you to wrap up warm this bitter weather, Dennis," she told him. "With two pairs of socks and the chest protector, for if anything happened to you, whatever would become of me in this world?"

"Let's not think of it," said Dennis.

"Let's not then," said Rosaleen, "For I could cry if you crooked a finger at me."

The local color pieces lack the dense web of associations, the amount of felt living, memory and contemplation that go into the more autobiographical stories. But in their bleak, abstracted way, they are splendid. Mexican stories, like the flawless "Maria Concepcion," have the beautiful and hollow ring of formal tragedy. "Hacienda" is a tale of some Russian filmmakers in Mexico to shoot a revolutionary epic—in real life the Russian director was Eisenstein—and through their tangled failures we begin to see what the camera captures, "the almost ecstatic death-expectancy which is in the air of Mexico," the peasant figures under a doom imposed by the landscape.

Some of her stories might be called political. Few apart from "Flowering Judas" bear directly on politics, but her historical and social sense is like a fine antenna, and certain pieces shimmer with the ominous presence of history. She has been haunted by the times. Shortly after the fall of France in 1940 she wrote: "For myself, and I was not alone, all the conscious and recollected years of my life have been lived under the heavy threat of world catastrophe, and most of the energies of my mind and spirit have been spent in the effort to grasp the meaning of those threats, to trace them to their sources and to understand the logic of this majestic and terrible failure of the life of man in the Western world."

There is a link between manners and politics, between our private, even our unconscious, selves and the world of public events. Politics is ordering people's affairs in certain regular patterns. Here, as elsewhere, there should be a balance between the patterns and the feelings they are supposed to organize and express; a proper tension between the forms of society and the instincts of its men and women. The characters in her two great political stories have let the tension between emotion and form slip and break. Laura, the heroine of "Flowering Judas," describes the resulting confusion: "It is monstrous to confuse love with revolution, night with day, life with death."

The gluttonous bulk of Braggioni [the Mexican revolutionary leader] has become a symbol of her many disillusions . . . she is, her comrades tell her, full of romantic error, for what she defines as cynicism in them is merely "a developed sense of reality". . . . But she cannot help feeling that she has been betrayed irreparably by the disunion between her way of living and her feeling of what life should be. . . .

This irreparable betrayal is also evoked in "The Leaning Tower," her superb short novel of Berlin in the early thirties. Through a series of terrifying images of shattered private lives, the story renders the drabness, the sadism, and the violence of Berlin in the inter-war years. The Germans manifest an extreme of the modern sickness; their desires and their actual lives, like skew lines, never intersect. They dream of far-off places, Pisa, Paris, Malaga, sunny, enchanted lands that look impossibly bright from the darkness of their defeated hopes. Here, as in *Ship of Fools,* is the rage, malice, and deception of the modern, the self-pity struggling in a last spasm to become pity, the outraged self-love striving to become love. ("Love me," say the Germans in *Ship of Fools,* "love me in spite of all! Whether or not I love you, whether I am fit to love, whether you are able to love, even if there is no such thing as love, love me!") The young American hero in "The Leaning Tower" senses that somehow the usual boundaries between people, even friends, fail to work; the Germans are too intimate. In their weakness they lean on an artificial ideal of harmony, the murderous illusion of a fellowship of race. They are misfits, cranks, political nitwits, torn between maudlin self-indulgence and grateful submission to the stupid splendors of authority. Violence hovers in the thin winter air: The young American looks at a fresh, swelling wound that will one day be a proud dueling scar and senses that he will never understand such things. Even trivial happenings connect to this undertow of violence. It comes as a shock to the figures in the political stories, but they are filled with suppressed, unfulfilled longings, and violence is really the end point, the final logic, of their crippled relationships. It is the external sign of an inner lack of grace. Even love, which of course everyone pursues, is often a subtle, veiled aspect of violence, its ritual counterpart. In the end of "The Leaning Tower," the American feels "an infernal desolation of the spirit, the chill and the knowledge of death in him."

What elusive, living spirit the modern age crushes, what natural rightness it destroys, is not altogether clear. Here and there are a few clean images and happy scenes, bright coins thrown into the threatening sea. They occur most often in the large number of stories dealing with Miss Porter's native Texas. Her Texas was the South, for it was peopled by Southerners from Virginia, Tennessee, the Carolinas, and Kentucky; and the values by which she judges the world derive from her family experiences in what she has called the Old Order. It must be understood, however, that the derivation is exceedingly subtle. (As well as selective: There are, for example, few traces in her art of her Catholic upbringing.) She has too much critical moral intelligence to become a genteel celebrant of the Southern heritage. There is

115

even less of that in her than in Faulkner. She is, after all, a Southerner in exile. Still, the Texas stories—or rather the family experiences they are distilled from—seem to be the ultimate source of her sense of things in their right proportions.

Just how subtle the derivation is may be seen in an autobiographical short novel, "Old Mortality," set in Texas in three spans of time between 1885 and 1912. There are many characters, each so vividly drawn that the story achieves the dense effect of a much longer work. The narrative is anecdotal, lingering over odd details and bits of family history in a deceptively casual way. The theme is every child's problem, making the stories grownups tell match reality as it begins to unfold. In this case the story is the rich tapestry of romance the family has woven around the figure of an Aunt Amy. As young Miranda's parents tell it, Amy's life touched their youth with poetry, "the nobility of human feeling, the divinity of man's vision of the unseen, the importance of life and death, the depths of the human heart, the romantic value of tragedy." Miranda and her sister examine the old, sepia-tinted photographs of Amy trying to reconstruct the legendary age of their parents' youth, the days of dark beauties pale as death, high-sounding words, eternal loves, and duels in the moonlight; for the children are held, as each new generation is, by the love of the living for what the faded relics and ribbons represent.

Growing up, alas, is a series of disillusionments. And in the final portion of the novel, Miranda returns home, a married woman now, to a funeral. On the train she meets old Cousin Eva, a spinster suffragette with a weak chin. Eva is the muckraking voice of the modern era, and she has a very different interpretation of the legends of magnolias and moonshine surrounding Amy and her circle. To Eva, the disenchanted modern, the legend is best debunked in terms of money and biology:

"It was just sex," [Eva] said in despair, "their minds dwelt on nothing else. They didn't call it that, it was all smothered under pretty names, but that's all it was, sex . . . so they simply festered inside, . . ."

116

Miranda is appalled by this modern portrait of corruption under the lace and flowers of the Old Order, but she realizes that Eva's debunking is no more credible than the family romance. Still, the talk with Eva chills her, and she yearns to feel once again the solid and reassuring presence of her father. A curious thing happens when everyone arrives home: Miranda sees that her pious father and skeptical Cousin Eva belong together in some mysterious way. They view the past by radically different lights, but it is their past together, and Miranda is excluded from their fellowship. The older generation has a complicity of experience that Miranda will never share.

Miranda ends by resenting the bitter love of her family, who

... denied her the right to look at the world with her own eyes, who demanded that she accept their version of life, and yet could not tell her the truth, not in the smallest thing. What is the truth, she asked herself, as intently as if the question had never been asked. . . . At least I can know the truth about what happens to me, she assured herself silently, making a promise to herself in her hopefulness, her ignorance.

The ironic last word closes the story with a snap and changes its whole meaning. Perhaps her truths about her own time will be like those of Cousin Eva and her father, the sort of truths that have meaning only for those who earn them with their lives, truths that to another set of eyes might be lies. Perhaps Miranda's memories will also be legends which another new generation will misunderstand and rebel against. At least what she wins will be her own truth; that will be something, but that will be all.

Thus "Old Mortality" shows some of the complexity of Miss Porter's relation to the Southern past she rebelled against. Much of that past is bogus, and what is worth saving, ironically, has to be re-created by each generation at a fearful cost. Some of the old truths are true; you find out which ones in the course of living a life.

I think her best stories are those of the Old South and Texas. In them, she creates, illumines, and places the tight family of the Old Order, with its accumulated weight of traditional living and its foolish conviction that the world would never change. The great theme of these stories is the initiation of young Miranda into a knowledge of the forces of cruelty, sexuality, and death. The symbolism of life and death is handled with power and delicacy—here, for example, in its detailed loveliness, is the description of what happens when the children are hunting and Miranda's brother shoots a rabbit that is with young:

Very carefully he slit the thin flesh from the center ribs to the flanks, and a scarlet bag appeared. He slit again and pulled the bag open, and there lay a bundle of tiny rabbits, each wrapped in a thin scarlet veil. The brother pulled these off and there they were, dark grey, their sleek wet down lying in minute even ripples, like a baby's head just washed, their unbelievably small delicate ears folded close, their little blind faces almost featureless.

From the spark of essential spirit that gleams through these stories from time to time, Katherine Anne Porter takes her stand. Morality and art are not the same for her—she is not *that* old-fashioned—but they meet in the question of order. The art that made these masterpieces is not primarily educative, though the stories are wise; it is not primarily enjoyable, though they give much pleasure. The special function of this art is to give shape to our existence: to achieve order and form and statement in a world "heaving with the sickness of millennial change." Even when her stories tremble on the edge of disintegration, even when they reveal the most unpleasant truths about ourselves and our age, they are replicas of life, complete and compelling. She has a triumphant ability to see a life and its surroundings as it is and as it might be: a knowledge of proper proportions. This is the sense of a great comic writer, of course, but the effect of most of these stories is relentlessly ironic, perhaps because proper proportions are so scarce in this world.

We feel, even of the weakest characters, that they are kin. She enables us to look on a figure with wonder and deep attention: When we see the mad Swede in "Noon Wine," we get an inkling of what it must really be like to be crazy, to play the harmonica in a dazed unhappy way over and over again in the noon sun.

And the power of the telling remains. You remember, not just the grace and precision of the sentences, but the actual experience of having listened to the voice of a character's inner imagination. In *Pale Horse, Pale Rider,* the First World War and the influenza epidemic blend together in a delirious dance of death, and as you follow Miranda's nightmares, you forget the incomparable style in the comprehension of how it is to be young and alive and in love in a world full of death.

(1965)

LESLIE A. FIEDLER

Adolescence and Maturity in the American Novel

Nobody nowadays is doing anything startling or new; the techniques that are being exploited are those that were revolutionary in the twenties; but the mass audience has stubbornly refused to catch up. This is hardly cheering to our younger authors, who tend to be a melancholy lot, having neither the comfort of commercial success nor the thrill of feeling themselves a gallant vanguard. They have tended, in self-defense, to find themselves special audiences for whom they specifically write and by whose acclaim they live; and while this strategy serves a purpose in sustaining them, financially and spiritually, it has tended to create a situation in which we have a series of competing "academies" rather than a conflict of the academic and the anti-academic.

Since it would be impossible to mention more than a few writers of the younger generation without simply compiling a catalogue, I shall limit myself to discussing particularly only two of the competing "academies," the two which seem to me in certain ways most important: one associated with *Harper's Bazaar,* the other with *Partisan Review.* I pick *Harper's Bazaar* to stand for a whole group which includes

Mademoiselle and *Vogue* and the ill-fated *Flair*, which attempted to be deliberately and whole-heartedly what the others had become partially and almost by accident, and which ended as a parody of itself and of the others. *Harper's Bazaar* is, of course, not primarily a literary magazine at all, but an elegant fashion magazine for women, read not only by those who can afford the goods it advertises but by many who cannot and who participate vicariously in its world of values, picking it up on the table of a beauty-parlor waiting room. Finding a story by, say, Truman Capote tucked away between the picture of a determinedly unbeautiful model and an ad for a brassiere, most of the readers of *Harper's Bazaar,* one assumes, must simply skip the meaningless pages, and, knowing this, the editors (writers themselves, or friends of writers) know that they can print anything they please.

But the conjunction of Capote and high style is not as accidental as it seems at first glance. We have been evolving in recent years a new sort of sensibility, defined by a taste for *haute couture,* classical ballet, baroque opera, the rites and vestments of Catholicism—and above all for a kind of literature at once elegantly delicate and bitterly grotesque. This new kind of sensibility, although (or perhaps because) it is quite frankly a homosexual one, appeals profoundly to certain rich American women with cultural aspirations, and is therefore sponsored in their salons and published decoratively in magazines that cater to their tastes. The development of new markets for the young writer with this sort of sensibility has gone in hand with the development of a kind of high bohemia, which moves freely from New York to Venice to Capri to establish a world that is international and anti-bourgeois without being political or sordid or sullen, like the older bohemias.

The most important writer of this group is Carson McCullers, the most typical Truman Capote (or his latest version, called Speed Lamkin or whatever, since in this world of evanescent youth the hungry generations tread each other down with astonishing rapidity). One can take the latter as almost a caricature of the type: the "queen" as American author, possessing a kind of beauty, both in person and as an artist, which belongs to childhood and early adolescence, and which withers before it can ripen; Southern in origin and allegiance; and gothic (a very refined gothic) in style, blending Edgar Allen Poe and Ronald Firbank in an improbable grafting.

Such writers also descend in a strange way from Faulkner, who provides them with a ready-made *paysage moralisée*, the landscape of the South as a natural symbol for decay and brooding evil. To the distrust and fear of woman in Faulkner, they respond according to their own lights; and what there is in the older writer of the agonizedly male has already been transmuted for them by two transitional writers, both women and both immensely talented, Katherine Anne Porter and Eudora Welty—who began the process of taming and feminizing Faulkner (he has had only one truly male follower, Robert Penn Warren, who falls outside the scope of my present essay), making possible the ingrafting of Henry James which produces the true Magnolia Blossom or Southern Homosexual style: pseudo-magical, pseudo religious, counterfeiting the symbolism of Faulkner in a rhetoric and rhythm derived from James.

I have used the word *counterfeiting* because I find this kind of fiction often merely *chic* behind its pretense of being subtle and advanced. Even Capote, who possesses considerable talent, has come more and more to *play* at being an author, to act out for the benefit of his own kind of society the role of the elegant, sad, futile androgyny—half reigning beauty and half freak. His novel *Other Voices, Other Rooms* already represents a falling away from the slight authentic music of such an early story as "Children on Their Birthdays," and some of his most recent work seems more and more just decor—like the quasi-surrealist window dressings of certain Fifth Avenue shops.

There has been a tendency for this school at its periphery, where it touches, let us say, Princeton, to combine in a perhaps foreseeable way with the formal emphasis of the "New Criticism," and to find expression in the more studied Jamesian effects of a writer like Frederick Buechner; but its realest triumphs are achieved in the fiction of Carson McCullers. Her first novel, *The Heart Is a Lonely Hunter,* published when she was only twenty-two, is heartbreakingly wonderful; the melancholy Southern town, the deaf-and-dumb protagonists all make their meanings precisely, scene and symbol fused into a single poetry without strain. The subject of Miss McCullers' work is the subject of her whole group: the impossibility of reciprocal love, the sadness of a world in which growing up means only learning that isolation is the fate of every one of us. Her central characters, those ambiguous boyish girls (Frankie and Mick; the names make the point) who stand outside of everything, even their own sex, lost in a world of freaks—these are strange new heroes of our time.

The *Partisan Review,* around which the second "academy" tends to polarize, is quite another matter. It is not an advertising journal that has stumbled into printing advanced fiction, but a review which began as a "little magazine" and has managed (thanks in part to angels, but chiefly to the stubborn devotion of its editors) to become an institution without ever having achieved a large circulation. One of the strangest things about *Partisan Review* is that, though its readers have never numbered more than about ten thousand, its name is confidently used in journals with one hundred thousand and two million readers as a symbol for certain values which do not have to be further defined. Certainly, it is resented, hated, and sullenly respected by a much larger number of people than have ever read it.

In its beginnings, it attempted to combine an allegiance to *avant-garde* aesthetic ideals and radical politics; at first, it was quite frankly a Communist publication, though its editors quite soon broke from orthodox Stalinism as the enemy of free culture. Its contributors are characteristically unhappy with each other and with the magazine itself; and they would resent to a man being spoken of as a group, as I am doing now. But they *do* have a good deal in common, not the least of which is their uneasy feeling of independence from each other, the sense that it is only their past which binds them unwillingly together. In politics, for instance, they have grown far apart, becoming variously Anarchists, Trotskyites, Social Democrats, New Dealers, and even Republicans—but they have all of them the complicated awareness of those who once lived inside of or close to the Communist movement.

They are "political" in the European sense of the word, a sense that does not even exist for most Americans. Not only do they have Marx, accepted or denied, in their blood, but also Freud in much the same way, as well as contemporary sociology, anthropology, and philosophy in general—so that they are likely to take sides passionately in arguments about, say, existentialism or other recent European ideologies. They share the fondness of the Southern group for James and Faulkner, but in some ways Kafka is closer to their hearts (Isaac Rosenfeld, for instance, made a major, not quite successful effort, to create a body of American work in his image), and they feel a real kinship with Dostoevsky and Tolstoy. Precisely because their cultural background is so complex, and also because they have almost all been forced somewhere between 1935 and 1940 to make a radical shift in their political allegiances and aesthetic ambitions, it has taken these writers a long time to grow up. Some critics have even found it comical or disheartening to learn that many *Partisan* writers spoken of as "young" are thirty or thirty-five or forty. But they are in truth, for the reasons I have tried to suggest, still young as writers when middle-aged as men, still *beginning*—not dazzling successes at twenty like Truman Capote. They have matured slowly, but they have matured; and this is exceptional in the American scene.

The best of the group is Saul Bellow, a novelist of exceptional talent and in many ways a typical figure. Like most of the writers I am describing, he is a second-generation

Jew (this is important, for Jews are just now taking a place of peculiar significance in American cultural life; and, as a history-ridden people in a history-less land, they stand in a different relationship to the past and to Europe than any other American group), an urban type, whose world is not the archetypal small town that from Twain to Sherwood Anderson and on to Faulkner has been the world *par excellence* of our fiction. Nor is his city the Big Town seen by the provincial, the bewildering un-home that has haunted the American literary mind from the moment of Pierre's wild trip to New York. Saul Bellow's Chicago (like the New York of Delmore Schwartz) is the only home of the essentially homeless, remembered not idyllically as the Garden but as the desert to which one woke at the moment of the Great Depression.

Bellow's controlling images and myths tend to be social ones; ideas, political and philosophical are not something intrusive in his work, but the atmosphere, the very condition of life. He feels most deeply where his thought is most deeply involved, and his characters come alive where they are touched by ideas. It is for this reason that the most moving passages in his books are discussions, the interchange of opinions and theories as vividly presented as a love scene or a fight. But his books are never "problem" novels in the sense of the socially conscious twenties. Even *The Victim* (which remains in many respects my favorite), though it takes off from the problem of anti-Semitism, does not aim at establishing the smug sense of our innocence and the other's guilt, but suggests in its muted fable the difficulty of being human, much less innocent, in a world of injustice.

With *The Adventures of Augie March,* Bellow has won for the first time the general recognition he has long deserved, though his two earlier books had won at least equal critical acclaim. Writers of this school have, I think, a special problem in reaching a mass audience to whom the commonplaces of their experience have an inevitable tinge of the remote and abstruse; and *Augie* is a deliberate attempt to break through to such a group out of the parochial world in which Bellow began. *Augie* itself is an uneven book, redundant and untidy, full of a strange tough-abstract poetry that becomes sometimes merely mannered; but it is held together finally by a versatile irony that moves from barely quizzical tenderness to wild burlesque. Ideally, the book should be read after the grey, tight, orderly *Victim* in order to understand the self-imposed limitations against which it is in revolt. In everything but self-understanding and control, it is a better book, richer, more ambitious, funnier, the saga of an improbable Huckleberry Finn: Huck as a metropolitan Jew, a wanderer through cities, fallen among Trotskyites and comedians of ideas as well as grafters and minor Machiavellians—but Huck still, the apostle of noncommitment, moving uncertainly but inevitably toward the "happy ending" of un-success. It is an explosive book, a novel powered by the atomization of its own world; and the world fragmented in its humor and violence is the world of the *Partisan Review,* which Augie may never have had time to read.

There are other lesser, but still interesting, writers in this constellation: Lionel Trilling, whose single novel was not quite successful, but who in two short stories perfected a new kind of moral-critical fiction; Delmore Schwartz, a poet and fictionist who evokes the Jewish-American milieu with a studied limpness, half-irritating, half-intriguing; Mary McCarthy, the most wickedly witty of the group, who satirizes the ideas of the *Partisan Review* itself at the point where they tend to die into banalities.

It is because the fictionists of this group are capable of seeing themselves with a characteristic irony, sad or brittle, because their world is complex and troubled enough to protect them from nostalgia and self-pity, that I see in them evidence of a movement toward a literature of maturity. Yet certain flaws endemic to the whole American scene reappear disconcertingly in the *Partisan* group and mar *Augie* itself. One feels sometimes that only the weaknesses of American literature survive from generation to generation; that the heritage of our writers is a series of vacuums, which by evasion or strategy they must bridge or bypass.

One waits still, for instance, for the American writer who can render as successfully as, say, any second-rank French novelist of the nineteenth century the complexities and ambiguities of sexual passion, of—(how absurdly hard it is for the American writer to say simply "love")—of *love*. The sentimental-love religion has died out of our serious fiction, leaving only a blank, a blank that the nympholeptic stereotypes which play the women's roles in Saul Bellow's book surely do not fill. Among certain *Partisan* writers, there has recently been an attempt to make out of Laurentian reminiscences and Reichian doctrines a new religion—not of love, of course, but of "full genitality"; yet this seems anything but mature.

Moreover, there appears to be a growing impatience inside the *Partisan* academy, superficially directed at the excesses of the newer criticism but actually aimed at the whole Jamesian cult of sensibility, and this threatens to end in a general scalping of all Paleface writers. Yet the urge toward this polar split between "honest crudity" and "elegant introspection" represents as deep a wound in the American aesthetic sense as the analogous distinction of Dark Lady and Fair Lady stands for in terms of our sexual consciousness. There is a kind of tough-minded provincialism implicit in the whole position: an impulse toward "moral realism," a fear of "Mystification" (i.e., of religion and metaphysics), which may at any moment explode in a reversion to the simplest redskin celebration of pure experience.

Against this temptation, Dostoevsky and Tolstoy and Kafka might well be expected to serve as antidotes; but it is hard to say how seriously these writers are finally taken and how far they are merely "culture" in the vulgarest sense of the word the souveniers of literary tourism. The "tradition" which sustains the *Partisan Review* remains, in a characteristically American way, partial and *willed*. Its canon develops not organically out of a given cultural past, but by forced breeding out of what a few strong-minded men *happen to know*. It is hard to see how such a situation can be avoided in a society distinguished by the indifference of the many to the making of its taste, and by an unbridgeable gap between its productive present and its only viable literary past.

The America which has survived westward expansion and the mass immigration of the last century can no longer live, except nostalgically, on the puritan-colored metaphysical tradition that was still able to nurture Hawthorne and Melville and Henry James. It is not only that America is comparatively young, but that it no longer possesses even the meager past it has lived; that it has, indeed, deliberately and joyously cast off that burden, so that each new generation must improvise not only its fate but its history. This is, on the one hand, an opportunity but, on the other, a curse; and, opportunity or curse, it cuts us off from European alternatives of Tradition and Revolt. To be sure, we use these terms frequently but somewhat comically to describe our pious allegiance to or disavowal of values some ten or fifteen years old; and our failure to confess this leads to the constant counterfeiting of new pasts and the restless revaluations that succeed each other among us with bewildering speed.

There has been in recent times a notorious attempt to invent a full-scale synthetic myth of an America of the Open Road to replace the defunct New England version of our country; but this was born as unreal as its predecessor has become, and, as it has grown less and less sympathetic to a second-generation, urbanized world, its sponsors have grown shriller and shriller. The sentimentality of the wholesale American Legend and its corresponding dream of an unlimited mass audience have not directly influenced most serious American writers; but, in their self-satisfaction at having resisted so second-rate a temptation, they are likely to fall prey to the subtler allures embodied in the exclusive little audience with its conviction of the superiority of its special taste. To write deliberately for the few, we have been learning, is as dangerous as writing for the many in a mass society. To shift from the latter aim to the former is to move from the child's desire to buy universal love with perfect obedience to the adolescent's resolve to compel universal recognition with perfect non-cooperation, a resolve that ends typically in complete submission to the mores of one's gang.

The mature writer must write, as he has always written, for neither mass nor sect but for that pure fiction the ideal understander, for whom we no longer have a name but who was once called the "gentle reader." In traditional cultures, that non-existent perfect reader was postulated in a set of values represented imperfectly but hopefully by a self-perpetuating body of critics. In America he has never been institutionalized, surviving only in the unwitting parody of the 'genteel reader," which at the end of the nineteenth century we rejected with scorn in favor of a more democratic but less useful concept, the "average reader."

The plight of the American writer is at best difficult; aware that the greatest books of our literature remain somehow boys' books, he seeks a way toward maturity. But between him and a mature relationship with his past lies our contempt for what is left behind, the discontinuity of our history; between him and a mature relationship with his public lies the impossibility of institutionalizing values in a democracy which regards taste as a vestige of aristocratic privilege; between him and a mature relationship with experience lies the fact that the only universally *felt* American morality arises from the *ersatz* religion of sentimentalism.

It is no wonder that our novelists have shuttled between the utopias of form and formlessness, pretending alternately that a technical point-of-view is a sufficient substitute for a moral viewpoint and that reported fact is the equivalent of judged experience. The images of childhood and adolescence haunt our greatest works as an unintended symbolic confession of the inadequacy we sense but cannot remedy. Perhaps it is impossible to attain a mature literature without a continuing tradition in the European sense: for it may be that no individual author alone and in a single lifetime can achieve an adult relationship to his culture and his vision of it. But we can, of course, never have such a tradition, only the disabling nostalgia for one; and quite rapidly the whole world is coming to resemble us in this regard. The essential fact of literature in our age is its inevitable "Americanization," as mass culture advances and the old systems of evaluation go down with the political structures into which they were ingrafted. In this sense, the Continental vogue of American fiction, which seems otherwise a merely fashionable exoticism or even a gesture of self-contempt and anti-intellectualism, represents the search of Western literature for its future. Even now, the writers of many other countries begin to stand to their own past in a relation as uneasy as our own; and in our novel they find raised nakedly at last the question that underlay the experimentation of the twenties, the "social consciousness" of the thirties, the search for formal security of the forties: "Can the lonely individual, unsustained by tradition in an atomized society, achieve a poetry adult and complicated enough to be the consciousness of its age?" To have posed that question for the world is the achievement of the American novel at the present moment.

(1955)

F. SCOTT FITZGERALD

Ring

For a year and a half, the writer of this appreciation was Ring Lardner's most familiar companion; after that geography made separations and our contacts were rare. When my wife and I last saw him in 1931 he looked already like a man on his deathbed—it was terribly sad to see that six feet three inches of kindness stretched out ineffectual in the hospital room. His fingers trembled with a match, the tight skin on his handsome skull was marked as a mask of misery and nervous pain.

He gave a very different impression when we first saw him in 1921—he seemed to have an abundance of quiet vitality that would enable him to outlast anyone, to take himself for long spurts of work or play that would ruin an ordinary constitution. He had recently convulsed the country with the famous kitten-and-coat saga (it had to do with a World Series bet and with the impending conversion of some kittens into fur), and the evidence of the betting, a beautiful sable, was worn by his wife at the time. In those days he was interested in people, sports, bridge, music, the stage, the newspapers, the magazines, the books. But though I did not know it, the change in him had already begun—the impenetrable despair that dogged him for a dozen years to his death.

He had practically given up sleeping, save on short vacations deliberately consecrated to simple pleasures, most frequently golf with his friends, Grantland Rice or John Wheeler. Many a night we talked over a case of Canadian ale until bright dawn when Ring would rise and yawn:

"Well, I guess the children have left for school by this time—I might as well go home."

The woes of many people haunted him—for example the doctor's death sentence pronounced upon Tad, the cartoonist (who, in fact, nearly outlived Ring)—it was as if he believed he could and ought to do something about such things. And as he struggled to fulfill his contracts, one of which, a comic strip based on the character of "the busher," was a terror indeed, it was obvious that he felt his work to be directionless, merely "copy." So he was inclined to turn his cosmic sense of responsibility into the channel of solving other people's problems—finding someone an introduction to a theatrical manager, placing a friend in a job, maneuvering a man into a golf club. The effort made was often out of proportion to the situation; the truth back of it was that Ring was getting off—he was a faithful and conscientious workman to the end, but he had stopped finding any fun in his work ten years before he died.

About that time (1922) a publisher undertook to reissue his old books and collect his recent stories and this gave him a sense of existing in the literary world as well as with the public, and he got some satisfaction from the reiterated statements of Mencken and F. P. A. as to his true stature as a writer. But I don't think he cared then—it is hard to understand but I don't think he really gave a damn about anything except his personal relations with a few people. A case in point was his attitude to those imitators who lifted everything except the shirt off his back—only Hemingway has been so thoroughly frisked—it worried the imitators more than it worried Ring. His attitude was that if they got stuck in the process he'd help them over any tough place.

Throughout this period of huge earnings and increasingly solid reputation on top and beneath, there were two ambitions more important to Ring than the work by which he will be remembered: he wanted to be a musician—sometimes he dramatized himself ironically as a thwarted composer—and he wanted to write shows. His dealings with managers would make a whole story: they were always commissioning him to do work which they promptly forgot they had ordered, and accepting librettos that they never produced. (Ring left a short ironic record of Ziegfeld.) Only with the aid of the practical George Kaufman did he achieve his ambition, and by then he was too far gone in illness to get a proper satisfaction from it.

The point of these paragraphs is that whatever Ring's achievement was it fell short of the achievement he was capable of, and this because of a cynical attitude toward his work. How far back did that attitude go—back to his youth in a Michigan village? Certainly back to his days with the Cubs. During those years, when most men of promise achieve an adult education, if only in the school of war, Ring moved in the company of a few dozen illiterates playing a boy's game. A boy's game, with no more possibilities in it than a boy could master, a game bounded by walls which kept out novelty or danger, change or adventure. This material, the observation of it under such circumstances, was the text of Ring's schooling during the most formative period of the mind. A writer can spin on about his adventures after thirty, after forty, after fifty, but the criteria by which these adventures are weighed and valued are irrevocably settled at the age of twenty five. However deeply Ring might cut into it, his cake had exactly the diameter of Frank Chance's diamond.

Here was his artistic problem, and it promised future trouble. So long as he wrote within that inclosure the result was magnificent: within it he heard and recorded the voice of a continent. But when, inevitably, he outgrew his interest in it, what was Ring left with?

He was left with his fine etymological technique—and he

was left rather helpless in those few acres. He had been formed by the very world on which his hilarious irony had released itself. He had fought his way through to knowing what people's motives are and what means they are likely to resort to in order to attain their goals. But now he had a new problem—what to do about it. He went on seeing, and the sights traveled back to the optic nerve, but no longer to be thrown off in fiction, because they were no longer sights that could be weighed and valued by the old criteria. It was never that he was completely sold on athletic virtuousity as the be-all and end-all of problems; the trouble was that he could find nothing finer. Imagine life conceived as a business of beautiful muscular organization—an arising, an effort, a good break, a sweat, a bath, a meal, a love, a sleep—imagine it achieved; then imagine trying to apply that standard to the horribly complicated mess of living where nothing, even the greatest conceptions and workings and achievements, is else but messy, spotty, tortuous—and then one can imagine the confusion that Ring faced coming out of the ball park.

He kept on recording but he no longer projected, and this accumulation, which he has taken with him to the grave, crippled his spirit in the latter years. It was not the fear of Niles, Michigan, that hampered him—it was the habit of silence formed in the presence of the "ivory" with which he lived and worked. Remember he was not humble ivory—maniacal ivory. He got a habit of silence, then the habit of repression that finally took the form of his odd little crusade in *The New Yorker* against pornographic songs. He had agreed with himself to speak only a small portion of his mind.

The present writer once suggested to him that he organize some *cadre* within which he could adequately display his talents, suggesting that it should be something deeply personal, and something on which Ring could take his time, but he dismissed the idea lightly; he was a disillusioned idealist but he had served his Fates well, and no other ones could be casually created for him—"This is something that can be printed," he reasoned, "this, however, belongs with the bunch of stuff that can never be written.

He covered himself in such cases with protests of his inability to bring off anything big, but this was specious, for he was a proud man and had no reason to rate his abilities cheaply. He refused to "tell all" because in a crucial period of his life he had formed the habit of not doing it—and this he had elevated gradually into a standard of taste. It never satisfied him by a damn sight.

So one is haunted not only by a sense of personal loss but by a conviction that Ring got less percentage of himself on paper than any other American author of the first flight. There is *You Know Me, Al,* and there are about a dozen wonderful short stories. (My God, he hadn't even saved them—the material of *How to Write Short Stories* was obtained by photographing old issues of magazines in the public library!) and there is some of the most uproarious and inspired nonsense since Lewis Carroll. Most of the rest is mediocre stuff, with flashes, and I would do Ring a disservice to suggest it should be set upon an altar and worshipped, as have been the most casual relics of Mark Twain. Those three volumes should seem enough—to everyone who didn't know Ring. But I venture that no one who knew him but will agree that the personality of the man overlapped it. Proud, shy, solemn, shrewd, polite, brave, kind, merciful, honorable—with the affection these qualities aroused he created in addition a certain awe in people. His intentions, his will, once in motion were formidable factors in dealing with him—he always did every single thing he said he would do. Frequently he was the melancholy Jacques, and sad company indeed, but under any conditions a noble dignity flowed from him, so that time in his presence always seemed well spent.

On my desk, at the moment, I have the letters that Ring wrote to us; here is a letter one thousand words long, here is one of two thousand words—theatrical gossip, literary shop talk, flashes of wit but not much wit, for he was feeling thin and saving the best of that for his work, anecdotes of his activities. I reprint the most typical one I can find:

> The Dutch Treat show was a week ago Friday night. Grant Rice and I had reserved a table, and a table holds ten people and no more. Well, I had invited, as one guest, Jerry Kern, but he telephoned at the last moment that he couldn't come. I then consulted with Grant Rice, who said he had no substitute in mind, but that it was a shame to waste our extra ticket when tickets were at a premium. So I called up Jones, and Jones said yes, and would it be all right for him to bring along a former Senator who was a pal of his and had been good to him in Washington. I said I was sorry, but our table was filled and besides, we didn't have an extra ticket. "Maybe I could dig up another ticket somewhere," said Jones. "I don't believe so," I said, "but anywhere the point is that we haven't room at our table." "Well," said Jones. "I could have the Senator eat somewhere else and join us in time for the show." "Yes," I said, "but we have no ticket for him." "Well, I'll think of something," and I had a hell of a time getting an extra ticket and shoving the Senator in at another table where he wasn't wanted, and later in the evening, the Senator thanked Jones and said he was the greatest fella in the world and all I got was goodnight.
>
> Well, I must close and nibble on a carrot. R. W. L.

Even in a telegram Ring could compress a lot of himself. Here is one:

> When are you coming back and why please answer
>
> Ring Lardner.

This is not the moment to recollect Ring's convivial aspects, especially as he had, long before his death, ceased to find amusement in dissipation, or indeed in the whole range of what is called entertainment—save for his perennial interest in songs. By grace of the radio and of the many musicians who, drawn by his enormous magnetism, made pilgrimages to his bedside, he had a consolation in the last days, and he made the most of it, hilariously rewriting Cole Porter's lyrics in *The New Yorker*. But it would be an evasion for the present writer not to say that when he was Ring's neighbor a decade ago, they tucked a lot under their belts in many weathers, and spent many words on many men and things. At no time did I feel that I had known him enough, or that anyone knew him—it was not the feeling that there was more stuff in him and that it should come out, it was rather a qualitative difference, it was rather as though, due to some inadequacy in one's self, one had not penetrated to something unsolved, new and unsaid. That is why one wishes that Ring had written down a larger proportion of what was in his mind and heart. It would have saved him longer for us, and that in itself would be something. But I would like to know what it was, and now I will go on wishing—what did Ring want, how did he want things to be, how did he think things were?

A great and good American is dead. Let us not obscure him by the flowers, but walk up and look at that fine medallion, all abraded by sorrows that perhaps we are not equipped to understand. Ring made no enemies, because he was kind, and to many millions he gave release and delight.

(1933)

GEORGE GRELLA

James Bond

Ian Fleming's James Bond is the most famous spy since Mata Hari. The indomitable secret agent reaches every level of literacy: Presidents to popcorn chewers. Not only has the author become a kind of subliterary lion in *Time, The New Yorker,* and *The Saturday Review,* which have devoted interviews and articles to his work, but his opinion was solicited on a major network show about the U-2 affair, the producers seeming to consider Mr. Fleming something like the Walter Lippmann of espionage.

Yet there is no puzzle to solve, no criminal to discover, no brilliant method to reveal. Fleming has no view of a corrupt society in the manner of a Cain, a Hammet or a Chandler; his style and outlook are facile and pedestrian. Unlike Mickey Spillane, he doesn't write pornographic thrillers. Unlike Graham Greene, he offers no metaphysical or psychological insight, no significant comment on the nature of good and evil. Eric Ambler, a genuine craftsman, gives us plausible incidents, people stumbling into affairs which are complex, ambiguous, and believable. Newer writers, such as John Le Carré in *The Spy Who Came in From the Cold* or Len

Deighton in the largely unrecognized *Ipcress File,* portray the life of a professional spy as unglamorous, poverty-ridden and full of odd danger—one never knows when his own organization may betray him, or how far a competing unit of his own government will go, or if he must kill someone on his side, or even what side he is on.

To put it plainly, James Bond, despite his lean good looks, his taste in food, wine and women, his high standing in the British Secret Service, his license to kill, is stupid. He disobeys orders and blunders into situations he should have anticipated chapters in advance. He is almost always known to the enemy as soon as he arrives, undercover, on the scene of action. He usually flounders around long enough for his adversaries to disrupt his elaborate plans and capture him.

His only genius lies in an infinite capacity for taking pain. He has suffered (and survived) bombing, shooting, stabbing, poisoning and automobile attack. He has managed to (barely) escape castration by carpet-beater; bi-section by buzzsaw; rocket blast; shark, barracuda and octopus attack; a near-fatal increase in height on a health farm stretching apparatus; and a dose of poison from the sex glands of a rare Eastern fish. Such bizarre punishment is oddly requited: Bond has enjoyed the charms of the expensive Tiffany Case; the Bahamian nature girl, Honeychile Rider; the mystic Solitaire; and the ineffable Pussy Galore.

No secret agent could behave with such incompetence and still achieve such high renown, such titillating rewards. Fleming's characters are grotesques, the much-publicized sex is chrome-plated, not at all shocking, and the plots are repetitive from book to book. The solution of the paradox of James Bond's popularity may be, not in considering the novels as thrillers, but as something very different, as historic epic and romance, based on the stuff of myth and legend.

Thus, the affectionate fondling of brand names, which readers cite as an example of authenticity, is a contemporary version of the conventional epic catalogue. It is important for the reader to know that Bond wears Sea Island cotton shirts, smokes a Macedonian blend of cigarettes, tells time by a Rolex Oyster watch, fires a Walther PPK 7.65 automatic in a Berns-Martin Triple Draw holster, drives a Mark II Bentley Continental, and so on, just as it is important for the reader of the *Iliad* to be told the immense detail of Achilles' shield. Instead of a catalogue of ships, Fleming gives us a catalogue of clothes, toilet accessories, or background material about some exotic place or some arcane field of knowledge. The catalogues reflect the culture: the long lists of brand names suggest the affluence of a capitalist civilization, just as Bond suggests the secure investment.

Bond fights epic battles, taking seriously what Pope used humorously in his mock epic, *The Rape of the Lock*—the epic game of cards. James Bond has won harrowing games of blackjack, baccarat, bridge, even canasta. Like Ulysses, he travels far, from Turkey to Las Vegas, the Mediterranean, the Caribbean, the Atlantic, even Miami Beach. He makes the obligatory trip to the underworld when he skindives in the Bahamas, travels through the sewers of Istanbul, visits the domain of Mr. Big in Harlem, negotiates Dr. No's cruel tunnel of terror. His name indicates further facets of his character: he is entrusted with the mammoth task of safeguarding an entire civilization; the free world depends on his actions.

In *Moonraker* the situation parallels the Perseus-St. George myth, an appropriate one for Bond's rescue of London from the great rocket of Sir Hugo Drax, the huge dragon menacing England. Drax has red hair, an ugly, burned face which even plastic surgery cannot mask, splayed "ogre's teeth"; the great burst of fire he hopes to run on London is the modern equivalent of the dragon's flames. Fleming employs an ironic reversal of one aspect of the Perseus myth: instead of rescuing Andromeda from the cliff where she is chained, Bond and his Andromeda, Galatea Brand, are nearly killed when one of the Dover cliffs, with some urging from Drax, falls on them. Of course Bond survives and, after escaping steamhosing and the lift-off of the Moonraker rocket (more fire from the dragon's nostrils), saves London. Alone among

Bond novels, the hero fails to get the girl at the end: as a modern St. George, it would scarcely be appropriate for him to win the fair maiden.

In *Live and Let Die,* Bond travels to New York to confront Mr. Big, a giant Negro who controls a black brotherhood of crime, gathering gold to aid the Soviet Union. With his Negro network, his voodoo cult, his clairvoyant mistress, Mr. Big is almost omnipotent; his followers believe he is Baron Samedi, the Devil himself. He even controls the fishes of the sea, summoning shark and barracuda to defend his island. But Bond hurls the epic boast, which we know will clinch his victory, "Big Man? Then let it be a giant, a homeric slaying." His boast is fulfilled; just as he and Solitaire are to be dragged over a coral reef and shredded, Bond's mine blows up Mr. Big's boat and Big is devoured by the fish he tamed, his immense head bobbing bodyless in the sea. Bond again saves Civilization, this time from the powers of blackness.

Goldfinger is probably the most obvious reworking of early myth. Auric Goldfinger, who drives a gold car, carries his money in solid gold, dreams of robbing Fort Knox, and likes his women gold-plated all over, is a reincarnation of King Midas. Midas was tone deaf and earned a pair of ass's ears for misjudging a music contest between Pan and Apollo; Goldfinger, when Bond first meets him, is wearing a hearing aid and sunning himself with a set of tin wings resembling a pair of long, slightly pointed ears. Midas' barber, unable to contain the secret of his master's aural adornment, whispered his message into a hole. Later a reed grew and told the secret to all passersby. James Bond, in Goldfinger's captivity, must foil the planned robbery of Fort Knox; he tapes his message to an airplane toilet seat, the only hole available, and thus transmits it to the outside world.

Fleming's best-known book, *Dr. No.* (there's a movie version too) is the most purely mythic of his works. Dr. No is the archetypal monster who casts a blight on the land and who must be conquered by the unquenchable spirit of life. He inhabits a lavish underground fortress in a guano island in the Caribbean, from which he misguides American missiles with intricate electronic apparatus. He has come to the British government's attention through complaints of the Audubon Society about the deaths of thousands of roseate spoonbills. Dr. No intimidates the natives and scares off the birds with a fire-breathing tractor made to resemble a dragon; his dragon is devastating the island of dung, killing the birds, the game wardens, all natural life. For his violation of nature, Dr. No must be punished by the grand spirit of affirmation, James Bond. Naturally Bond's mission fails at first; he is detected and captured by the evil doctor. After a rich meal and an opportunity to enumerate and use the deluxe living accommodations of the island fortress, Bond is subjected to an agonizing series of tortures in a tunnel of horrors, including an ordeal by fire and by water. He manages to crawl through the bowels of the island (anthropomorphically, the bowels of the monster as well), and kill Dr. No's pet giant octopus, displaying all the while superhuman strength and stamina. He buries Dr. No alive in a small mountain of guano. He has brought back the fertility of the land by ridding nature of the destroyer. As his reward, he spends a night with Honeychile Rider, the nymph of the Bahamas, who knows the secrets of snakes, spiders and seashells. His heroic reward is the possession of the nature spirit herself; it is richly deserved. James Bond has redeemed the Waste Land.

The much-touted background which distinguishes the Bond novel, the close attention to real places and real names, the bits of esoteric information, are all products of an expensive research organization. Aside from their epic function, the lists of names lend only a spurious authenticity which is negated by other lapses from realism. Not only do people like Dr. No and Mr. Big inhabit an unreal world, but even their surface reality is questionable. Fleming's painstaking tour of Manhattan with Bond in *Live and Let Die* proves only that he can read a New York City map. Mr. Fleming is maladroit at transcribing American English; his Negro dialect echoes *Porgy and Bess*. His Americans, from cabdrivers to CIA agents, speak like graduates of non-U public schools. In *Diamonds Are Forever,* Bond thinks the tails attached to automobile antennas are beaver tails. No one in America hunts beaver for their tails or for anything else and not even teenagers fly squirrel tails (which don't look at all like beaver tails) from their cars any more. It's been thirty years since jaded Café Society types slummed in Harlem; Fleming seems to think it's still fashionable.

But no matter; we are dealing with myths. Vivienne Michel, the breathless French-Canadian girl who narrates *The Spy Who Loved Me,* may be intended as a representation of the typical James Bond fan. Most of the book concentrates on her rather unexciting sexual reminiscences in an odd fusion of *True Confessions* and *McCall's.* She is rescued from a pair of gangsters in an Adirondack motel by the coincidental appearance of our agent. After first fumbling the job (he can't kill in cold blood, he explains, forgetting that he's hired for that job and that in another book he's detailed a couple of these jobs), Bond triumphs. He and Vivienne couple hygienically (in air-conditioned comfort, on Beautyrest mattresses, with Sanitized toilet facilities), and Vivienne comments on the action, "He had come from nowhere like the prince in the fairy tales, and he had saved me from the dragon. . .and then, when the dragon was dead, he had taken me as his reward." Vivienne doesn't have Bond's powerful Bentley, she drives a "cute little Vespa." She lists a variety of brand names, but hers consist of clothes and motel appliances. Her comments about the dragon indicate that she, at least, recognizes what's up.

In Fleming's most recent novel, *On Her Majesty's Secret Service,* Bond saves England from biological warfare waged by Ernst Blofeld, the elusive chief of SPECTRE. He narrowly escapes death and matrimony. Blofeld murders Bond's bride of a few hours and escapes, no doubt to reappear in a future novel. Bond, though hardly chaste, still must be unmarried, celibate in his fight against evil. Since there can be no Son of Bond, Blofeld does agent 007 a great service.

Mr. Anthony Boucher, an astute and prolific critic of thrillers, complained in a *New York Times* review of the book, that only bad shooting enabled Bond to escape his enemies. Mr. Boucher is correct, but he criticizes the book as a poor thriller, neglecting the myth: since Bond leads a charmed life, no one can ever shoot him dead.

Perhaps centuries from now, scholars will trace assiduously those references to Yardley soap, Kent brushes, Lanvin perfume, Sanitized toilet seats. Perhaps there will be a variorum Fleming, and "Fleming men" as there are "Milton men." Theses may be written on the epicene role of M, clearly a father figure (yet why unmarried? and that maternal sounding initial is rather damning). For James Bond is the Renaissance man in mid-century guise, lover, warrior, connoisseur. He fights the forces of darkness, speaks for the sanitary achievements of the age, enjoys hugely the fruits of the free enterprise economy. He lives the dreams of countless drab people, his gun ready, his honor intact, his morals loose: the hero of our anxiety-ridden, mythless age: the savior of our culture.

(1964)

FRANCIS HACKETT

Main Street

Can you imagine Henry James deposited for five or six years in McHenry, Illinois, or Sun Prairie, Wisconsin, or Eldora, Iowa? Or can you imagine George Meredith coming to anchor in any of these hard-shelled villages? Or, for that matter, Joseph Conrad? A Kalmuk village might easily engage Conrad, or a London village hold Henry James, but there is something about the American town of small size that says no to the idea of these artists. The small American town, that is to say, presents a fictional problem all its own, and one can only imagine Henry James pathetically groping for the handle as one imbecilly gropes for a strange door-handle in the dark.

The immense interest of *Main Street* is not simply that Mr. Sinclair Lewis has written his best novel, but that his best novel should cope with this flatness and hardness and thinness which is the small, new American prairie town. He calls it Gopher Prairie, Minnesota, and because it is Minnesota the facts group around Swedes rather than Germans, around the Cities rather than St. Louis or Chicago. But his village is not a special village. It is, as he himself says, a representative specimen, standing for something to be found anywhere and everywhere, in the length and breadth of the Middle West. It is, so to say, the heart of American Philistia, the perfect nodulation of the plutocratic middle class. It has its college graduates, its clergymen, its Reds, its Whites, its Single Taxers, its Protective Tariff disciples, its smart set, (who has not heard of the Four Hundred of Chillecothe, Illinois?), its clubwomen, its bankers and bakers and butchers and undertakers, its doctors and lawyers and odd-job men and deadbeats and Joans of Arc? But the collection, the agglomeration, of all these is, necessarily, a specimen of pluto-democratic American society, earmarked by *The Saturday Evening Post*. Man, of course, does not live by Fords alone. Even among the dreariest of American institutions and under their heavy multiplicity and monotony there does sprout an occasional surprising difference. That Mr. Lewis shows. But his Gopher Prairie stands out precisely because it is like all the other Gopher Prairies. And in being grasped with such cruel fresh firmness as Mr. Lewis the whole nation may be felt to squirm.

The method is H. G. Wells's. To Gopher Prairie—the one that is part of the author's own being, the one he grew up with and the one to which he has brought his biting observation—Mr. Lewis has applied not merely the imagination of the artist, but the ravenous curiosity of the political animal. And to that ravenous curiosity, like his master Wells, Mr. Lewis has sacrificed much of the mood of art. To put in evidence his full theory of this nation of villagers Mr. Lewis has been ready all through his book to represent his men and women as actually saying those things about themselves and their socio-political situation which, perhaps, they ought to say, but don't. He has, indeed, a briskness and naturalness of discourse which almost induces one to believe that Gopher Prairie can be articulate. But the articulateness is Mr. Lewis. He has a stinging perceptiveness of practically everything that pertains to the jays and super-jays of this United States. He knows the Busy Booster. He knows the "gentleman hen" who loves art. He knows the hearty people whose sympathies are warm, but stationary. He knows the self-effacing couple who are worth several millions and who take themselves and their Gopher atmosphere to Pasadena—the last way-station en route to those new, decorous, expensive cemeteries which cater only to hearse-automobiles. Mr. Lewis possesses the 'orrible details about the town's bad boy, the town's diabolic gossip, the wife of repressed sex instinct who is like the moist plant that envelops flies. He understands and exposes the ghastly boredom diffused by the Baptists, the Congregationalists, the Methodists and all the other gentry who have a vested interest in the conformity of nonconformity and the dissidence of dissent. Mr. Lewis pinions these professional Christians. He also pinions the cut-up, the bright reforming librarian, the person who does a stunt at the party, the person who makes the "servant problem" and later discovers it. But while he is much too mobile to accept the matter as settled, when he exposes boredom or triteness or inflexibility, he does—like H. G. Wells, or, to be fair all round, Wells does, like Sinclair Lewis—push the classificatory tendency so far that the whole fascinating circumstance of personality is subordinated.

It is subordinated even in Will Kennicott, the doctor, and Carol Kennicott, the doctor's wife. At times Will Kennicott is very real—sound, generous, reliable, wholesome, facetious, executive, crude and the rest. He does all the things that ought to make him real. He amputates in a farm-house at night, Carol giving the ether. He goes hunting, in all the sports-goods that are needed to bring about the death of two or three rabbits. He talks about cars and other tangible objects in a bright stream of slang that shines like the coffee-urn in an American restaurant—and pours forth the same staleness. Mr. Lewis apprehends every necessary convincing detail. And yet, captious though it may sound, this rich chunkiness of detail does not establish the insideness of Kennicott, or give us that entente with him which is the triumph of imagination. Toward the end, when Kennicott comes to see his wife in Washington and dimly perceives that there is in the world such a thing as another personality, we have a glimpse of his being. But this is a small macaroon to satisfy the reader's long hunger.

The woman of the story (for this is The Story of Carol Kennicott) is placed more gently and tenderly, but not in any degree more securely. She is a super-jay who reacts against Gopher Prairie as a person coming in out of the fresh air reacts against stale travelers in a day coach. This Mr. Lewis depicts admirably. But her repeated efforts to maintain a full personality against the tribal fear of personality Mr. Lewis fails to encircle because he gives these efforts a sort of sociological twist. Her stabs at the new library, the new theater, a friendship with the pale-gray lawyer, or the Greek-faced tailor's assistant, her attempts to take an interest in Kennicott's work—these could not be more vivid, but they would gain depth of intelligibility if Mr. Lewis himself had more interest in the specific "otherness" of this undeveloped, striving person.

The same exterior vision is seen in the get-it-over-the-footlights emphasis on the stage Swedes who come in and out. And even the conscientious imagism of the nature-descriptions is not the same as feeling.

But *Main Street* is pioneer work. Some formulae it does help to perpetuate. Some garishness and crudity it does unpleasantly employ in its anxiety to be effective and pat. But while the novelistic hen does not necessarily lay better if surrounded by strong artificial light, the light in *Main Street* is on the whole natural, honest and oh so amazingly illuminating. No one who reads *Main Street* can remain a stranger to Gopher Prairie. There are things about Swedes and the Kennicotts that perhaps Sinclair Lewis is not interested in knowing or cannot ever know. He, like the rest of his country, is touched with utilitarianism, wants his analysis to answer "do" rather than "be." But even if he pelts himself at taste and hits it too hard occasionally, his novel is immeasurably better, better-experienced and seasoned and lived and thought and felt, than most of the American novels. Out of his "land of dairy herds and exquisite lakes, of new automobiles and tar-paper shanties and silos like red towers, of clumsy speech and a hope that is boundless," he has created a reality. And while he is much too tender to it, in the end, he has given American herd-life something, of which it had seemed scarcely capable—a literary domicile.

(1920)

FRANCIS HACKETT

The Age of Innocence

Someone told me that *The Age of Innocence* was "a dull book about New York society in the seventies." This is amusing. It is, undoubtedly, a quiet book, and quietness is dullness to the jazz-minded; but most of those who'd call it dull would really have found it confusing and disturbing, and would therefore wish to dismiss it as "boring." It is really a book of unsparing perception and essential passionateness, full of necessary reserve, but at the same time full of verity.

Mrs. Wharton has definitely widened her critical sense of "good society" in the U.S.A. Is it in sympathy with Elsie Clews Parsons that she has come to talk in terms of pattern and ritual, to relate the taboos of Fifth Avenue to the taboos of Primitive Man? I do not wish to accuse Mrs. Wharton of anthropology, which sounds pedantic, or of gleaning a theory from Elsie Parsons, which sounds derivative; but this novel is thoroughly arousing precisely because a person who had so often exhibited discriminations and disparagements belonging to a certain social order has at last, so-to-speak, bolted the party. And is there not, on this account, an absence of a rather habitual irritable sensitiveness? In this book, at any rate, Mrs. Wharton opens to life a free and swinging door. Those who enter it are, for the most part, the people of fashionable New York and Newport; but no longer does Mrs. Wharton seem to attach to them an extra-fare importance. They happen to be padded externally and internally, but in *The Age of Innocence* Mrs. Wharton inspects this class upholstery not as an excellence, but as a relevant detail. And just because she is a born appraiser, not a romantic bargain-hunter in psychological values, her acuteness serves her well when turned upon her compact phenomenon, the fashionable village of New York fifty years ago.

Mrs. Wharton is not unamiable in her version of this particular village. She simply observes, or rather observes with parching wit, that with all its advantages of place and time and money it is, or was in 187–, a tight tribal community, run with the usual tribal preoccupations of ancestors, ancestresses, and property.

Only three of New York's dynastic families, Mrs. Wharton indicates, could be said to be well-bred in the European sense, and only one of these, the ineffable van der Luydens, had kept from slithering into bankruptcy or imbecility or whiskey or some other form of dust to dust. The rest of the tribe ran from first-rate second-rates through the bullying financier Beaufort down to the splashing Mrs. Struthers—and "once people had tasted of Mrs. Struther's easy Sunday hospitality they were not likely to sit at home remembering that her champagne was transmuted Shoe-Polish." The note of the community, however, as *The Age of Innocence* perfectly captures it, is one of correctness, prudence, and gentility—which is what you would expect from men who had milked their aristocracy from banks and railways and commission houses, and women who had stored it in brown-stone houses and places on the Hudson. As to the special economic background of New York's prudence and timidity Mrs. Wharton is not unduly speculative, but she leaves no doubt as to the general principles of this village. First to lock the chastity of its women in the safety-deposit vault of well-provided matrimony and maternity; secondly, to make of matrimony itself a decidedly tribal function from church wedding to churchyard; and thirdly to extrude from the inner circle by a simple movement of the involuntary social muscles any male financially, or any female matrimonially, dubious. The male promiscuousness, in other words, could never be commercial. It might provide a smart little house on Lexington Avenue for a smart little woman, but it could not get into the wrong columns of the newspaper so far as finance was concerned.

Into this tight circle, which Mrs. Wharton defines so neatly, there returns from darker Europe one of those "strange women" of whom all villages are suspicious. Ellen Olenska was indeed a New Yorker. She is a young woman who has had a Polish count for husband, "a half-paralyzed white sneering fellow—rather handsome head, but eyes with a lot of lashes. Well, I'll tell you the sort: when he wasn't with women he was collecting china." This man, Olenski, she has left in Europe (he keeping the marriage settlement) and she wants to renew life in the circle from which she had departed as a child. In this effort she is sponsored by her grandmother, the striking and powerful old Mrs. Mingott, who had been "only Catherine Spicer of Staten Island," but who had come in control of her late husband's money and had gone her way with "a kind of haughty effrontery that was somehow justified by the extreme decency and dignity of her private life." She is a personality, fearless, outspoken and full-flavored; and of her "monstrous obesity" Mrs. Wharton makes picturesque use. This strong lady adopts the cause of the Countess Olenska, but New York decides to snub her, and only the invocation of the dynastic van der Luydens turns disaster to triumph.

This whole situation is measured by Mrs. Wharton through one of New York's "carefully-brushed, white-waistcoated, buttonhole-flowered gentlemen." At the moment of Madame Olenska's return Newland Archer is tacitly engaged to her cousin, beautifully named May, a classic example of the right thing from every point of view, with "frank forehead, serious eyes and gay innocent mouth." Newland Archer is extremely complacent about this young lady to whom he sends lilies-of-the-valley every day and whose "soul's custodian" he is to be. But he thinks much of family solidarity. At the first sign that "New York" may denigrate Ellen, May's cousin, he shows himself in the Opera box with both of them, and decides to take a strong line. The strong line has its deep emotional significance to Ellen, who sees in Archer something besides a prig.

The finest projection in *The Age of Innocence* is the hieroglyphic world of this correct young engaged couple, Newland and May. "In reality they all lived in a kind of hieroglyphic world, where the real thing was never said or done or even thought, but only represented by a set of arbitrary signs; as when Mrs. Welland, who knew exactly why Archer had pressed her to announce her daughter's engagement at the Beaufort ball (and had indeed expected him to do no less), yet felt obliged to simulate reluctance." Newland and May, as he himself recognizes, breathe "an atmosphere of faint implications and pale delicacies." And yet, while he smiles at it, he only smiles intellectually. "Few things seemed to Newland Archer more awful than an offence against 'Taste,' that far-off divinity of whom 'Form' was the mere visible representative and vicegerent." But the pale and serious face of Madame Olenska speaks to him of something outside the tribal fidelities—something, even, outside the purity of May.

The plight of Madame Olenska is treated by Mrs. Wharton with extremely skillful reserve. We have, to be sure, the village-wedding of Newland and May at Grace Church, described with a certain pointedness; and we have the van der Luydens' dinner for the Duke of St. Austrey in New York handled with a lack of reverence: but Newland Archer, and ourselves, are left to make our own inferences from the divorce accusations of Olenski against Ellen and a tutor, and the palpable pursuit of Ellen by the financier Beaufort. It is only when Ellen's words of gratitude "fell into his breast like burning lead" that Newland realizes the depths of his tribal complicity and the passion of his feeling for Ellen.

He is married to May. And just as his will is aroused to his love for Ellen, and hers for him, May plays her trump card—and the same card twice. That final clamor of hieroglyphics, when Archer sees *why* Madame Olenska is given a farewell dinner, is a masterly creation, exhibiting the tribe as "full of the twists and defences of an instinctive guile."

Is Mrs. Wharton as sure of touch in depicting Newland as in depicting the romantic Ellen? I found her first views of him so slighting and frigid that his later capacity for rebellion taxed my faith. But the inevitable end, "She cannot fade, though thou hast not thy bliss," seemed to me imaginable—one of the few instances imaginable.

The Age of Innocence is spare and neat. It is also quick with a certain kind of dry sympathy and at times like a tongue of fire. The "best people" are, after all, a trite subject for the analyst, but in this novel Mrs. Wharton has shown them to be, for her, a superb subject. She has made of them a clear, composed, rounded work of art. In thinking that this old New York society is extinct, succeeded by a brisk and confident generation, Mrs. Wharton is amazingly sanguine, but this does not impair her essential perceptions. She has preserved a given period in her amber—a pale, pure amber that has living light.

(1920)

GEOFFREY T. HELLMAN

Look Homeward, Angel

Unheralded, *Look Homeward, Angel* will hardly remain unsung. Stamped with the approval of no book-of-the-moment club, lacking even the customary blurb-writer's accolade, it is an extraordinarily fine novel, not to be mentioned in the same breath with all the forgotten blue-ribbon winners of the past few years. In it Mr. Wolfe tells the story of the Gant family of Altamont, North Carolina. Oliver Gant, a dead wife behind him, comes to Altamont and marries Eliza Pentland, his opposite in every way. Gant is a dreamer, unconventional, poetic, but at the same time full of a very earthy vigor, to put it mildly; Eliza is dull, insensitive, strong, above all, practical. Imbued with a Forsyte-like mania for money and property, she knows what every lot in town is worth, foresees land developments, saves every penny to be used in buying up real estate, turns her own home into a boardinghouse, forcing her family into smaller and smaller quarters to make room for the increasing number of lodgers.

Thus she saves her husband and children (there are seven) from the poverty which Gant's shiftlessness would otherwise

155

have reduced them to, but at the same time deadens their spiritual and intellectual development. Eugene is the exception; his unusual mind, which even his mother cannot disregard, wins him the privilege of continuing his education at an age when his brothers and sisters are struggling to earn a living. As the book continues, he supplants his father as central character, and *Look Homeward, Angel* becomes less a family chronicle revolving about the rebellious Gant and more a character study of his equally rebellious but more complex son. Mr. Wolfe takes Eugene from birth through early manhood; in passages that range from what is generally known as "rare lyric beauty" to the most downright realism imaginable, he shows him in every conceivable mood.

Look Homeward, Angel has been criticized for its style and its lack of structural form. Whenever Mr. Wolfe feels like it, which is fairly often, he launches into episodes, descriptions, and proclamations of his own that could be cut out without impairing the architectural unity of his book. Such deletions, however, would rob it of its gusto, and anyone in favor of making them is the sort of person who thinks that *Moby Dick* would be a good book if it weren't for Mr. Melville's digressions. Totally unnecessary characters and events inspire magnificent passages in *Look Homeward, Angel*. Mr. Wolfe lavishes his enthusiasm upon people who enter on one page and make their final exit on the next. Of a salesman he writes:

> Enormous humor flowed from him like a crude light. Men who had never known him seethed with strange internal laughter when they saw him, and roared helplessly when he began to speak. Yet, his physical beauty was astonishing. His head was like that of a wild angel—coils and whorls of living golden hair flashed from his head, his features were regular, generous, and masculine, illuminated by the strange inner smile of idiot ecstasy.

Mr. Wolfe has a quality that is rare enough in itself and is practically never found (as it is here) combined with literary ability, taste, and a scholarly background: relish. He has, in addition, an ironic wit and a sincerity that should prevent his emotional passages from seeming affected to even the most violent prose-poetry haters.

(1929)

GRANVILLE HICKS

The Edwardians

The title of *The Edwardians* is doubly apt, in that the novel not only concerns itself with life in the reign of Edward VII, but also and more particularly with those sophisticated and discreetly unconventional members of the aristocracy in whose company the monarch found pleasure. The setting is Chevron, which, as the publisher's blurb takes unnecessary pains to assure us, is really Knole, the ancestral home of the author. The leading character is the young Duke, Sebastian, who is first presented at the age of nineteen, complaining that nothing ever happens. On that very week-end, however, he falls in love with Sylvia, Lady Roehampton, and listens to Anquetil, an explorer, who urges him to break away from the routine life to which he is by birth committed. Sylvia is the stronger attraction, and Sebastian sows the appropriate crop of wild oats with the splendor that his position demands. Disappointed by Sylvia, he turns to a member of the middle class, and is confronted by an even stodgier morality. The coarseness of a farm girl and the bohemianism of an artist's model are more than his aristocratic stomach can bear, and, finding his love for Chevron his strongest emotion, he contemplates a conventional marriage. He meets Anquetil, however, on the day that George V is crowned, and is persuaded to devote the next three years to an expedition with him. Viola, Sebastian's sister, has carried on a quieter but more successful revolt, and, Sebastian is surprised to learn, plans to marry Anquetil on his return.

A summary of the novel indicates its character and the intention of its author. Taking that intention as a standard, one can find many pleasant things to say about the book, even to the point of agreeing with the American critic who calls it "the true and delightful history of an era and a class." Miss Sackville-West, an intelligent, well-informed and witty woman, has shaped her story with precision and economy. A study of the principles according to which she shifts her point of view shows clearly her skill of construction. Comparison with any work of Galsworthy's, but more especially with *The Patrician,* provides a measure of both her knowledge of the class she portrays and her ability to adumbrate the life of a class in the lives of individuals. Her phraseology is sophisticated and pointed. Indeed, keeping adverse criticism within the limits imposed by Miss Sackville-West's aims, one could perhaps find fault only with certain awkward and unnecessary comments which the author makes as author.

If, then, the novel fails to satisfy the reader, criticism must press beyond the performance to the intention behind it. Not long ago we were told, and most of us believed, that the traditional novel was bankrupt. It seemed as if Victorian genius had fully exploited the possibilities of the novel of character and manners, with its patternless structure and its approximate realism. The novel, it appeared, must change, and in the work of Joyce, Lawrence, Proust and Mrs. Woolf even the more cautious critics saw the transformation taking place. Now Proust is dead, Lawrence is dead, Joyce seems to be galloping into darkness with one foot on Pegasus and the other on a hobbyhorse, and Mrs. Woolf has written *Orlando,* which may not be an absolute calamity, but is surely an omen of defeat. And what is perhaps more, half a dozen of the more brilliant young men and women have, instead of carrying on the revolution, invested their talents in new exemplifications of the old forms.

One ought, of course, to avoid the supposition that the traditional English novel is dead merely because its requiem has been sung. But it may be observed that so far no one has succeeded in revivifying the older forms and making them the vehicles of his genius. *The Edwardians* will do as an example of what is happening. Let us admit that it is free from the more obvious faults that mar the work of Galsworthy, Bennett and Wells: Miss Sackville-West does not underscore her characters as Galsworthy does; her work is not formless and unselective as Bennett's is; she is not a propagandist like Wells. All this can be granted, and it may yet be maintained that she has accomplished no more than, if she had accomplished as much as, these novelists. There is not a single point at which she has enriched our experience of life. She has shown us, presumably quite accurately, the manners of a class with which most of us are not familiar, and we may add to our stock the information she conveys as we might file away a newspaper clipping; but she has not recreated the lives of the Edwardians as Proust has recreated the lives of a comparably aristocratic group. What we find in her work is, in the words of Ramon Fernandez, "the substitution of an order of conceptual exposition for the order of living production, and of rational proofs for esthetic proofs."

Such failures as this lead one to reaffirm the dogma of the bankruptcy of the traditional novel. The more interesting problem now is the attitude of the young writers. It is not necessary to argue that Miss Sackville-West or any other writer should imitate Joyce or Proust; it is enough to suggest that an example has been set which Miss Sackville-West and her contemporaries might follow. We see today, more clearly than we could a few years ago, that Joyce and the rest did not create a new kind of novel, a new kind that could immediately supplant the old. What they did was to show that talent and determination and ingenuity could find more adequate ways in which to say, freshly and convincingly, whatever there was to be said. If they did not show, once and for all, how good novels were to be written in the twentieth century, they at least showed—and this was perhaps more important—that good novels could be written.

Their example seems, at the moment, to have counted for little. The younger writers, with three or four American exceptions and perhaps one or two British, are playing safe. They do not lack talent, but they do lack courage. As a result of their malingering, the situation of the novel is only slightly more hopeful than it was fifteen years ago. Recognizing this, one can neither greet *The Edwardians* with enthusiasm nor dismiss it as utterly unimportant; one can only regard its sleek success as a misfortune, almost an affront. It is not sure how much Miss Sackville-West's talents, real as they are, would accomplish if she were to undertake an ambitious experiment, but even failure, of a certain sort, would entitle her to more profound admiration than can be bestowed on the present work.

(1930)

IRVING HOWE

The Country of the Pointed Firs

Standard opinion has not done justice to Miss Jewett—not
since James Russell Lowell wrote that she had composed
"idylls in prose, and the life they commemorate is as simple
as its main elements, if not so picturesque in its setting, as
that which has survived for us in Theocritus." Parrington
called her Brahmin, which is surely an absurd tag for the
daughter of a Maine country doctor; he probably meant to
say that her work didn't satisfy his appetite for social realism.
Van Wyck Brooks, while purring over forgotten ladies who
dabbled in polite literature, said almost nothing about Miss
Jewett, though she wrote, as it happens, one of the few
first-rate works of prose we can claim for nineteenth-century
America. F. O. Matthiessen, in his little book on Miss Jewett,
drew a warm and charming vignette, but barely touched on
criticism. By contrast, Carlos Baker in the more recent
Literary History of the United States has the good sense to
praise her as an artist—but then proceeds to cancel out his
praise by exiling her to that literary wilderness known as
"regional fiction."

Sarah Orne Jewett was a writer of deep pure feeling and a

limited capacity for emotional expression: there is always, one senses, more behind the language than actually comes through it. In her best work she employed—it was an instinctive and inevitable choice—a tone of muted nostalgia. She knew that the Maine country she loved so well was slowly being pushed into a social impasse: it could not compete in the jungle warfare that was American life in the late nineteenth century. But even as this knowledge formed and limited her vision of things, she did not let it become the dominant content of her work, for she understood, or felt, that the obsolete also has its claim upon us. She was honest and tactful enough not to inflate her sense of passing and nostalgia with the urgencies of a heroism that could only have been willed; in her bare, linear stories about country people strugling to keep their farms alive, she made no false claims, for she saw that even when one or another figure in her Maine country might be heroic there was nothing distinctively heroic in the spectacle of a community in decline, a way of life gradually dying. But she knew—it was an enviable knowledge—that admiration and love can be extended to those who have neither the vocation nor the possibility for heroism. She paid a price, of course. In a country where literature has so often been given over to roaring and proclaiming and "promulging" it was nearly impossible for so exquisite an artist—exquisite precisely because she was, and knew she was, a minor figure—to be properly valued.

At first glance *The Country of the Pointed Firs* bears a certain structural resemblance to Mrs. Gaskell's *Cranford*. In both books a young woman who has tasted urban knowledge returns to a quaint, outmoded village which represents pre-industrial society, and there observes the manners of its inhabitants with a mixture of fondness and amusement. But charming as *Cranford* obviously is, it does not seem to me nearly so good as Miss Jewett's book. Too often Mrs. Gaskell is content to bask in the soft glow of eccentricity and oddity, so that her narrator leaves Cranford pretty much the person she was. But Miss Jewett's "I" registers the meaning of Deephaven with an increase of force and insight that is beautifully arranged: for her the experience of arriving and leaving becomes an education in mortality.

The people in *The Country of the Pointed Firs* are eccentrics, a little gnarled by the American weather and twisted by American loneliness; but it is not for a display of these deformities that Miss Jewett presents them. She is interested in reaching some human core beneath the crusted surface and like so many other American writers, like Anderson and Frost and Robinson, she knows the value and pathos of the buried life. That is why it is harmful, despite the fact that her stories are set in the same locale, to speak of her as a regional writer; for regional literature, by its very premise, implies a certain slackening of the human measure, a complacent readiness to accept the merely accidental and unusual.

With infinite delicacy Miss Jewett moves her light from one figure to another: the shy fisherman William who late in life returns to the interior country to claim his love; the jilted Miss Joanna Todd who in the immensity of her grief cuts herself off from humanity and lives alone on a coastal island; the touched sea captain who remembers journeys to places that never were; and most of all, Mrs. Almiry Todd, the central figure of the book, sharp-tongued, wise, witty, a somewhat greyed version of George Eliot's Mrs. Poyser. (As Mrs. Todd recalls her dead husband, "She might have been Antigone alone on the Theban plain. . . . An absolute, archaic grief possessed this countrywoman; she seemed like a renewal of some historic soul, with her sorrows and the remoteness of a daily life busied with rustic simplicities and the scents of primeval herbs.") The book is set in a dramatic present that is necessarily somewhat fragile, but it resounds with full echoes of the past: tradition lives as an element of experience, not a proposition of ideology. ("Conversation's got to have some root in the past," says an old lady, "or else you've got to explain every remark you make, and it wears a person out.")

Like other books dealing with a relatively simple society, *The Country of the Pointed Firs* gains organic structure from its relaxed loyalty to the rhythms of natural life. The world it memorializes is small and shrinking, and the dominant images of the book serve only to bound this world more stringently: images of the ranked firs and the water, which together suggest the enclosing force of everything beyond the social perimeter. But meanwhile a community survives, endowed with rare powers of implicit communication: to say in this world that someone has "real feelins" is to say everything.

Finally the book is a triumph of style, a precise and delicate style such as we seldom find in nineteenth century American prose. The breakdown of distinctions between prose and verse which occurs under the sponsorship of romanticism and for a variety of reasons is particularly extreme in America, where it produces two such ambiguous figures of genius as Melville and Whitman—this breakdown hardly affected Miss Jewett. Very probably this is one reason she remained a minor figure while Melville and Whitman were, occasionally, major ones. But at the moment there is much to be gained from a study of her finely modulated prose, which never strains for effects beyond its reach and always achieves a secure pattern of rhythm. Listen to this sentence with its sly abrupt climax: "There was something quite charming in his appearance: it was a face thin and delicate with refinement, but worn into appealing lines, as if he had suffered from loneliness and misapprehension." Or to the lucid gravity of this sentence: "There was in the eyes a look of anticipation and joy, a far-off look that sought the horizon; one often sees it in seafaring families, inherited by girls and boys alike from men who spend their lives at sea, and are always watching for distant sails or the first loom of the land." Or to the wit of Mrs. Todd as she places her minister: "He seemed to know no remedies, but he had a great use of words."

The Country of the Pointed Firs is not a "great" book; it

isn't *Moby Dick* or *Sister Carrie* or even *The Great Gatsby*. It cannot sustain profound exegesis or symbol hunting. In fact, all it needs is appreciation. But living as we do in a country where the grand too easily becomes synonymous with virtue and where minor works are underrated because major ones are overrated, it is good to remember that we have writers like Miss Jewett, calmly waiting for us to remember them.

(1954)

IRVING HOWE

By Love Possessed

By Love Possessed is a mediocre and pretentious novel written by an experienced craftsman. This judgment seems so obvious that under ordinary circumstances it would hardly require elaboration. But the circumstances are, clearly, not ordinary. That the novel has been a fabulous popular success; that it should have succeeded, as one gathers it has, in impressing people as a work of wisdom and significance; that it has been praised by the middlebrow reviewers in terms a critic might reserve for, say, Moby Dick—all this suggests the presence of a new cultural problem.

The problem, as it happens, has less to do with the book than with its public life. Simply as a novel, By Love Possessed seems already to have been lost in the smoke of a gathering Kulturkampf; almost everyone who writes about it finds himself referring to what othr people have said, and rightly so, since it exists as a fact in our culture rather than as an independent work of art. Mr. Cozzens, a writer deficient in the more tender sentiments but well-equipped with a sense of the sardonic, will not be the last to appreciate the ambiguousness of his long-delayed triumph.

167

The middlebrow critics have seized upon the novel as a rallying-cry in their persistent campaign to discredit literary seriousness. Their choice is a shrewd one. For *By Love Possessed,* as I shall try to show, not merely exemplifies what they want but, more important, allows them to feel virtuous in wanting it; the values of Cozzens, while not really theirs, are peculiarly useful to them. Thus Mr. John Fischer, editor of *Harper's* and a man who seems to regard literary criticism as a personal threat, presents Cozzens as the champion of the "classical mind," literary sensibleness, moral rectitude and traditional American virtue. It follows, for Mr. Fisher, that Cozzens has been deliberately—no, outrageously—slighted by "the magisterial critics whose encyclicals appear in the literary quarterlies ... This note is also struck by many other reviewers as they pronounce *By Love Possessed* to be "great," "a masterpiece," and (most revealing, since it comes from Clifton Fadiman) "mature." All of which, but particularly the stress upon "maturity," forms part of what Dwight Macdonald has called the Middlebrow Counter-Revolution.

Now, happily, Macdonald has struck back. In the January *Commentary* he prints a witty dissection of the verbal fuzziness and moral inadequacy of *By Love Possessed;* and despite his failure to do justice to Cozzens' earlier work and his implicit use of a standard of prose style — lucid, sharp and epigrammatic—that is not always relevant to the novel as a genre, Macdonald scores heavily. We may now expect angry rebuttals, and since any quarrel is better than our present cultural somnolence, let me add a bit of fuel to the fire.

Cozzens began his career with several pieces of juvenilia and then wrote two short works, *S.S. San Pedro* and *Castaway,* both of which are livelier in technique and less stagnant in moral assumption than his later books. In *S.S. San Pedro,* which portrays the break-up of a ship's community when an aging captain loses his grip and no one takes over his authority, Cozzens showed a notable gift for disciplined narrative. In *Castaway* he wrote a fable about a man alone in an empty department store who, despite the presence of material necessities, quickly disintegrates. The writing in *Castaway* can be very good; the sentences are formed with a care for effects of rhythm and color that one seldom finds in Cozzens' later, more portentous novels; and the book as a whole is perhaps the only one in which his capacity for descriptive notation is fully controlled by his motivating ideas.

After these experiments Cozzens turns to what might as well be called his dominant manner. He now becomes a quite conventional novelist, either uninterested in or unable to use the twentieth century advances in techniques; he strives for and often achieves a strong, efficient but rather flavorless style. It is a decent, workmanlike style, neither exalted nor corrupt, and generally most useful when approaching the tone of anonymous objectivity. It serves far better for locating objects in the external world than for projecting a vision of life through accumulation of metaphor or nuances of inflation. It is a style, in short, that is likely to reassure prople who find modern literature bewildering.

Structurally, Cozzens worked out a scheme that does represent a certain deviation from—though hardly an improvement upon—the conventional novel. What seems particularly to interest him as a writer is the weight of social and moral pressures that a community brings to bear upon one of its significant members, generally a professional man who both leads and serves it. It is this idea of friction that is central to Cozzens' work, far more so than the patterns of drama or the risks of tragedy. As a result he does not generally use plot in his novels, at least in the traditional sense of a coherent action moving through time and guided toward climax and resolution. Instead, he concentrates on the moment before climax. We are brought very quickly to this moment and then are stopped for a series of dogged investigations of group after group, representative figure after figure, as each of these impinges on the protagonist and multiples the pressures to which he is subject. Meanwhile the action, to

169

the extent that there is one, hangs suspended, waiting for Cozzens to amass the necessary data that might have come more dramatically and organically through a use of plot.

Before trying to indicate the strengths and weaknesses that follow from this procedure, let me add that Cozzens' interest in the relationships between a group and its major figure does not become the occasion for investigating a conflict between his hero's private self and public role; Cozzens would probably reject such a split as evidence of romanticism. He is not much concerned with the idea of the self, and he certainly does not share the exalted valuation most modern novelists place upon its inviolability. I suspect that he would regard the whole notion of personality—which in modern literature often means the capacity of the self to mold at least part of one's social being—as a positive nuisance.

What leads Cozzens to his typical subject matter is, first, a quite American fascination with the routines and demands of professional life (he tinkers with legal details the way your neighbor does with an old car) and, second, a view of moral experience. The first of these does not come, as it might with a writer like John O'Hara, to a feeling that what people do is more interesting than what they are; Cozzens, for long stretches of his work, seems honestly unable to notice much difference between the two. As a result, whenever anything more than appetite or duty is involved, he is quite poor at establishing the motives of his characters, and his psychology has a way of disintegrating into the ragtags of home-made behaviorism. Like certain other American novelists, he seems to feel that a conclusive insight has been achieved when he refers to sex as an "itch."

Cozzens repeatedly turns to the theme that the accumulation of experience (which in his novels often means learning to get a job done because it has to be done) shatters moral presuppositions—and shatters them to the point where a serious effort to realize the intentions behind them forces one to violate their surface claims and indeed, to engage in what might seem to be dubious conduct. For working up a novel this notion is about as good as most others, though in Cozzens' later books it hardens into a truculent ideology which seems to me both morally dispiriting and esthetically crippling. But of that, more in a moment.

In one of his least well known novels, *Men and Brethren*, published in 1936, Cozzens managed to put these technical devices and moral notions to good use. *Men and Brethren* is a compact novel free from the disastrous ambition to write the Big Book that would mar Cozzens' later work. It focuses upon a few days in the life of an Episcopalian minister who is suddenly beset by a variety of crises: some he meets by falling back upon his sanctioned asceticism, others by an unconventional yet morally effective use of his special powers (he quietly arranges an abortion for a distressed parishioner), and in at least one case by knowingly funking his responsibility. One reason Cozzens' formula works in this novel is that the assumptions about a minister's conduct are so rigid and familiar that not much space is needed for blocking out the ways in which the other characters may claim his attention or violate his solace. The result is both economical and pleasing.

As one might expect, the typical structure and situation of Cozzens' novels yield typical strengths and weaknesses.

Many of his books are freighted with heavy loads of information about the professional activities of their heroes (in *By Love Possessed* this becomes an almost *Time*-like display of inconsequential accuracy). The American respect for technology becomes in Cozzens an unconcealed admiration for the man who uses his mind for precise utilitarian ends and who is impatient with other ideas about the value of thought. Though at any given point a Cozzens novel tends to resemble a sociological casebook in which the data have been neatly assembled but not finally grasped, he does manage, more often than not, to put his specialized information to some novelistic use. If, as Gertrude Stein said, remarks don't make literature, then neither does information; but information can help authenticate a locale and root characters in the circumstances of their lives. No novel has ever been spoiled merely by an accurate statement of fact.

Cozzens is at his best when closely examining those moments of abrasion that inevitably arise because a man's competence at his work brings him into unpredictable difficulties with colleagues and friends. And in general, he often succeeds in the novelist's elementary task of creating the illusion of verisimilitude. One believes that his world is "there" though one almost never believes that he has plumbed or understood it—or even felt for it—with that imaginative mastery which marks the first-rate novelist.

The weaknesses are also recurrent. Cozzens' device of sliding from section to section, or flashback to flashback, in order to show the convergence of pressures upon his heroes, almost always creates difficulties. Either this sort of section seems merely illustrative of the novel's larger intent, so that we plough through it merely to discover its relation to the main theme, or it becomes a piece of sprawling representation, in which tyrannical informativeness leads to the exhaustion of interest.

Similar troubles beset Cozzens in his characterization. Since so much of the material in his novels is supplied in order to clarify and hasten a central crisis, the subsidiary figures have a way of wilting into lifelessness; and when Cozzens endows them with a few pat idiosyncracies, he usually does no more than aggravate the problem.

The leading characters, in turn, are frequently sentimentalized, not through the usual identification with suffering and sensitiveness, but through a perverse admiration for their ordinariness of spirit, their rudeness of manner, and their contempt for tenderness of feeling. When Hemingway struts about to show how tough he is, he usually irritates us with his need for wearing a silly mask; when Cozzens tries to show how hard-bitten and illiberal his attitudes are, he can be very convincing.

As he has written book after book, Cozzens has taken for himself the role of an irritated spokesman for the values of a snobbish and soured rationalism that approaches nineteenth-century American Know Nothingism. Nor does the fact that he commands an extensive vocabulary and various kinds of specialized knowledge keep him from indulging in such attitudes. In American culture, on the contrary, these often go together.

Some years ago, in the Winter 1949 *New Mexico Quarterly,* Stanley Edgar Hyman noted that " . . .Cozzens is the novelist of the American white Protestant middle class, the chronicler of its doing and values, and his work represents those values so thoroughly as to make all of his books . . . exercises in making peace with the world as constituted."

Hyman then cited instances in Cozzens' novels where the cheap terms of prejudice toward Negroes, Jews and foreigners were used either with tacit approval or taunting ambiguity. Here, for example, is old Doc Bull, the hero of *The Last Adam:*

Time was when Sansbury was a white man's town. Look at the Roman covent there . . . . What the hell are these monks and priors and novenas of the Little Flower doing in New England? Same with a lot of Jew artists, like Lincoln over in the Cobb place . . . . Early American house! Why doesn't he go restore himself a synagogue in Jerusalem?

Reading that last line, one suddenly notices that these are the very accents of Jason Compson in *The Sound and the Fury,* but with this crucial difference: Jason is the villain while Doc Bull is the hero, Faulkner's contempt for Jason is unmistakable while Cozzens admires Doc Bull as the embodiment (strong as a bull) of the vitality of the human race.

Still, does Doc Bull (also a bull-thrower) really speak for Cozzens? I doubt that Cozzens finally shares his sentiments, or shares them at more than the level of mind where his main concern is to taunt "sentimental liberals"—though it had better be noted that such remarks are repeated by the "positive" characters in several of Cozzens' novels and that in

By Love Possessed the hero, Arthur Winner, reflects upon a Jew lawyer from New York in these terms:

Was something there of the patient shrug, something of the bated breath and whispering humbleness? .... Did you forget at your peril the ancient grudge that might be fed if Mr. Woolf could catch you once upon the hip?

A lovely allegory—the Christian Winner and the Jewish Woolf!

But despite such passages, I think it would be a mistake to charge Cozzens with the garden variety of prejudice. It would also be letting him off a bit too easily. For something more complex is at work in his novels, something that, in the name of his need always to be hardheaded and never to be "taken in" by the illusions of ordinary men, makes him cultivate a stance of the wilfully bigoted spirit—a stance for which one cannot even claim the spontaneity of genuine prejudice. It is all part of a literary pose, Cozzens' desire to regard himself as an advocate of outspoken, uppity, no-nonsense, tough-spirited and crotchety skepticism of mind. In American folk-lore this is usually associated with New England, but in Cozzens' reduced version it is really much closer to the village philosophizing, the cracker-barrel wisdom that has played so sorry a part in American literature.

II

By Love Possessed is a desperately ambitious book, an effort—one last throw of the dice against the cruelty of neglect—to create a *summa* of craft and wisdom. And as usually happens when a writer decides to compose a masterpiece, it succeeds mainly in magnifying his deficiencies.

For a book that is so ambitious, *By Love Possessed* is also remarkably uninventive, almost to the point of self-mimicry. In its central situation and thematic development, it is little more than an inflated reworking of *Man and Brethren,* with the difference that the priest of the earlier novel is replaced by a lay confessor, Arthur Winner, the lawyer who sustains the weak and suffers their aggression. Given both the drift and limitations of Cozzens' mind, this substitution is hardly to be regretted.

By Love Possessed reflects Cozzens' ambition in two other ways: a generous concentration upon the surface motions and mechanics of sex (not love but the "itch" possesses most of his characters), and an indulgence in large amounts of quasi-philosophical reflection that indicate a sudden interest in the later and less fortunate works of William Faulkner. I doubt that the sex is meant for sensational effect or is the main reason for the book's success, but it does seem likely that the philosophy has genuinely impressed the reviewers. We live in so anxious a moment that people seem to have a greater need for spiritual direction than for personal pleasure.

Because of the ambition that shapes it, By Love Possessed succumbs to a technical fault so common in recent American novels as almost to constitute a failing in national character. Straining for a "rich" inclusiveness, Cozzens tries to absorb far more material than he can handle, and at times By Love Possessed begins to resemble that dreary native genre: The Novel as County History. As he moves in upon his small town, Cozzens tells us a great deal more than we need or care to know about a large number of characters, all of whom, one can but hopefully assume, will have some effect upon the fate of Arthur Winner.

The result is a classical example of what Henry James called "the misplaced middle." Having expended more than half his space on preparatory side-panels and flashbacks that his theme does not require but toward which his ambition goads him, Cozzens then finds himself faced with a need for suddenly driving toward a melodramatic climax—otherwise, the book might never end. And this means, in effect, to "misplace" the middle of his book.

One repeatedly asks oneself: why is this incident here? why are we given the details about the homosexuality of the man who plays the organ at the Episcopal church? why do we need to know about the childhood of Winner's repressed secretary? or the sordid little affair of her brother? is any principle of selection, of controlled intelligence, at work here? Most readers of popular fiction never dream of asking such questions, for if they did, they would soon be reading other kinds of books. But they are questions that a critical reader is obliged to raise.

Far from being a mere triviality of "academic criticism," this analysis leads directly to a central weakness of the novel: the characterization of Arthur Winner. It would require a figure of genuinely heroic proportions to sustain the weight of preparation that Cozzens has accumulated, a figure whose brilliant energy and mind would persuade us that all this documentary scurrying has been worth the trouble. But the joke of it is that Cozzens means Winner to be simply a decent and ordinary American, a mature and responsible citizen who can almost be defined by the absence of heroic traits.

A sadder joke still is that Winner does not even satisfy these modest requirements. He is a mediocre figure, incapable of thinking clearly, who fails to understand the impulse to meddling that lies behind his fretful benevolence. (Though, to be fair, neither does Cozzens.) He is also, as Dwight Macdonald has remarked, something of a prig who "delights in demonstrating his superiority on small occasions." He is often given to rudeness, which Cozzens has a way of confusing with manliness. And worst of all, he is a cold fish, about whose one sexual adventure Cozzens writes, though without realizing how badly this damages the image he means us to have of Winner: "Far from coveting his neighbor's wife, he rather disliked her, found her more unattractive than not." By love possessed, indeed!

Had Cozzens really understood what he had made in Winner it might have been possible to build a 570-page novel about him, though the tone and implication would have had to be radically different. As it is, Cozzens tries to compensate for the porousness of Winner by surrounding him with passages of reflective prose intended to give the novel philosophical body. If ever rhetoric did the work of imagination, it is in *By Love Possessed,* though mere quotation could never suggest the pretentiousness and emptiness and elephantine coyness of Cozzens as thinker. Still, here are a few examples of what Mr. John Fischer has called Cozzens' "clarity and grace":

Ah, how wise, how sure, how right, was that genius of the language whose instinct detected in the manifold manifestings of the amative appetite (however different-seeming; however apparently opposed) the one same urgent unreason, the one same eager let's-pretend and so, wisely consented, so, for convenience covenanted, to name all with one same name! Explaining, sweet unreason excused; excusing, sweet let's pretend explained. The young heart, indentured (O wearisome conditions of humanity!) to reason, pined, starved on the bare bitter diet of thinking. One fine day, that heart (most hearts) must bolt. That heart would be off (could you blame it?) to Loveland, to feeling's feasts.

With this rich prose there is also deep wisdom:

An irreplaceable she was, in ordinary practise, replaced with almost ludicrous ease and dispatch. When his serious object was matrimony, a man was never long in perceiving there were still good-enough fish in the sea, and plenty of them.

And strong feeling:

Deaf as yesterday to all representations of right, he purposed further perfidy, once more pawning his honor to obtain his lust. Deaf as yesterday to all remonstrances of reason, he purposed to sell himself over again to buy venery's disappearing dross.

And relentless realism:

. . . there had been awkward occasions when the animal (disregarded by the hour and teased too far) reacted of a sudden, put to the shilly-shally so long imposed its own unpreventable end. Arthur Winner Junior— confusion in the moonlight: dismay among the roses!—was obliged to conceal as well as he could a crisis about which his single shamed consolation was that Hope, anything but knowing, would never know what had happened.

And a tender awareness of mortality:

On the agreeable, admiring amusement, on the bemused tenderness, on the warmed heart, how cold a hand laid itself! The hand was doubt's, was dread's, was death's—could this be mine to keep? Ah, no; this is beyond moral man's deserving.

And finally the distillation of profound experience, the moral of the story, spoken to Winner by his law partner:

Boy, never try to piss up the wind. Principle must sometimes be shelved. Let us face the fact. In this life we cannot do everything we might like to do, nor have for ourselves everything we might like to have.

Here, at last, we come to the heart of the matter: what has so won the hearts of the public and the reviewers? Surely not the sex, which can be had almost anywhere in popular fiction. Surely not the story or characterization, which are no better or worse than you might find in any number of unnoticed novels. Surely not the style. . . .

The answer, I think, is the implied meaning, the "philosophy," which the last quotation makes explicit but toward which the whole context of the book inexorably moves.

Cozzens is a writer who resists all optimistic and meliorist illusions about man; he will not be deceived by romantic expectations or transcendental fancies; he knows that the body is flesh in decay and love is appetite momentarily sated. He knows about the hard contingency of facts; indeed, facts are his specialty. He recognizes the fallen nature of man without succumbing to notions about redemption or grace. For he is an independent old-fashioned American, and this is a country where people understand what happens when you try to piss up the wind. It is a great economy: to reach the resolution of tragedy without having traveled the painful road of the tragic experience.

Yet it may be that there can be no tragic resolution without the preceding experience. The idea of limit—which is the one thing Cozzens permits himself to celebrate—may mean nothing without the excess of yearning to break past it. And American common-sense realism about that critter, man, may prove to be the ultimate delusion.

For our historical moment, however, the Philosophy of Limit, with its reiterated stress upon the direction of the winds, has a peculiar and powerful appeal. It speaks to a society weary of ideals and dubious of hopes; it helps console people in their prosperous frustration; it offers conservative widsom in a moment of liberal twilight.

And here I must disagree with Dwight Macdonald who describes *By Love Possessed* as a Novel of Resignation in which "the highest reach of enlightenment is to realize how awful the System is and yet to accept it *on its own terms.*" Macdonald confuses the impact which the book has upon readers with the meaning it conveys to them: he fails to see that the solace of resignation can be provided only by a novel that does not deal in categories of resignation.

For the audience that finds *By Love Possessed* a significant comment on the condition and problems of its life, a novel of resignation would be painful, perhaps too painful. It would have to acknowledge that there is something about which to feel resigned, it would have to confront realities of disappointment and unfillment. *By Love Possessed,* however, creates the effect of resignation not by preaching it but by implicitly denying that there is any cause for it, not by offering apology but by providing absolution. *That is the way life goes and, man being what he is, that is the way it must go*—such is the message which the novel brings to the suburban reader who, amid the floating malaise of his or her life, hangs to the pattern of Arthur Winner's "responsibility." Such is the lesson it brings to the middlebrow reviewer who,

179

like Arthur Winner, has also learned something about the frustration of the will among benefits of prosperity. And that is why Clifton Fadiman praises the "maturity" of *By Love Possessed*: he too has been acquainted with the winds.

But let it be said for Mr. Cozzens that he has not tried to adapt himself to the mood of the moment, he has not favored the *Zeitgeist,* he continues to say today what he had been saying for years. It is the weary *Zeitgeist* that has finally limped round to him. And, indeed, a civilization that finds its symbolic embodiment in Dwight David Eisenhower and its practical guide in John Foster Dulles has been well prepared for receiving the fruits of the Philosophy of Limit. It is a civilization that, in its naked and graceless undelusion, deserves as its laureate James Gould Cozzens—Novelist of the Republic!

(1958)

IRVING HOWE

Herzog

Where shall a contemporary novel begin? Perhaps unavoidably: with the busted hero reeling from a messy divorce and moaning in a malodorous furnished room; picking at his psyche's wounds like a boy at knee scabs; rehearsing the mighty shambles of ambition ("how I rose from humble origins to complete disaster"); cursing the heart-and-ball breakers, both wives and volunteers, who have, he claims, laid him low; snarling contempt at his own self-pity with a Johnsonian epigram, "Grief, Sir, is a species of idleness"; and yet, amidst all this woe, bubbling with intellectual hope, as also with intellectual gas, and consoling himself with the truth that indeed "there were worse cripples around."

This is Moses Herzog, hero-patsy of Saul Bellow's extremely, if also unevenly, brilliant new novel. Herzog is a representative man of the sixties, eaten away by those "personal relations" which form the glory and the foolishness of a post-political intelligentsia. He is a good scholar, but cannot complete his books. He rips off imaginary letters to great men, finessing their wisdom and patronizing their mistakes. He is a lady-killer, "aging" at forty-seven and worried about his potency. He is a loving father twice-divorced, who each time has left behind him a child as token of good will. He is a true-blue Jewish groaner, and perversely, groans against fashionable despair. Inside or outside our skins, we all know Herzog: *Hypocrite lecteuur—mon semblable—mein shlemiehl.* Hungering for a life of large significance, eager for "a politics in the Aristotelian sense," he nevertheless keeps melting into the mercies of women, each of whom, in sequence, really understands him.

Herzog is Bellow's sixth novel and in many ways the most remarkable. All of his books—whether melancholy realism, moral fable or picaresque fantasia—represent for him a new departure, a chosen risk in form and perception. Bellow has the most powerful mind among contemporary American novelists, or at least, he is the American novelist who best assimilates his intelligence to creative purpose. This might have been foreseen at the beginning of his career, for he has always been able to turn out a first-rate piece of discursive prose; what could not have been foreseen was that he would also become a virtuoso of fictional technique and language.

Behind Bellow's writing there is always a serious intention, but as he grows older he becomes increasingly devoted to the idea of the novel as sheer spectacle. His last few books comprise a hectic and at times ghastly bazaar of contemporary experience; they ring with the noise of struggle; characters dash in and out, glistening with bravura; adventures pile up merrily, as if the decline of the West had not been definitely proclaimed; the male characters plunge and rise, mad for transcendence; the women (a little tiresomely) are all very beautiful and mostly very damaging. And the language spins.

Before and, I hope, after everything else has been said, *Herzog* should be praised as a marvelously animated performance. It is a book that makes one greedy for the next page, the next character. Racing ahead like a sped-up movie, the action covers a brief time in the life of Herzog and nimbly reaches back and forth to segments of his immigrant childhood in Montreal, his failed marriages, his intellectual spiralings, and his recent lady-hopping. The minor figures are drawn as sharp caricature, without the distraction of psychological probe or nuance, and sometimes, when Bellow's zest becomes compulsive, a little over-focused. There are foul-mouth lawyers, boiling with drug-store wisdom, professional chicanery and "potato love"; a couple of tough-spirited aunts; a sadly ineffectual father fumbling at bootleggery; a professor who loves, solely but purely, his monkey. There are Herzog's ladies of the season: Sono, a Japanese doll who soothes the spirit and, Oriental-style, washes the back of Master Moses in an Upper West Side bathtub while cooing at him in baby French, "mon professeur d'amour," and Ramona, bravely marching into middle age with an overload of "understanding" and graduate credentials in sex, who "entered a room provocatively . . . one hand touching her thigh, as though she carried a knife in her garter belt."

And then the demons, the evil spirits: Madeleine, the wife who betrays; Valentine Gersbach, the best friend with whom she does it.

A talentless buffoon-double of the talented hero, Valentine Gersbach (what a name!) booms out the latest highbrow cant in his great bearish voice and ends by lecturing to Hadassah clubs on Martin Buber. Toward Valentine, Bellow is merciless, yet one is seldom troubled by this open display of aggression; for there is no pretense in this novel that we are being shown a world which exists, self-sufficient, apart from the neurotic inflammations of the central figure. Gersbach is a clown, a windbag, a traitor, the kind of man who makes intellectuals wish they were dead when they hear him parroting their words; yet he is utterly alive, one waits for him to reappear on the page, and finally even he wins a moment of humane redemption: secretly, angrily Herzog watches Gersbach bathing his (Herzog's) little girl and must admit to himself that the act, though done by a betrayer, is yet done with tenderness.

Madeleine is drawn with pure venom, a sentiment capable of generating in writers, as in other men, great quantities of energy. She is, naturally, a beauty; she piddles in Russian intellectual history and Catholic conversion; she out-maneuvers the slumping Herzog not merely at sexual games (where she has, after all, the advantage of youth) but also in intellectual competition. When Herzog complains about her extravagance, her arrogance, her paranoia, she replies with the great modern rationale: "Anyway, it'll never be boring." A moony schoolgirl meets Madeleine, and describes her in a phrase embodying the great modern cant: "She gives a sense of significant encounter." With her postures of depth, screeches of enthusiasm, learned references and distinguished airs, Madeleine is the female pseudo-intellectual done, and done in, once and for all. The portrait is unjust, an utter libel, but a classic of male retaliation.

Herzog himself is not, in the traditional sense, a novelistic character at all. He is observed neither from a cool distance nor through intimate psychological penetration. We experience him intensely, entering his very bones; yet, trapped as we are in his inner turmoil, we cannot be certain that finally we know him. For Bellow has not provided a critical check: there is no way of learning what any of the other characters, by way of Jamesian correction, might think or feel about Herzog. Bellow offers not a full-scale characterization but a full-length exposure of a state of being. We do not see Herzog acting in the world, we are made captive in the world of Herzog. The final picture is that of Herzog in cross-section, bleeding from the cut.

In one sense, then, there is a complete identification between Bellow and Herzog: the consciousness of the character forms the enclosing medium of the novel. But in a more important respect Bellow manages skillfully to avoid the kind of identification which might lead one to conclude that he "favors" his central character or fails to see through his weaknesses and falsities—a fault that could radically distort the line of vision by which everything is to be considered. That Herzog cannot accurately perceive the other figures in the novel and that we are closely confined to his sense of them, is true and in ways I shall later suggest, a limitation. But not a crippling limitation. For it soon becomes clear that, while totally committed to Herzog's experience, Bellow is not nearly so committed to his estimate of that experience.

Things, to be sure, do not always work out neatly. There are sections in which the malice toward Madeleine gets out of hand, so much so that one suspects Bellow of settling private scores. And while the device of having Herzog compose imaginary letters is often amusing—"Dear Doktor Professor Heidigger, I should like to know what you mean by the expression 'the fall into the quotidian.' When did this fall occur? Where were we standing when it happened?"—one becomes somewhat irked at being unable, at times, to grasp which of the letters are serious, that is, Bellow's opinions, and which are not, that is, Herzog's conniptions. Ambiguity? No doubt. We all know about this prime blessing of modern literature; but there are occasions when the uses of ambiguity can themselves be ambiguous, shading off into confusion or evasiveness.

For the most part, however, *Herzog* marks a notable advance in technique over Bellow's previous books. He has become a master of something that is rarely discussed in criticism because it is hard to do more than point toward it: the art of timing, which concerns the massing, centering and disposition of the characters and creates a sense of delight in the sheer motion of the narrative.

Bellow has also found a good solution to a technical problem which keeps arising in the contemporary novel. Most readers, I imagine, groan a little when they see a novelist wheeling into position one of those lengthy and leaden flashbacks in which, we know in advance, the trauma will be unveiled that is to explain the troubles of time-present. These flashbacks, by now one of the dreariest conventions of the novel, result in a lumpiness of narrative surface and blockage of narrative flow. But Bellow has managed to work out a form in which the illusion of simultaneity of time—a blend of past with the present-moving-into-future—is nicely maintained. Instead of the full-scale flashback, which often rests on the mistaken premise that a novelist needs to provide a psychiatric or sociological casebook on his characters, Bellow allows the consciousness of his narrator to flit about in time, restlessly, nervously, thereby capturing essential fragments of the past as they break into the awareness of the present. Through these interlockings of time—brief, dramatic and made to appear simultaneous—he creates the impression of a sustained rush of experience.

Bellow began his career as a novelist of somber intellectuality: his impressive early book *The Victim* asks almost to be read as a fable concerning the difficulties of attempting a secure moral judgment in our day. With *Augie March* he made a sharp turn, casting aside the urban contemplativeness and melancholy of his previous work, and deciding to regard American life as wonderfully "open," a great big shapeless orange bursting with the juices of vitality. Though in some ways his most virtuoso performance, *Augie March* suffers from a programmatic exuberance: it is fun to watch the turns and tricks the suddenly acrobatic Bellow can execute, yet hard to suppress a touch of anxiety concerning his heart-beat.

With *Augie March* Bellow also began to work out a new fictional style, for which there may be some predecessors— just possibly Daniel Fuchs and Nathanael West—but which in the main is an original achievement. By now it has come to be imitated by many American Jewish novelists as well as by a few gentiles trying wistfully to pass, but not of these manages it nearly so well as Bellow himself.

What Bellow did was to leave behind him the bleak neutrality of naturalistic prose and the quavering sensibility of the Jamesian novel: the first, he seemed to feel, was too lifeless and the second insufficiently masculine. Beginning with *Augie March*—but none of this applies to his masterful novella, *Seize the Day*—Bellow's prose becomes strongly anti-literary, a roughing up of diction and breaking down of syntax in order to avoid familiar patterns and expectations. The prose now consists of a rich, thick impasto of verbal color in which a splatter of sidewalk eloquence is mixed with erudite byplay. Together with this planned coarsening of texture, there is a great emphasis on speed, a violent wrenching and even forcing of images, all the consequence of his wish to break away from the stateliness of the literary sentence. Analytic refinement is sacrificed to sensuous vigor, careful psychological notation to the brawling of energy, syntactical qualification to kinesthetic thrust. (One is reminded a bit of action painting.) Psychology is out, absolutely out: for to psychologize means to reflect, to hesitate, to qualify, to modulate, to analyze. By contrast, the aim of Bellow's neo-baroque style is to communicate sensations of immediacy and intensity, even when dealing with abstract intellectual topics—to communicate, above all, the sense that men are still alive. Toward this end he is pre-pared to yield niceties of phrasing, surface finish, sometimes even coherence of structure.

It is a style admirably suited to the flaming set-piece, the rapid vignette, the picaresque excursion. But it is not so well suited to a sustained and complex action, or a lengthy flow of experience, or a tragic plot, or what George Moore, in discussing the nature of fiction, called the "rhythmic sequence of events." In *Augie March* there is a run of action but hardly a plot; in *Herzog* a superbly-realized situation but hardly a developing action; and in both of these novels, as well as in *Henderson,* not much of a "rhythmic sequence of events." That is why, I think, none of them has a fully satisfying denouement, an organic fulfillment of the action. In principle these books could continue forever, and that is one reason Bellow finds it hard to end them. He simply stops, much against one's will.

Finally, Bellow's style draws heavily from the Yiddish, not so much in borrowed diction as in underlying intonation and rhythm. Bellow's relation to Yiddish is much more easy and authoritative than that of most other American Jewish writers. The jabbing interplay of ironies, the intimate vulgarities, the strange blend of sentimental and sardonic which characterizes Yiddish speech are lassoed into Bellow's English: so that what we get is not a sick exploitation of folk memory but a vibrant linguistic and cultural transmutation. (Precisely at the moment when Yiddish is dying off as an independent language, it has experienced an astonishing, and not always happy, migration into American culture. In two or three decades students of American literature may have to study Yiddish for reasons no worse than those for which students of English literature study Anglo-Saxon.)

One of the most pleasing aspects of *Herzog* is that Bellow has brought together his two earlier manners: the melancholy and the bouncy, the "Russian" and the "American," *Seize the Day* and *Augie March*. *Herzog* is almost free of the gratuitous verbalism which marred *Augie March*, yet retains its vividness and richness of texture. The writing is now purer, chastened and a great deal more disciplined.

There is a similar marshaling of Bellow's earlier themes. For some years now he has been obsessed with that fatigue of spirit which hangs so dismally over contemporary life. *Seize the Day* shows a man utterly exhausted, unable so much as to feel his despair until the wrenching final page. *Augie March* shows a man composing a self out of a belief in life's possibilities. Of the two books *Seize the Day* seems to me the more convincing and authentic, perhaps because despair is easier to portray than joy, perhaps because the experience of our time, as well as its literature, predisposes us to associate truth with gloom. In any case, what seems notable about Herzog is that nothing is here blinked or evaded, rhetoric does not black out reality (Herzog declares himself "aging, vain, terribly narcissistic, suffering without proper dignity"); yet the will to struggle, the insistence upon human possibility, is maintained, and not as a mere flourish but as the award of agony. Herzog learns that "...To look for fulfillment in another...was a feminine game. And the man who shops from woman to woman, though his heart aches with idealism, with the desire for pure love, has entered the female realm." Not, perhaps, a very remarkable lesson, but worth learning when the cost comes high. More importantly, Herzog says about himself, wryly but truthfully, that he is a man who "thought and cared about belief." To think and care about belief: that is the first step toward salvation.

For all its vividness as performance, *Herzog* is a novel driven by an idea. It is a serious idea, though, in my judgment, neither worked out with sufficient care nor worked into the grain of the book with sufficient depth. Herzog, he tells us, means to write something that will deal "with a new angle on the modern condition, showing how life could be lived by renewing universal connections, overturning the last of the Romantic errors about the uniqueness of the Self, revising the old Western, Faustian ideology...." This time clearly speaking for Bellow, Herzog declares himself opposed to

The canned sauerkraut of Spengler's "Prussian Socialism," the commonplaces of the Wasteland outlook, the cheap mental stimulants of Allienation, the cant and rant of pipsqueaks about Inauthenticity and Forlornness. I can't accept this foolish dreariness. We are talking about the whole life of mankind. The subject is too great, too deep for such weakness, cowardice. . . .

And in the magazine *Location* Bellow has recently written an attack on the "the 'doom of the West' [which] is the Established Church in modern literature." It is a Church, he says, which asserts the individual to be helpless among the impersonal mechanisms and sterilities of modern life; it cultivates self-pity and surrender; and it is wrong.

Bellow has touched on something real. Talk about "the decline of the West" can be elitist rubbish. The posture of alienation, like any other, can collapse into social accomodation. Cries of despair can become mere notes of fashion. Where the motif of alienation in the literature of modernism during the nineteenth and early twentieth centuries signified an act of truth, courage and sometimes rebellion too, now it can easily become the occasion for a mixture of private snobbism and public passivity. Yet may not all ideas suffer this sort of outcome in a culture which seems endlessly capable of assimilating and devitalizing everything? Suppose Bellow's assault upon alienation becomes fashionable (it is not hard to imagine the positive thinkers who will hasten to applaud): will it not then suffer a public fate similar to that of the ideas he attacks?

Bellow is being just a little too cavalier in so readily disposing of a central theme of modernist literature. Surely, as it was manifested in the work of writers like Joyce, Flaubert, Eliot and Baudelaire, the sense of alienation expressed a profound and even exhilarating response to the reality of industrial society. (An imagining of despair can be as bracing as a demand for joy can be ruthless.) And does not the sense of alienation, if treated not as a mere literary convenience but as a galling social fact—does this not continue to speak truthfully to significant conditions in our life?

I raise these matters because Bellow, as a serious writer, must want his readers to consider them not merely in but also beyond the setting of his novel. When, however, one does consider them strictly in the context of *Herzog*, certain critical issues present themselves. There is a discrepancy between what the book actually is—brilliant but narrow in situation and scope—and the sweeping intentions that lie behind it; or in other words, between the dramatic texture and the thematic purpose. In the end one feels that *Herzog* is too hermetic a work, the result of a technique which encloses us rigidly in the troubles of a man during his phase of withdrawal from the world. The material is absorbing in its own right; it is handled with great skill; but in relation to the intended theme, it all seems a little puny.

Bellow has conceived of the book as a stroke against the glorification of the sick self, but the novel we have—as picture, image, honest exposure—remains largely caught up with the thrashings of the sick self. One wants from Bellow a novel that will not be confined to a single besieged consciousness but instead will negotiate the kind of leap into the world which he proclaims, to savor the world's freshness and struggle against its recalcitrance, perhaps even to enter "politics in the Aristotelian sense."

Meanwhile, critics and readers, let us be grateful.

(1964)

MATTHEW JOSEPHSON

Virginia Woolf

The dilemma of the novel as an artistic medium has been most lucidly resumed by that young Parisian philosopher and erstwhile chieftain of the Superrealists, M. André Breton: *"The Marquise went out at five o'clock*—there," he says, in effect, "is the formula with which all your novels begin." They end of course, with her coming back, more or less, somewhere, at some time, and in some state or other. In the interim (which must be about an inch and a quarter in thickness of paper), she has had presumably interesting encounters or interviews: she has fallen in love, or she has been seduced, or broken an ankle, or lost money at the races, or endured a thousand and one other plausible experiences, so long as all these phenomena offer a *story*. Now, though the medium of prose fiction, newest of all literary media, has had great popular fortune in the four hundred years since Bocaccio's *novella,* and especially in the last two centuries, it has shown every sign, during our own generation, of approaching an esthetic saturation point. Even the correspondence schools teach us that the quantity of situations, "triangles," intrigues, is limited; and if the partially critical reader seems sometimes surfeited with recent examples of prose fiction, then the talented or ambitious writer, who is a prospective novelist, is even earlier surfeited, and must start from the problem: how to write a novel *without telling a story.*

The muscular French and Russian realists of the nineteenth century had their own solution, to be sure: by telling a story-with-a-moral; that is, by being interesting and rather positive social philosphers. Their procedure was quite definitely taken over by men of letters such as H. G. Wells (in his earlier phase) and John Galsworthy, who did what they could, tolerably well and without novelty. But at some point in the twentieth century, immediately before or during World War I, the widespread moral certainties which had buoyed up the prolific realists were generally lost. It is at this point that innovators such as Virginia Woolf, James Joyce, Gertrude Stein and the unjustly forgotten Dorothy Richardson—I leave aside the question of priority—may be said to enter the literary scene and confront the dilemma earlier announced.

Since the novels of Mrs. Woolf, long conceded to be infinitely talented, sensitive and of a brilliant technique, are now accorded a permanent place in modern literature, and given, despite their artistic heresies, the honors of a collected popular edition—it is almost like becoming a member of the Academy—one is prompted to review her career a little and to trace her interesting mutations and her progression, during some fifteen years in which she has wrestled with the problems of her craft.

She was virtually born to letters, her father having been Sir Leslie Stephen—O grave and dull Victorian, may he rest in peace!—and her grandfather, the perennial, the irrepressible Thackeray himself. There was "atmosphere" in her house, as in that cultured house which Henry James evokes for us in *The Spoils of Poynton;* moreover, she and her sister had as their friends certain bright young men, Mr. Clive Bell (who married the sister), Mr. G. Lytton Strachey, Mr. John

Maynard Keynes, and ultimately Mr. Leonard Woolf (who married her). I mention these names, now so resonant, of the members of the "Bloomsbury Group," to indicate the surrounding conditions of intelligence, consciousness and critical alertness under which Virginia Woolf made her first essays. Nor must we forget that in the London of those days there was the presence of the aged Henry James, a great and mystifying teacher of the craft of fiction, who had been discouraged by our fathers from clinging to these shores.

The first novel, *The Voyage Out* (1915), was "promising," one is forced to say. It was gracefully written, successfully conceived, and announced a finely imaginative writer who built character and situations out of "suggestion," rather than by the way of massive realism, a writer in the tradition of Turgeniev, let us say, or of Henry James in his *Daisy Miller*. It distinguished itself from other works by its capable, significant development of atmosphere, South American and exotic at that; but in this department it fails to surpass its good models, or even Mr. E. M. Forster's *A Passage to India,* with which it obviously invites comparison. A first novel that was not easily forgotten, on the whole; one that very few of us would have been ashamed to write. It is, perhaps, most perplexing and disappointing that *Night and Day,* the long novel that followed two or three years later, was in almost every sense a failure; and I can scarcely believe that it really follows Virginia Woolf's first, interesting venture. It is as if she had been advised to abandon her arts of "suggestion" and to attempt a conventional novel in the grand old style, dealing with the *fiançailles* of three or four marriageable and rather pendantically literary persons, whose troubles, resistances and solutions make up such a mild Victorian comedy of manners and of petty social differences as the British novelists had been writing for better or worse and for a century or more.

For such an academic labor, this hypersensitive woman, who could write passages of the purest English style, simply did not have "her heart in it." In these pages, everything

went rigid, trivial or flat. I remember, then, the delightful
surprise with which I read, toward 1921, one of her short
tales or sketches, entitled "In a Garden," of a somewhat later
period, and included in the collection called *Monday or
Tuesday*. These smaller pieces, in her ripened manner, were
written, like *Jacob's Room* (1922), in the years that followed
World War I.

II

Like nearly all intelligent Europeans, Virginia Woolf had
undergone a great personal revolution during the war years.
The upheavals and the new social alignments, the emergence
of new philosophies and new or old despairs, all took a direct
effect. There were also the frightfully immediate emotional
aspects: for it is my impression that Mrs. Woolf's son died in
the War. . . .

All sorts of things were in the air, which was charged with
so much hope, dread and anguish, as we remember. There
was Bolshevism and Americanism, Futurism and Dadaism;
there was an excitement for change and experiment, while
Mr. Ezra Pound and Mr. Wyndham Lewis exploded or
"blasted" with innovations borrowed from the young French
artists. One was oppressed, now by the sense of a cruel
insecurity, of the end of a world, now by the sure need of
returning to a few cherished objects or principles, above all,
to the sense of beauty. Virginia Woolf, too, renewed or found
herself; she became in her prose what we had best call, for
the sake of definiteness, an "impressionist."

I am sure that just as music deeply influenced the
Symbolist literature of the 1870-1890 era in Europe, so the
painters of the post-Cézanne school made their great mark
upon the writers who rose out of the War. The picture of life
that formed itself in Mrs. Woolf's mind was now of
something breathless, fleeting, wonderfully deceiving; something of infinitely changing or dissolving substance and tint;

something impossible to organize or penetrate, except subjectively, through the inevitable limits of the human temperament. Inconceivable now to write novels-with-plots, by the Victorian formula. Where she had once been a gently ironic commentator on life, manners, character, she now became a supremely sensitive and passive mechanism, a sensorium receiving reality avidly, and emitting it in "blobs of color," as Mr. E. M. Forster terms it, in "gasps and drones," in streams of similes, unfinished sentences, hectic catalogues, unanchored proper names. The extension of her technique, the new kind of awareness she shows, may be indicated best by the following passage from *Jacob's Room:*

....To show how very little control of our possessions we have—what an accidental affair this living is after all our civilization—let me just count over a few of the things lost in one lifetime, beginning, for that seems always the most mysterious of all losses — what cat would gnaw, what rat would nibble—with three pale blue canisters of book-binding tools? Then there were the bird cages, the iron hoops, the steel skates, the Queen Anne coal scuttle, the bagatelle board, the hand organ—all gone, and jewels, too. Opals and emeralds, they lie about the roots of turnips. What a scraping, paring affair it is to be sure! The wonder is that I've any clothes on my back, that I sit surrounded by solid furniture at this moment. Why, if one wants to compare life to anything, one must liken it to be being blown through the Tube at fifty miles an hour—landing at the other end without a single hair pin in one's hair! Shot out at the feet of God entirely naked! Tumbling head over heals in the asphodel meadows like brown paper parcels pitched down a chute in the post office!

There is confusion here, as in the spectacle seen all about; and yet it is seen by an imagination in love with the concrete. When most felicitous, Mrs. Woolf is even robust, like Lady Wortley-Montagu or Fanny Burney; and at her best moments there are, in her extravagance of metaphor as in her dissociations, inescapable meanings and implications. After all that has passed, "life, London, this moment of June," is to be seized, to be lived rapturously, even; and if one is an artist, to be evoked in all its color, fullness, and especially its time-qualities or fluidity.

In *Jacob's Room* a "new type of fiction has swum into view"; but little clear understanding has spread of just what changes or advances this new prose fiction implies. We may say that the intention of the artist was to be neither "representative" nor historical, just as Cézanne, for example, in his paintings sought to evoke life while fleeing the photographic. Replacing our hypothetical "Marquise" who "went out at five o'clock," with the remembered youth and student Jacob, we may add significantly that he is dead before the book opens, and so can do nothing the "Marquise" might do. Again, it is interesting to ponder over the very title of the book: *Jacob's Room*. We are in a room, filled with the presence of the dead youth, with the *things* of him. We never meet him or live with him, as in Dumas. He is known only through his effect upon the people and objects around him. He is recollected; and we know only that he lived here, that he loved, that he studied—there is great intellectual drama even in his reading of the *Phaedrus*. It is all an exquisite dirge, filled with the most precise images, the freshest perceptions; and in the end Jacob has been blocked out or sculptured out of the airiest, the most intangible things: out of dreams, hints, half-remembrances, secret gestures, fragments of sentences, and out of prose rhythms. For the novelist, abandoning "plot," and employing the new poetics (which certain of here above-mentioned contemporaries also use), has sought to weave a series of impressions, "suggestions," moods and states of mind, indirectly induced in the reader, as by music, about a luminous center, an idea. In this case, the idea is the figure of Jacob within the restless flow of time.

III

If *Jacob's Room* seems, to a retrospective view, a veritable masterpiece, to be set up permanently beside certain larger and smaller ones of modern literature, then *Mrs. Dalloway*

(1925), is an even more complete, brilliant, zestful affair. It is a moment in the life of all London, a day which the chimes of Big Ben punctuate, over which the Houses of Parliament loom, and whose restlessly flowing and ebbing colors, shapes, *disjecta,* are clustered about the person of Mrs. Dalloway. To respond to the spirited yet mysterious movements and changes of pace of this prose, we too must be imaginative and sensitive, so that the delicate symphony, the whole adroit, cinematic arrangement, possesses us completely. Mrs. Dalloway is, presumably, a superb example of English civilization and beauty; out of the vague movements of persons and events around her there comes the culmination of a certain melodrama and tragic bafflement, from which she returns swiftly, warily, almost like an acrobat, with a revived sense of life, of its beauty and also of its fatality and cruelty.

There is something evasive and almost too *raffinée* about this artist; we must agree with her, for instance, that "It's not catastrophes, murders, deaths, diseases, that age and kill us; it's the way people look and laugh, and run up the steps of omnibuses." For Virginia Woolf is tremendously feminine, aggressively feminine in her intelligence, her perceptions, her intuitions; her plea for the fullest enjoyment of the sense of life and the sense of beauty is an intensely feminine view. She would build up again the purely feminine intelligence, with its genius and its limitations, one feels in reading "A Room of One's Own"; and to understand her fully one must read that beautiful essay.

The limitations, that is, the evasiveness, overrefinement, oversuggestiveness, seem to come out rather more freely in *To the Lighthouse* (1927), which completes the triad of short novels in the impressionistic genre. (I use the term "impressionistic" here, not to denigrate, but in a rather free and general sense, since it calls to mind the tendency traditionally opposed to the literal and "representative" type of art; other terms applied to Joyce, Gertrude Stein, Virginia Woolf and writers of their school, such as "symbolist," are apt to be confusing; "modernist" is misleading and detestable.) Reading this novel, the portrait of a Mrs. Ramsay, it is as if I have seen Virginia Woolf's cultured English lady once too often, and have become callous toward her. Too much pregnant taciturnity; too many of those famous English silences. If one's interest declines perceptibly, so does the grasp of technique waver a little; emotion is quietly tortured away in a too tenuous prose, which is all in short breaths or gasps—largely, monotonously in iambs, to be perfectly candid. There is, in this book, at least one long, beautiful chapter of interlude, "Time Passes"—after the death of Mrs. Ramsay—which gives uncannily the sense of passing time and forms a kind of Einsteinian poem in itself. *To the Lighthouse* seems weaker in interest, the interruptions and dissociations less skillful, or artistically justified, yet it represents still a very high order of art.

Of *Orlando* (1930), not included as yet in the collected edition of Virginia Woolf, I have said nothing. Its scheme of fantasy and variation is plainly a departure in a new direction, successful enough in its way, yet giving no light on the questions of craftsmanship here studied. Sometimes the artist, by venturing into bypaths of his medium, may discover enough secrets of self-renewal for a fresh start; sometimes he may lose himself. . .

Mr. Arnold Bennett has observed of Mrs. Woolf's novels that not only is their moral basis undiscernible, but that they "seriously lack vitality." And it seems true, after all, that much of the "new type of fiction" written during the 1920s has sacrificed some important principle of energy, in its pursuit of the suggestive, the pervasive, and of pure form. Joyce, to be sure, had this principle of energy in *Ulysses;* but one hopes that some new and different personality will arise, who knows as well how to use the full orchestra, while leaving behind the terrible, end-of-the-century moods which Joyce crystallized. Mrs. Woolf's particular contribution lies in her remarkable extension of the zone of sensibility; at her best, she has the most penetrating, the most candid vision, yet she has kept her sense of beauty—a sense which too many of our facile young exploiters, here, of Middle Western corn fields and farm kitchens have either lost or never acquired. With the sense of beauty, literature, even the modern novel, may survive.

(1931)

STANLEY KAUFFMANN

Lady Chatterley's Lover

Thirty-one years after its initial private publication in Italy, the unexpurgated final version of *Lady Chatterley's Lover* appears in this country. An abridged edition of this version was published here in 1930; the first version (of the three Lawrence wrote) appeared here in 1944. Now the general public may read what has heretofore been available only to contrabandists and scholars with access to locked library shelves.

The novel's publication inevitably raises the issue, not only of intrinsic literary merit but of censorship. First, is the book censorable? The answer is: Indeed, yes. In the light of current legal and extra-legal practice, its language and many of its scenes come well within the usual scope of the suppressors. No doubt there are books containing language and scenes perhaps even more daring that have been untouched, but the law does not have to indict A, B, and C in order to indict D. Luck and notoriety are more operative in these matters than logic.

Ulysses apart, this is the most notorious novel of the twentieth century, prosecuted from Poland to Japan. As late as 1953 an English magistrate inveighed against the *expurgated* version (the only one permitted there) as "absolute rubbish." Now Grove Press has decided to test the unexpurgated book here and is getting a quick reply to the challenge. In Washington a criminal law test has already begun; in New York the Post Office Department has seized mailings and will shortly decide whether the book is mailable.

For those of us who doubt the moral superiority, let alone the keener literary taste, of police chiefs and postal inspectors, the great snare in proceedings of this sort is a kind of surprised tedium. The serious writer and reader are concerned with the exploration of human relationships, therefore always at least to some degree concerned with sex, and are jolted out of their concern in a curious way by the obtrusion of police and postmen. The first reaction is often to smile; it seems almost as anachronistic and silly to become angry as to rush out and shout "Votes for women!" How can one fight seriously, one feels, about a matter which has so long ago been taken to the barricades and which has for so long been settled in one's own mind?

Yet—and this must be faced at least—the fight goes on: because the police-postal mind goes on and has, besides its superiority in numbers, one huge advantage. It can define obscenity. Dogmatism always has an advantage over the free-ranging mind. Some of us are stuck (one might say) with the passionate belief that obscenity cannot be defined, that what disturbs one man will be perfectly acceptable to another, that no universal moral yardstick is ever possible. The tendency to deprave and corrupt is usually taken as the touchstone of obscenity. Well, if it is any help, I can report to the Post Office that I have just finished this book and would not be a whit purer if I had not read it.

Very possibly the matter of censorship will never be settled until we look past the immediate battle which, even if won, really cures nothing, and examine the source of the urge to censor. Its conduit is, almost always, the ecclesiastical channel, but perhaps this is only another instance of the wisdom of the church (all churches) in recognizing and using human truths. The reluctance to abolish capital punishment lies, probably, not in concepts of justice but in latent sadism; just as probably, the reluctance to abolish censorship arises fundamentally not from a desire to protect our fourteen-year-old daughters but from repressions that society puts on our own sexual lives and thoughts. The sexually happy man or woman is not deeply interested in or conscious of police notions of decency.

This is not to say that even the healthiest parent will necessarily want to put *Lady Chatterley* into the hands of his early adolescent son or daughter, any more than he will want his son to lift a weight that he could handle at twenty or his young daughter to marry immediately and have children. But he resents being told that he may not give the book to them—even mail it to them—when he sees fit; may not, in fact, buy it for himself.

The law insists not only that it can decide what is proper for me to read (and I may be a lot less tolerant than you), it implicitly assumes that if it didn't protect me, I would do nothing else but buy pornographic books and see pornographic films. Its attitude is that of Latin civilizations toward their women—if it weren't for the duenna, they would certainly misbehave. A nice compliment to their wives and daughters; a nice compliment by the law to you and me.

Sometimes it is granted that you and I could be trusted but that most people need protection, and so we must put up with the inconvenience for the sake of the majority. That the weak-willed exist is inarguable; equally so, that we all have our weak-willed moments. Certainly, too, in the absence of censorship laws, cheapjack publishers and film producers would rush to exploit the new liberty. But can one honestly visualize mass corruption as the result? The mere increase and availability of salacious material would tend to surfeit its audience. Nudity soon bores; and the makers of pornographic pictures soon elicit only pity as they so fruitlessly struggle for variety.

Undoubtedly there are members of society who might be seriously affected by exposure to pornographic materials, but it is hardly rational to gear society to the level of its weakest members, like a wartime convoy. In any event, can such highly susceptible persons be protected merely by censoring books and films? Is it not then also necessary to ban lingerie shop windows and the wearing of perfume in public and dancing? Is it not illogical to do less? And is it not madness to abolish freedom because some would abuse it? Do we ban French-fried potatoes because a few of us have ulcers?

Some of the censor's best blows are struck, I believe, by his enemies, because they cannot agree on one basic principle: all censorship—of any kind—is untenable and immoral. It is they, the opponents, anxious to prove that they are "decent" even though they are liberal, who hamstring themselves. They oppose, let us say, restrictions on serious literature but they affirm stoutly that there must be some control over trash. (And who is to differentiate? And suppose there are people who want to read trash. What about *their* civil liberties?) Or certain works may be circulated to adults but not to children, the decisive factors being availability and price. Trade books and the theatre must not be censored, low-priced, paper-bound books and films must be controlled. (And the whole sneaky war of adolescents versus their parents must be perpetuated, a war which the adolescent always wins. Adolescent interest in sex cannot be censored out of existence. As with liquor, home influence is the only real safeguard.)

Worst of all, in my view, is the liberals' argument that books like *Lady Chatterley* are not sexual, they are Beautiful. Surely, they say, the magistrate must see that this novel is spiritual, not physical. This, to me, is the most wrong-headed of defenses and self-defeating. The erotic passages in *Lady Chatterley* are most certainly intended to evoke erotic responses. Not something mistily lovely but distinctly sexual. The artist has as much right—even necessity—to evoke that response in a reader as he has to evoke appreciation of a landscape. If Lawrence doesn't make you feel in your very glands what it meant to Connie and Mellors to find at last a satisfactory sexual partner, then he has failed as an artist.

There is the crux of the matter. Let not the defenders of *Lady Chatterley* claim that it is, by postal definition, a "pure" work. It is a sexually stimulating work (among other things) and rightly so. To lose that point is to betray Lawrence. What must not be conceded to the Post Office and others is that sexual stimulation is necessarily, or usually, synonymous with depravity and corruption. Or as Mr. Justice Stable said in his charge to the jury in a recent English obscenity case, "Is the act of sexual passion sheer filth? It may be an error in taste to write about it. It may be a matter in which perhaps old-fashioned people would mourn the reticence that was observed in these matters yesterday. But is it sheer filth?"

Certainly there is, as noted earlier, such a thing as pornography—by derivation "the writing of prostitutes." Most of us have seen examples of it which seem to have no *raison d'être* besides almost mechanical sexual stimulation; and as soon as we are old enough to appreciate a context, we reject it as having little to do with sexual realities or even desirabilities. At best it becomes funny, not inflammatory. Must society cripple serious artists in order to obliterate the relatively minor nuisance of pornography? If centimeters of bare skin are the criterion, we will not only have to burn crates full of *Tillie and Mac* but also the canvases of such an utterly sexual artist as Renoir.

There is no viable, no *moral* middle-ground in this matter. Opponents of restriction on the artist's freedom are forced to fight also for the freedom of the pornographer. Anything less is to appease the beast by feeding him scraps that only keep him alive to attack you. You may throw him garbage, but it strengthens him, nevertheless.

The matter is uniquely complicated in this instance because of the personality of Lawrence. In spite of his life-long tribulations with censors, he was himself considerable of a prude. He called *Lady Chatterley* a "phallic novel, but tender and delicate"; but he called *Ulysses* a "dirty" book. Norman Douglas said (as quoted in Nehls' excellent composite biography): "Lawrence was no Bohemian; he was a provincial, an inspired provincial with marked puritan leanings. He had a shuddering horror of Casanova's *Memoirs;* he was furious with a friend for keeping two mistresses instead of one, and even with the Florentine boys for showing an inch or two of bare flesh above the knee—'I don't like it! I don't like it! Why can't they wear trousers?'; my own improprieties of speech he ascribed to some perverse kink of my nature."

Thus we find that *Lady Chatterley* must be defended against its own author's private state of mind as found in others. Well, history is largely the record of God-sure people butchering people who are differently God-sure, so it is a relatively minor irony that a literary rebel should want to impose bonds on other rebels. To protect Lawrence's work, we must see what he did not see; that the only sure route to freedom for him is via the freedom not only of Joyce and Casanova but of *Fanny Hill,* as well.

The previously suppressed passages of *Lady Chatterley's Lover* are so numerous and so integral that no criticism based on the abridged version can have validity. Euphemism and ellipsis are maiming to a work which depends for its effect not only on certain sexual actions and reactions but also on a vulgar vocabulary. To "love" a woman did not mean the same thing to Lawrence as its ruder four-letter synonym. It is this confrontation of what may be called the facts of the facts of life that is an essential of this work. Whether this confrontation is artistically successful (as distinct from being morally permissible) is another, interesting subject.

Two of the most commonly held assumptions about this novel are that it is a symbolical work and that it is the story of a triangle. In my view, both these assumptions are wrong. It is an explicit *roman à thèse,* with nothing left symbolical, everything carefully spelled out; and it is the story of a quadrangle.

Lawrence's thesis, well-known, is that civilization is destroying the human spirit: that the intellect, as well as the machine, is the enemy of life: that we stand in this century (H-bomb or no) on the brink of destruction: and that only a return to a full life of the emotions can save us from withering and death. But these ideas are not merely symbolized in this book; every major character fully articulates his point of view. Nothing is left hinted at, shadowy or suggestive. Even Clifford's war wound is an absolute fact, completely utilized on the topmost level of the book, not a symbol like Jake's in *The Sun Also Rises*. The factories beyond the park, the dreariness of the Midland towns, the currents of English and world society, the meaning of Mellors' revolt, all these and more are dealt with in the explicit propagandistic vein of Ibsen and Zola at their most hortatory—as far removed from, say, the symbolic methods of Melville or some of Lawrence's other work like *The Plumed Serpent* and *The Fox* as is imaginable. The poetry in this book, where it exists, lies in the emotional states arrived at openly by the characters, not in any symbolic illumination of forces beneath the surface of life.

This explicitness is further augmented by the quadrangle—by the pairing of Mrs. Bolton, the nurse, with Clifford as a balance for the pairing of Mellors with Connie. In this unabridged version it is clear that, in his impotent, lately childish fashion, Clifford is as sexually involved with his nurse as his wife is with the gamekeeper. The relationship is necessarily different for physical reasons, but the outcome, in character development, is much the same. He becomes a fuller, more competent man. It is surely laboring the term "symbolism" to apply it to this patent (and literal) man-handling of the aristocrat by this deep-breasted working woman. Clifford himself, if not the critics, knows what has happened to him.

These two points aside, the most remarkable thing about

the novel is that it seems considerably more than thirty-one years old. Consider that 1928, the year of its first publication, was also the year of *The Sound and the Fury* and that *The Sun Also Rises* was already two years old, and you see not only an illustration of the difference between the novel's development here and in Britain; you see plainly that Lawrence is a man from the past coming forward, not an innovator. The Hemingway and Faulkner novels, from their first words, exist as themselves, unselfconscious and new. *Lady Chatterley* seems a late Edwardian novel, still trailing bits of plush as it pushes onward. To the present-day reader, it has a good deal of the air of *fin de siècle* rebellion—glimpsed twenty-five years later but still the same Free Love Marching and Chowder Society. And it is this air that gives the repeated use of earthy language a tone of forced bravado rather than of healthy shock and peasant candor.

There are, too, a couple of nervousnesses in the book. First, although a major portion of the story deals with Connie's movement from the sterility of the educated upper classes to the pulsing elemental animalistic life of Mellors, Lawrence lacked the courage to make Mellors a pure animal, an O'Neill Hairy Ape. Mellors is not only a person of some intellect and education, he is also—with a nice bow to British proprieties—an ex-officer. The bet, therefore, is carefully hedged. Lawrence seems to have been afraid to make Mellors the ordinary countryman that a gamekeeper would usually be either because of a taint of conventional "appropriateness" left in his soul or because of a belief that an ordinary countryman would have made an uninteresting character. If either of these hypotheses is true, does that not impair his basic thesis? And if Lawrence felt he had to endow Mellors with some intellectual quality in order for Connie to be attracted to him, does not that too impair the thesis that salvation and worth reside in the sheerly elemental life?

The second nervousness is in relation to politics. The theme of Communism mutters through the novel like thunder on the horizon. It is discussed by various characters.

Mellors has "bolshevist books" in his bedroom. (In the first version of the novel the gamekeeper ended up as secretary of the local Communist Party.) Lawrence, with his extraordinary dog-like powers of scent, early sniffed the titanic changes for the world inherent in the Soviet revolution but lacked the intellectual courage or penetration to make decisions about them, pro or con. He could neither completely face them nor forget them.

Other curiosities might be noted. I do not understand Clifford's allowing his friends to use broad language in the presence of his wife, and I simply do not believe the way in which Connie's father jokes about her, sexually, with Mellors. There is an unsteadiness of control in points of view throughout the book, best exemplified by a little disquisition on the novel (by the intruding author) in chapter nine. Several times we are made aware of the author's chronic anti-Semitism—a fact largely glossed over in discussions of this love prophet.

But—and it is a large antithesis—in spite of its technical defects, its persistent air of hothouse freedom, its touches of fierce inverted snobbism, the novel finally triumphs over its faults. Its power derives from two factors, I believe. The first is Lawrence's total subscription to his work. This only seemingly contradicts the nervousnesses discussed above. The point is that *all* of Lawrence—imperfections and cripplings included—is thrown into his work, and his burning commitment carries him through the slightly ridiculous passages and the flaws. His fervor, born of revolt against smug morality and supercilious intellectualism, may be too vindictive to be whole-souled, but it is sufficient to sustain him through scenes that would sink a lesser man.

Second, his prophecies and beliefs seem to have been substantially validated by the passage of time. Civilization has not become, in as neat and pat a way as he thought, the slave of the machine; the wearing of red trousers by the villagers would do little for them now; but the pace and trend of modern life have to some degree anesthetized human feelings: have made large emotional experience very difficult in the Western world. The fight against intellectual conformity is much promulgated now, but the threat of emotional conformity is perhaps more important—since few people were ever intellectual non-conformists anyway. The sense of life as emotional adventure, as the opportunity to bare one's breast to the thorn and thus sing, is a diminishing one in our pre-packed, deep-freeze world. It may be that this is the root loss, the biggest price we have paid for technology and organization and factual knowledge; and it may be that only in the emotional man revived will it be possible to approach fullest truth. Of these beliefs Lawrence is a hobbled but dedicated spokesman.

That he is, in the most rigorous view, a great writer is worth doubting. That he is an important one is past question. The paradox of Lawrence, I believe, is that—unlike truly great artists—the more you have liberated yourself the less he means to you. Norman Douglas was perhaps cruelly accurate:

I think the writings of Lawrence have done good; his influence was needed by a large class of our fellow-creatures. He has done good negatively as a warning to thinkers and writers; positively, because his work is in the nature of a beneficent, tabu-shattering bomb. . . . Scholars amd men of the world will not find much inspiration in his novels. Lawrence opened a little window for the bourgeoisie. That is is life-work.

(1959)

STANLEY KAUFFMANN

Tropic of Cancer

Henry Miller's *Tropic of Cancer* is now published in this country in an unlavish edition of 318 pages set in big type at the price of $7.50—and this in spite of a large first printing. The interest of the price is that here it relates to the content of the book—not, as is usual, to its length or format. The publisher knows that the public knows the book's reputation and is willing to pay much more than is currently charged for books of similar production cost. This gives, from the start, a different atmosphere to its publication. Rather than call it cashing in on prurience, let us say that the publisher is asking the purchaser to make a contribution to a defense fund in case of legal prosecution, although no provision is made for refunding, say, three dollars per copy if the publisher is unmolested.

The book itself, first issued in 1934 in Paris (in English) is an autobiographical first novel recounting the experiences, sensations, thoughts of Miller, a penniless American in the Paris of the early thirties. It is not so much a novel as an intense journal, written daily about what was happening to him daily, full of emotion recollected in proximity, as he scrounged for food, devoured books, conversed volubly, and flung himself into numerous beds. It is formless, in the sense that it could have continued indefinitely, but then Miller is an enemy of form. He writes of a Ravel compositon:

> Suddenly it all dies down. It was as if [Ravel] remembered, in the midst of his antics, that he had on a cutaway suit. He arrested himself. A great mistake, in my humble opinion. Art consists in going the full length. If you start with the drums you have to end with the dynamite, or TNT. Ravel sacrificed something for form, for a vegetable that people must digest before going to bed.

The "full length" is Miller's ideal. Frankness of fact and devotion to truth are not always concurrent, but Miller has, within his powers, both of these. He says on an early page: "There is only one thing which interests me vitally now, and that is the recording of all that which is omitted in books."

He had been a husband and a hireling in various jobs in New York and elsewhere, always a hungry reader with literary ambitions, when at thirty-nine he broke loose and, without money, went alone to Paris to write. He swore he would never take a job again. In fact he takes two in this book—as a proofreader on the Paris *Tribune* and as an English teacher in Dijon. But the point was made—he had broken away.

Essentially that is what the book is: a mirror-image of the testimony which is given at revival meetings. There you can hear about men who got right with God; this man got right with art and sex and the use of his brain and time. Like all converts, he is on fire. Like all converts, he simply will not leave your lapels alone. Thus he is a bit tedious. Because he came fairly late in life to a personally valid ethic, he cannot believe that anyone he talks to has ever done it before him.

The book is a fierce celebration of his enlightened freedom, which is to say his acceptance of real responsibilities instead of merely respectable ones. But in the course of this paean he exhorts us mercilessly with such discoveries as: sex can be fun; America is commercialized and doomed; civilization must refurbish its values or perish. (Edmund Wilson has called the book "an epitaph for the whole generation that migrated to Europe after the war.") All this now suffers, of course, from the passage of time. These burning messages have been the commonplaces of novelists, most of them inferior to Miller, for at least a couple of decades. But could these views have been startling even in 1934? This was eight years after the publication of a much more widely read novel of Americans in Paris, *The Sun Also Rises.* Hemingway is as unlike Miller as is imaginable in temperament, but surely the new liberty and the dark apocalypse are in his book.

How Miller rages at us. And what is his chief complaint? That we are not like him, living like him, desiring and perceiving like him. A prime function of art is criticism, and if the artist in question has merit, he certainly *is* a superior person and modest coughs are out of order. But the smuggest bourgeois has no smugness like that of the self-consciously liberated bohemian. It tainted Gauguin and D. H. Lawrence; it infects Miller.

He is often compared to Whitman, which must please him because he thinks Whitman "that one lone figure which America has produced in the course of her brief life" (despite the fact that he began by worshipping Dreiser). There is considerable basis for the comparison, especially in attitude. Miller sees no democratic vistas and certainly does *not* hear America singing, but he, too, is a buddy of the universe and privy to its secrets, calling on the rest of us to be as open-shirted and breeze-breasting as himself. Also there is in Miller, although on a much lower level than in Whitman, a feeling of settled iconoclasm, of artistic revolt made stock-in-trade. There are attempts at bardic sweep, some of them successful, and there is Whitmanesque rejoicing in the smack of wine and flesh.

Sometimes Miller uses language stupidly (he calls Paris "more eternal" than Rome). Sometimes, as in the rhapsody on Matisse, he writes a symbolist poem with a heat that carries us across its weaker passages. Or he can transmute sensation into images that propagate like guppies. For example, one day, broke and hungry, he finds a concert-ticket and uses it.

My mind is curiously alert; it's as though my skull had a thousand mirrors inside it. My nerves are taut, vibrant! the notes are like glass balls dancing on a million jets of water. I've never been to a concert before on such an empty belly. Nothing escapes me, not even the tiniest pin falling. It's as though I had no clothes on and every pore of my body was a window and all the windows open and the light flooding my gizzards. I can feel the light curving under the vault of my ribs and my ribs hang there over a hollow nave trembling with reverberations. How long this lasts I have no idea; I have lost all sense of time and place. After what seems like an eternity there follows an interval of semiconsciousness balanced by such a calm that I feel a great lake inside me, a lake of iridescent sheen, cool as jelly; and over this lake, rising in great swooping spirals, there emerge flocks of birds of passage with long slim legs and brilliant plumage. Flock after flock surge up from the cool, still surface of the lake and, passing under my clavicles, lose themselves in the white sea of space. And then slowly, very slowly, as if an old woman in a white cap were going the rounds of my body, slowly the windows are closed and my organs drop back into place.

I have quoted this at length because it is a good cross-section of his style. "The tiniest pin" and "after what seems an eternity" and careless spewing; but the "old woman in a white cap" is orphic.

This is Miller. Narrative is not his forte; his characterizations are sketchy; his philosophy is jejune. It is in pressing his whole existence against the warm wax of his prose and leaving there its complete imprint that he is at his best—in following every quiver of sentience to its source or destination with phrases that sometimes add up to a gorgeous fabric. Karl Shapiro, in an introductory essay streaked with gibberish, says that "everything [Miller] has written is a poem in the best as well as in the broadest sense of the word." This is a sentimental and foolishly inclusive judgment, but it points in the right direction.

Shapiro says that Miller writes with "complete ease and naturalness" about sex, as Lawrence and Joyce did not. To me, there is (speaking only of this book) much less sex than bravado. As far as specific language is concerned, Lawrence thought there was something thaumaturgic in four-letter words and had Mellors speak them therapeutically. Joyce wrote down the words that his miraculous surgery of the psyche revealed. Miller employs them—mostly *outside* of dialogue—to demonstrate somewhat ostentatious emancipation and contempt for slaves of convention.

Anyway, to talk about complete naturalness in the use of those words by a member of our society is arrant nonsense. The only person who could use them completely naturally would be a mental defective unaware of taboos. The foulest-mouthed longshoremen knows that he is using naughty words and is wallowing in them. Miller uses them in an exultation very much like that of a college boy away from home for the first time.

Proof of his lack of naturalness about it lies in his avoidance of earthy language whe he talks about his great love, Mona. Virtually every other girl in the book, well or lightly regarded, is referred to at some time or other as a c--t. Making Mona an exception seems to show not only some residual puritanism but exhibitionism in the other cases. In fact, before one is far along in the book, the plentiful four-letter words become either irritating or tiresome. I thought of Robert Graves' remark that in the British army the adjective "f---ing" has come to mean only a signal that a noun is approaching.

Lawrence Durrell, no more reluctant than numerous other foreigners to tell Americans what their best works are, says that "American literature today begins and ends with the meaning of what [Miller] has done." Further: "To read *Tropic of Cancer* is to understand how shockingly remantic all European writing after Rousseau has become." (Durell, of all artists, must know that "romantic" is a qualitative not a pejorative term.) These statements are typical of the—to

215

me—inflated praise that this book has evoked. I hazard a couple of guesses at extrinsic reasons for this. First, when a gifted man writes a prosecutable book, it is often over-lauded as a tactical move by those interested in the freedom of letters—especially those who hold that sex is Beautiful, not sexy. Second, possibly these statements are, as much as anything else, a tribute to Miller's purity of commitment, to his abhorrence of the pietisms of Literature and the proprieties of the Literary Life, to his willingness—if not downright eagerness—to suffer for the right to live and write as he chooses. His is no small spirit, it is just not as large as some have told us.

Here, then is his first novel, available (*pro tem*, at least) in his own country twenty-seven years after its publication abroad. Durrell believes that its place is next to *Moby Dick*, which seems to me a hurtful thing to say about a frisky minnow of a book that ought not to be compared with leviathans. Far from being "the jewel and nonpareil" of American literature (Durrell again), Miller cannot be put near such twentieth-century novelists as Dreiser, Fitzgerald, early Dos Passos, early Hemingway—let alone Faulkner—without unfair diminution.

This book belongs, modestly but securely, in the American tradition of profundity-through-deliberate-simplicities that has its intellectual roots in Thoreau and continues through such men as Whitman and Sherwood Anderson until, in a changed time, it thinks it needs to go abroad to breathe. Miller stands under his Paris street-lamp, defiantly but genially drunk, trolling his catch mixed of beauty and banality and recurrent bawdry—a little pathetic because he thinks he is a discoverer and doesn't realize that he is only a tourist on a well-marked tour. We see him at last as an appealingly zestful, voracious, talented hick.

(1961)

ALFRED KAZIN

The Human Comedy

Running through Saroyan's work, and now the hero of *The Human Comedy*, is the figure of a telegraph boy—a modern American Mercury, riding his bike as Mercury ran on the winds, with a blue cap for an astral helmet and a telegraph blank waving the great tidings in his hand. Like most of us, Saroyan comes from that class to which a telegram is never a message, but always an intimation of disaster or great change, the first sounding of some awful ceremony. But here, as Saroyan saw it as a boy, the ceremony is seen through the eyes of the telegraph messenger, and it makes him an ubiquitous folk-character and something of a priest. As he brings news to men he symbolically brings them to each other; as he flits along the American towns, he beats his wings as if to embrace all the lonely Saroyan souls in them. Everything proximate to this boy is part of the human comedy; and he is everywhere. Homer Macauley stands for youth, for expectancy, for the keenness of an adolescence spent in the offices at night, where the sense of danger is gulped down like midnight coffee, and where each ticking brings some special knowledge. But he stands even more for the easy Saroyan knowledge of America, and the easier access to it; he stands for the struggle between his native innocence and the world's experience; and that is the point of the story.

This boy unites the American strands in himself; he carries them all. In his life can be heard the pulsing of all the telegraph keys over America—the silvery piping of all those interlocked metals and wires, the grim, visored men listening to the beat of each other's hands, listening to that telegraph heart beating over America. All the locked doors open to this boy; all the reverberations of the national experience are to be heard in him. But he is not only an agent; he is a hero; and his education is the drama of the book, his learning to cry, like Blake: "O Rose, thou art sick!" He is Saroyan's white dove, singing his songs of innocence and being soiled by the world's experience. Everything about him is pure, mock-Grecian in its sunniness and youth. Part of him is Oliver Optic—a grubby American hero supporting his widowed mother and little brother by carrying messages after school; pure and undefeated, but with no time to play, losing the dream girl to the rich brat across the aisle. Yet the town he lives in is Ithaca; his California is an old earth, but the last, as it were, to be settled by men; the last to have retained the old American innocence, the yea-saying power; and he has a little brother named Ulysses.

Ulysses' little adventures are to Homer's as the adventures of the classical Ulysses were to the adventures of Homer's imagination. Ulysses is in the chrysalis, or the purely physical, stage of the world's disillusion; he has only preposterous little adventures. He goes with an idiot friend to the public library and they stare at the covers; he gets caught in a bear trap at a shop while people watch painfully thorugh the window, and the aimless frolic of Ulysses' life is defined by the Dadaist touch of deadly simplicity which Saroyan adds when the child is freed: "The crowd in front of the store cheered, but not effectively, as they were unorganized and had no leader." Or you may see him, as in one of Don

Freeman's friendly head drawings, staring up at the ceiling, just wondering.

But Homer has entered into the human realm; everything he sees on his rounds leads him from the songs of innocence to the songs of experience; and where he saw only Blake's lamp, and was the lamb, he now sees the "tyger burning bright." But this is an exaggeration, for there are no tygers in Saroyan's conception of the human experience; there is only a wistful attrition of sadness. He does not even see deceit, ugliness, violence—they are not in Saroyan's world; he merely brings the messages of death from the War Department to the locked houses. (Saroyan, a quick fellow, is perhaps the first American writer to have made imaginative use of America's participation in the Second World War.) He talks to old Grogan at the telegraph office, a sot; he hears the sweetly delirious Saroyan lovers, lovers who can never find each other; he is hungry and tired, and painfully conscious of his family's poverty. And he wants to know—"*Did he who made the lamb make thee?*"; when he weeps, as a man weeps, he is still more eager to keep his capacity for tears than to revert to his old innocence. "Otherwise I'm just as good as dead myself." That is the height of Homer's experience, the drama in his dismay—he wonders, he wants to know. And now the process is reversed—the tiger that was never a tiger has become a sweetly bleating lamb; the resolution is Love. When he goes to his mother, the youngest, the wisest Penelope in the world, he is comforted, as the Saroyan people are forever comforted, when she confides:

Everything is changed—for you. But it is still the same, too. The loneliness you feel has come to you because you are no longer a child. But the whole world has always been full of that loneliness. The loneliness does not come from the War. The War did not make it. It was the loneliness that made the War.

There it is, and there is Saroyan. Having been baptized in the perilous streams of Postal Telegraph, Homer the human foundling is now swimming in goodness and innocence and the easy Saroyan heartbreak. Everyone talks of Love; everyone relapses, like little Ulysses, into being a darling little chick. Even old Grogan hears the heavenly spheres singing together. And Homer's experience in life now becomes like the singing Saroyan describes in a café where some soldiers are gathered around the piano. "Their singing wasn't particularly good, but the feeling with which they sang was not bad at all." The feeling in Saroyan is never bad at all: at times, in fact, it is quite wonderful. I never knew, I must confess, how effective a writer he was until I read *The Human Comedy*. He had told me that he was wonderful; now I believe it. But they call this a "novel"? A novel has to have some conception of resolution, some dramatic structure, some sense of process and understanding of conflict. There has, surely, to be something more than this humming flute-music, this succession of exquisite little scenes, all so expert in charm, so calculated to break your heart. What we have here is the Saroyan gallery at its best, a kind of definitive one-man show. Where he once created moods, he now creates characters; but the characters, lovable as they are, only add up into one big mood. That is why the book falls away so soundlessly at the end, where a real novel, structurally composed, would break up when imagination failed. Saroyan's imagination never really fails him; it just remains small, mimetic and careful. Each character is a moment, each is like the separate glistening pebbles that F. M. Ford once described in Hemingway's style; they all glisten with their wonder at life and Saroyan's wonder over them. They are "marvelous," in the Saroyan manner, in the sense that the whole world is marvelous—when evil is not so much ignored as gently named, with gentle stubbornness dismissed; when the secret of each person's charm is his conviction that he is separate and original; when the tone of the human comedy is sweet dismay lost in the reverberations of love.

Years ago, on the East Side of New York, there was a wonderful café owned by a wonderful man who played wonderfully on the Hungarian cymbalon. The cymbalon is never admitted into the orchestra, but when people are together late at night, and there is a feeling of peace in the air, it can sing very powerfully to the human ear. The cymbalon is no doubt an inferior instrument, too exclusively personal; but it has a remarkable characteristic—it plays heart-throbs. Its tremolo is fantastic; the air shivers with it. Reading Saroyan I thought of that wonderful man coming to a table. He plays on his cymbalon; he is enraptured, and his hair falls over his eyes. He paints the Hungarian scene that every cymbalon plays—the trees reflected in the water, perpetual twilight and easy longing. And what does he sing of? He sings of love. At that moment, with the tremolo beating in the drowsy café air, he makes you see that life is not life, at least not the grimness of it, but the human appeal, the heavy languorous call of love. At that moment he means it, with the cymbalon throbbing before him. At that moment he really means it.

(1943)

STEPHEN KOCH

Narcissus and Goldmund

In every college of the land, the Hesse boom has hit peak phase and become so powerful that it has even knocked Camus off his "portable pedestal." Ever since Timothy Leary pronounced *Steppenwolf* his favorite work of literature, Hesse has been standard psychedelic equipment, along with water-pipes, day-glow art, the Maharishi, Jim Morrison and the *I Ching*. There is even a new electronic rock group on the west coast called Steppenwolf.

Guruhood is nothing new for Hesse—I know Germans in their middle sixties who devoured each new book during their own adenoidal phase—and the role fits him rather well. His art springs from an unshakably profound infatuation with adolescence, and his vision of youth is underwritten by his incapacity to break loose from youth's fascination. His only interesting material is the passions of twenty-five and under: the pangy vertigo of limitless prospects, of the utterly pure, corny tenderness of narcissism, or the wild thrill of discovering feelings that are entirely new, *never* felt before. When he turns to other materials—as he does in the inexpressibly boring final two thirds of *The Bead Game*, he can be a fusty drag, with all his limitations showing. Like everything else in his work, Hesse's thought is irretrievably adolescent, so that in his chosen role of artist of ideas, he is invariably second-rate, although unlike the other prophets of the New Age, he is never less than second-rate. His thought is never cheap, never trashy, but neither is it ever intellectually exalting, the way the professorial, unfashionable Mann so often is. Almost without exception, Hesse's ideas are derivative, schoolboyish, traditional to the point of being academic, influenced by all the right people, and boringly correct. Life, for example, is divided into Many Dualisms which cause Much Unhappiness. There is Intellect versus Passion; Thought versus the Senses; Good versus Evil; Self versus All; Male versus Female; Yin versus Yang. It is a Terrific Experience to Transcend these Dualisms and Make them Fuse. Likewise, the Self is limiting; it is a Terrific Experience to surrender to Self and confront the All. The intellect is inhibiting, so it's a Terrific Experience to forget your brain and let the Senses take over. Good and Evil are all mixed up together, but they are both Terrific Experiences. The All is wonderful. Each of us has a Steppenwolf inside. The World-Soul is androgyne. Sex can be *wild*.

So, it goes, book after book, the Great Ideas chasing the Terrific Experiences home to their all-too-obvious destinations. Flawed though it sometimes is, Hesse's aesthetic sense is different and better than this; it does sometimes rise to extraordinary levels, does transform itself into "something else," as the kids say. The final third of *Steppenwolf* is one of the great moments in modern literature, a moment original to the point of being in a class by itself, and one with an importance to future art which is not to be patronized.

This disparity between his intellectual and aesthetic capacities is one of the most noticeable facts about Hesse, one of those boring dualisms with which he himself was afflicted. It is this dualism which is the subject of the newly translated *Narcissus and Goldmund*, the medieval romance Hesse wrote just after he finished *Steppenwolf*. Like

Siddhartha, Narcissus and Goldmund is set in the remote past, though in this case not in Gautama's India but in medieval Germany, It is about the Artist versus the Intellectual. The intellectual in question is a monk named—what else?—Narcissus, and the artist is his pupil, Goldmund, as sensuously passionate as his teacher is analytic and cold. They thus make an all-too-perfect pair. In a fit of adolescent piety, Goldmund has decided to follow his frigid, beautiful mentor into a life of asceticism until the brilliant, sterile Narcissus perceives that his pupil's Tao, his "thing," is a creative lust for the female. At this moment, the book reaches an almost grotesque symmetry:

"Why yes," Narcissus continued "Natures of your kind, with strong, delicate senses, the soul-oriented, the dreamers, poets, lovers are almost always superior to us creatures of the mind. You take your being from your mothers. You live fully . . . . You are in danger of drowning in the world of the senses; ours is the danger of suffocating in an airless void. You are an artist; I am a thinker. You sleep at the mother's breast; I wake in the desert. For me the sun shines; for you the moon and stars. Your dreams are of girls; mine of boys. . . ."

"Your dreams are of girls; mine of boys. . . ." This sentence tears the heart from the mystery of *Narcissus and Goldmund,* because this novel is not really about the Artist versus the Intellectual at all. It is about wanting women. Escaping the all-male environment of the monastery, Goldmund embarks on his career of screwing girls, and that is the substance of the book. Lise, Marie, Lydia, Rebeckah, Lene, Lisbeth—Goldmund finds women everywhere, in every castle and field and town. There is a woman on every page, and every one of them loves Goldmund. The book is thus a strangely unsalacious but blissful male idyll. If *Siddhartha* is a cool canticle raised to the ideal of Ego Transcendence, *Narcissus and Goldmund* is a jangling rage in praise of heterosexuality. Goldmund is defined and created through women, who are the substance from which he derives his reality. They are his air; he breathes and devours them. And he creates through them.

Goldmund becomes a sculptor. He riots through his existence, leaving behind him a trail of girls, in Eliot's phrase, "sore but satisfied." He sees the face of the Madonna. He grows old. At the end of the novel, the aging prodigal returns to the monastery, where Narcissus, also aging, is still sterile, intellectual, and secretly queer. After one last fling, Goldmund dies:

> And now the sick man opened his eyes again . . . and with a sudden movement, as though he were trying to shake his head, he whispered: "but how will you die when your time comes, Narcissus, since you have no mother? Without a mother one cannot love. Without a mother, one cannot die."
>
> What he murmured after that could not be understood. Those last two days Narcissus sat by his bed day and night, watching his life ebb away. Goldmund's last words burned like fire in his heart.

Even gossipy America has kept surprisingly well the open secret that throughout his life, Hesse was an overt homosexual. (The standard English biography by Ernst Rose doesn't give the slightest hint.) The fact casts another strange light on this book about woman-lust, and on the final destitution of its "intellectual"—the narcissist whose dream is of boys. It was surely as Narcissus that Hesse saw himself—mentor to youth, using his wisdom to liberate their sensuous creativity and thereby forcing them beyond him.

In 1916, Hesse was analyzed by a pupil of Jung—he was thus, so far as I know, the first major artist ever to be analyzed—and he surely accepted the Jungian message about maternity and death which he puts into the dying sculptor's mouth. The novel's last cliché about the words burning like fire is too weak to suggest the obvious fact that *Narcissus and Goldmund* is not only about Goldmund's ebullience, but also about Narcissus' despair.

That despair is never felt within the dualistic structure of the book. True enough, one does feel Narcissus fighting his impulse to fall in love with Goldmund, and senses him inverting those impulses into thought. But the Narcissus—Goldmund syzygy is by and large maintained by a coolly symmetrical, organizational principle which makes the book's structure Narcissus-like while the details are Goldmund-esque in their sensuous, "psychedelic" richness. (An "oceanic" richness often awash in oceanic cliché, not terribly far from the prose of the *East Village Other:* "Suddenly in the middle of a page, he'd sink back into himself and forget everything, listening only to the rivers and voices inside himself, while they drew him away into deep wells filled with dark melodies. . . ." etc., etc.) Such a nifty paradox overlooks the fact that the book's best moments are neither "intellectual" nor especially womanizing, but are blasted with cold chaos. Goldmund stabs a murderous highwayman to death. He wanders across the terrain of the plague; he walks into a musty house where the dead family is still sitting in its chairs. He stumbles onto the corpse of a little boy, its tiny fists clenched in rage.

Hesse's habitual dualism is trivial academic rubbish: rubbish derived from a truth, perhaps, but still rubbish. Wittgenstein, it is said, aestheticized philosophy; Proust philosophized aesthetics. Both were homosexual, and so what? Nothing, except the obvious platitude—which is *this* book's obvious destination—that Narcissus and Goldmund and all they stand for are all mixed up together, bound together in their opposition.

But despite his faults, Hesse is a graceful and generally unpretentious artist. What can be said about his current bondage in the hands of the hippie philistines? A large part of Hesse's huge new audience reads nothing *but* Hesse, preferring non-literary means for most of its Journeys to the East. It is an immense, energetic and ignorant audience with a wild capacity to co-opt the creative energy of high art (look, for example, at the way rock has swallowed in one avid gulp the whole ethos of "serious music") and its charm and energy seem so vast that it repeatedly seems on the verge of subduing unto itself the whole world of making and emotion.

This capacity for cultural co-option scares the hell out of a lot of people, myself sometimes included. American culture is at the point of turning into a vast Children's Crusade, and Hesse is actually one of the best of its leaders. He should thus be discussed not only as an artist, but as a teacher. I shudder at what he would think if he knew how many in his audience think *Steppenwolf* expresses the view that Mozart "and all that stuff should drop dead." And yet, to turn to Orientalism and mysticism which Hesse feeds, though it is clearly dilettantish, naive, and often damnably vulgar, I don't despair that some of the new *chinoiserie* may play some part in lifting the culture to a new stage of growth.

In *Steppenwolf*, Harry Haller—that poor, up-tight nineteen-year-old in drag as a middle-aged man—steps into Pablo's magic theatre and discovers his own irresponsible youth. I sometimes think that at the moment, not Harry but American culture is reeling through the Magic Theatre, rediscovering its own narcissistic youth in the midst of unearned Dionysian opulence. The new, arrogant *embarras de richesses* of what is happening now is, undeniably, a liberation. It may even be a healthful one. Who can deny that the culture is almost screaming for re-creation, or deny that the job will have to be done by people from that vast generation with everything on its side except that "intellect" which Hesse misrepresents in *Narcissus and Goldmund*. For the hippies are absolutely right: we are at a critical moment in the history of culture; we *have* been brought to a point of no return. But they don't see the intellectual challenge implicit in that fact, nor that the prime question is whether anyone can rise to it. I don't see any evidence that anyone can. Certainly, Hesse can't and he is the most intelligent of the new doyens. But this ultimate sensitive schoolboy—this Compleat Guru—is never going to make it. The problem is bigger than he is: it is Nietzschean in its demands, and until minds that can cope with *that* begin to emerge—and in numbers—our famous Liberation is likely to remain stuck in the noisy futile vitality whose source is neither chaos nor lust, but childishness.

(1968)

JOHN LEHMANN

Somerset Maugham

In *Cakes and Ale*, the narrator, purporting to analyze the secret of the great reputation of Edward Driffield, the Hardy-like novelist Somerset Maugham had invented, came to the conclusion that "what the critics wrote about Edward Driffield was eyewash. His outstanding merit . . . was his longevity. Reverence for old age is one of the most admirable traits of the human race and I think it may safely be stated that in no other country than ours is this merit marked."

It seems to me a near certainty that the glamor of longevity, of *having survived*, was an extremely important element in the extraordinary reputation that built itself up around Maugham in the last two decades of his life. In the first obituaries to appear in Britain, his death has been treated as the death of a Great Writer. And yet, while waxing lyrical over his "ironic sense of the human comedy," his "mastery of technical means and ends," his superb skill as a story-teller and his "capacity to probe life to its very depths," the obituarists have betrayed an uneasy feeling that perhaps a large part of his reputation was like Driffield's, "eyewash."

This schizophrenia among the critics is by no means new. In *Enemies of Promise* (published 1938), for instance, Cyril Connolly, while treating Maugham as a sage and a key figure in modern writing, has to admit that there is something wrong with his prose as an example of the vernacular, colloquial style. "The vocabulary is flat," he points out, and the figures of speech with which his paragraphs are peppered, "while not yet officially cliché, are phrases so tarnished as to be on the way to them," they "rattle like peas being shelled into a tin."

Maugham's reputation, in intellectual circles, went up and down like the fever chart of a malarial patient, at one moment the awe-struck enthusiasts appearing to gain the upper hand, at another those who dismissed him as unworthy of serious study. What never varied, ever since the publication of his novel, *Of Human Bondage,* in 1915 (by which time he had become a successful and fashionable playwright), was an enormous public eager to gobble up his books and add to his fortune.

It is only fair to say that Maugham himself had few illusions about his own limitations. *The Summing Up* must be one of the most candid books ever writen by a popular author about his gifts and achievements. "I had no ambition to be a stylist," he wrote. "I know I had no lyrical quality . . . poetic flights were beyond my powers." "I made the best of the very limited powers given to me by nature." "It is impossible that my work should have the intimacy, the broad human touch that the great writers alone can give." What he believed was valuable in his own capacities was his gift of story-telling and his power of observation—without moral judgment. "I could put down in clear terms what I saw. . . .It seemed to me I must aim at lucidity, simplicity and euphony." And in making that confession he pointed to his debt to the French civilization in which his earliest years were passed. There was undoubtedly an element of truth in the claim, made at one time, that he was the "English Maupassant." The amoral attitude, the clinically dry observation of his human specimens were novel, even revolutionary in his own country when he started to write.

At the same time, I am inclined to think that too much has been made of his training in St. Tomas' Hospital as an influence on his writing. He certainly took an immense interest in the work of a house surgeon, but surely because the dispassionate analytical view already appealed to him temperamentally. One of the greatest romantics in the whole of world literature also underwent his training in a hospital: John Keats.

Will Maugham be read as widely and as keenly in fifty years' time as he is now? A contemporary, even a much younger contemporary, is likely to make himself ridiculous if he answers such questions too confidently. One can, however, try certain definitions, or elimination tests. I do not think there is much doubt that the great preservatives of authors' reputations are, first, style; second, imagination; third, wit (or humor). How often has one said, or felt, that such-and-such a writer's plots creak, characters are wooden, moral judgments are hopelessly dated, but that his work is nevertheless redeemed by his marvelous style, creative use of language; or imaginative intuition about states beyond the rational and the everyday; or by his absolute wit.

Now, in the case of Maugham it is perfectly clear that the plea for style fails. Maugham himself, to a considerable extent, admits it. He did not outgrow his clichés—perhaps he did not give them a thought. *The Razor's Edge* (1944), which in many ways was the most seriously intended work of his later age, can offer almost as many specimens as his earlier works. Even the most tiresome, minor-prophetic later works of D. H. Lawrence, which have an obvious, exasperating design upon the reader, are en-ambered in a lyrical prose which makes one ready—or very nearly ready—to forgive the insistent Message.

Imagination? There is nothing of poetry in Maugham, no transcendence, no perceptive vision such as makes Kipling,

230

for instance, so much more than the recorder of an imperial moment in British History. He explored no hitherto concealed depths of human psychology, and such descriptions as there are in his works of the subtler yearnings of the human soul are entirely conventional.

Nor can one say that wit, in the sense in which it abounds in *The Importance of Being Ernest,* or even in Aldous Huxley's *Crome Yellow* or *Those Barren Leaves,* is a marked characteristic of his work. His disillusioned irony about human foibles is nearest, it seems to me, that he gets to the distillation of a preservative fluid. It is always bitter, it always tastes of ashes. It was no accident, I cannot help thinking, that he originally wanted to call *Of Human Bondage* by a title chosen from Isaiah, *Beauty from Ashes;* nor that his narrator, his I-figure, more than once adopts the name of Ashenden.

Take the story "Red," one of the first he wrote when he returned to the short story after the success of *Of Human Bondage,* and one of the first to have a South Seas background. The idyll of Sally and Red is about as near as Maugham ever got to rhapsodic description of young love. He wanted the reader to be carried away by the beauty of it, to point up the grotesque irony of their failure to recognize one another when they are both old and fat and coarsened by life. They are his Haidée and Don Juan—or he would like them to be. And he nearly brings it off; but if read carefully there is something almost embarrassingly tinselly and meretricious about the high romantic passages. "Here love had tarried for a moment like a migrant bird"—"the fragrance of a beautiful passion hovered over it"—"his mouth was like a scarlet wound,"—etc. etc. No, it won't do as the prose of a Master; but it *will* do as an after-dinner story by an extremely skillful raconteur who has seen a great deal of the world—and seen through it.

Maugham has frequently been admired for his suprise dénouements. And yet, though they administer an effective dramatic shock, they never disturb on any profounder level.

His originality, his power of holding the reader's attention, consists largely in putting conventional stories in exotic settings. The basic plots of the stories in *The Casuarina Tree* are really magazine clichés. They are saved from being nothing more than that by their Eastern colonial trappings, by the cunning twists of their unfolding, and by the remorseless cold irony of the story-teller's eye. And when Maugham allows a slight twinkle to creep into that cold eye, it is nearly always cruel; as in the portrait of Alroy Kear in *Cakes and Ale*. There is an underlying indifference to human suffering, a bluntness of sensibility in the secret service adventures of *Ashenden*. It is distasteful; but it is not the point. In the introduction to that work, Maugham wrote:

It is quite unnecessary to treat as axiomatic the assertion that fiction should imitate life. It is merely a literary theory like any other. There is in fact a second theory that is just as plausible, and this is that fiction should use life merely as a raw material which it arranges in ingenious patterns.

In the making of those ingenious patterns Willie Maugham was never at a loss. When all criticisms have been made on other aspects of his work, this particular power of his remains indisputable.

(1966)

PHILIP LITTELL

Life with Father

Nearly twenty years ago, when I made Clarence Day's
acquaintance, his rheumatism wasn't much more than fifteen
years old, and once in a while he could still dine out. Even
then, though, he was pretty lame, and when we went in to
dinner something had to be done to make is possible for him
to sit at the table. Not much, but it had to be done
accurately. He had to take charge. His directions were clear,
brief and few. Once he was properly seated, he forgot his
lameness and kept the rest of us from remembering it. His
way of taking it was impersonal, as though it were an
external object. He paid it as much attention as it needed,
not more, not less, and that was that.

Though these dinners were small, and most of the guests
his old friends, he didn't say a great deal. Yet I don't believe
he often struck people, whether old friends or newcomers, as
unwilling to talk his share. Some otherwise quite decent
listeners behave as if they had taken their ply long ago, put
silence on like a shirt which must never be changed. Clarence
Day was silent because he happened to be hearing things that
happened to interest him. Shy he might be, but his silence

did not come from this cause. He seemed attentive, slightly expectant. The little he did say, whether it was caricatural or witty or gaily exclamatory, was apt. It helped the talk forward. People were glad they'd said whatever it was that made him say what he said. Two other things I remember as likely to catch a newcomer's notice. Just under the top skin his color changed quickly, like an excitable man's. And though I knew, having been told, that he would never get better, I kept on expecting him to be entirely well the next time we met.

The key to such an expectation is this: though Clarence Day has had to live like an invalid, on his body's account, since about 1900, he has now and always did have the point of view and the interests of a man in perfect health. Even today, whenever I go to see him, though I can tell city from country, outdoors from indoors, it would not surprise me to find him beside a lively brook, propped against a tree trunk. The place where you do find him has a view that is nearly all trees, rocks, grass and sky. The high couch where he enjoys life is parallel to the wall of his sitting room, a few feet from windows looking north over Central Park.

When you come in he doesn't turn his head, doesn't usually say anything till you are at the foot of his couch, in the field of his straight-ahead vision. His gaze bids you welcome. His smile assumes that your arrival is among other things a joke shared between him and you. His first words are never a greeting. They wipe out the interval between this visit and the one before. They take up an interrupted talk, continue an unfinished letter. Sometimes he waits—I can never guess the proportion of intentional to unconscious in these waitings—till he's found out whether this time you have anything on your chest that you want to get rid of. Something you say, something odd in your get-up, may touch him off into an extravagant burlesque, improvised, never thought of before, new as the moment. Or he may take fewer words to be himself in. After the talk has been going on for a while, and his mind begins to play with a subject—Maeterlinck, for example, if you have brought him

piety resembles them. They are done with affection and gusto, with here and there a touch of lovely, unsweetened tenderness, always with kind, unflinching eyes and the friendliest laughter. And while we read we also laugh, often uncontrollably, in outbursts. for these are two of the funniest books written in our time, and written in a prose whose ease is deceptive. It is written for the ear, it sounds like the best talk, it has a casual air, its nonchalance invites you to ignore the subtlety of its cadences. Delightful books they are, these two, books you like as though they were alive, books that are alive with energy and collisions and the running water of happiness.

In a book about the writer's own people there is always a risk that we may not see them quite as he sees them. The only part of *Life with Father* where I dissent from the author's view is the chapter called "Father Interferes with the Twenty-third Psalm." Here Clarence Day tells us how he felt as a small boy about the Bible in French. Among the French words that upset him and made him laugh was *"irrité"* where the English Bible says "wroth." Instead of the Lord being wroth, *le Seigneur* was *irrité*. The patriarchs were *irrité* when they ought to have been wroth. This was unsatisfactory. It lowered the patriarchs. It reduced their stature. "If they were full of mere irritation all the time," Clarence Day felt, "they were more like the Day family." I don't feel that way at all. What *Life with Father* shows us is not irritation. Nearly every chapter in the book does, I admit, lead us up to and into and then away from an outburst of temper. It is from explosion to explosion that the story moves on its quiet feet. Life in the Day family was a series of detonations. Mr. Day lost his temper often and tremendously. But he was not irritated. Men several sizes smaller thin-lipped ungenial men, they are the ones who get irritated. Mr. Day was wroth.

(1935)

ROBERT LITTELL

The Enormous Room

I feel as if I had been rooting long, desperate hours in a junk heap, irritably but thoroughly pawing over all sorts of queer, nameless garbage, rotting tin cans, owl's skeletons, the poisonous fragments of human apparatus rusting into morbid greens, yellows, oranges, and yet as if after prodding about among these and other objects best touched only with a stick, I had come away at last with some lumps of curious, discolored but none the less precious metal.

Could any sensitive person be locked up in a small, filthy French prison with a riff-raff of suspected spies and write an honest book which did not give something of this effect? I doubt it. Mr. Cummings is honest. He is also sensitive, so sensitive that the lightest tremors of life make his tongue, like some cubistic seismograph, record them in a cryptic, half insane dance of words.

This sensitiveness has a tinge of self-pity, which the indignant letters of the introduction do nothing to diminish. Mr. Cummings was arrested while with a section of the Norton Harjes Ambulance Corps at the front, and shipped off to the prison for political suspects at La Ferté Macé on charges none too clear, but apparently not more serious than that a friend of his had written home in a revolutionary vein disliked by the censor. He does not take this fate easily, of course, but too often his bitterness is venomous. It also leads him into a rather unpersuasive account of his own ease and dignity. We find him replying "imaginatively," speaking "gently," "briefly and warmly," "deliberately," or "with perfect politeness"; he makes a verbal "sortie"; here he bids "a vivid adieu," there he "cares no whit." He imagines himself threatened with a firing squad, and, being asked "when he preferred to die," replying "Pardon me, you wish to ask when I prefer to become immortal?" With many other such touches he builds up, I cannot say how unconsciously, a not very flattering self-portrait.

Before leaving to the psychologist these clues toward a reconstruction of Mr. Cummings's mind, let me add to them a few of the words and phrases he particularly likes to use in describing the world that surrounds him. He is fond of "divine," "thrilling," "very," "insane," "infinite," "neat," "gentle." Things seem to have an enormous meaning for him when, using a shorthand of his own, he describes them as "neatly hopeless' or "utterly delightful," when he calls the darkness "gentle" or "very tremendous," or silence "violent and gentle and dark"; when a face seems to him "intensely sexual," when a "roar bulges," or a "racket bulges in the darkness." A "din" to him is "minutely crazy," or has a "minutely large quality." How many guesses as to Mr. Cummings's meaning are we allowed when he hears a voice that is "moldly moldering molish"? Is there anything to be said, by anyone not a symbolist, an expressionist, or other verbal cutter-across-lots, for "a sharp, black, mechanical cry in the spongy organism of gloom"; for "female" or "sonal" darkness?

Do such expressions mean that reality has tortured their author's nerves into a snarl? Can the other parent of such obvious children of disorder be any kind of light? Before you go on to the good things Mr. Cummings has done, read this bit carefully and roll it on your tongue.

. . . a lithe pausing poise, intensely intelligent, certainly sensitive, delivering dryingly a series of sure and rapid hints that penetrate the fabric of stupidity accurately and whisperingly; dealing one after another brief and poignant instupidities, distinct and uncompromising, crisp and altogether arrowlike.

If one gives one's imagination (in this case out of Nerves by Dictionary) a free rein, this sort of thing is not hard to do. Such a horse shies easily at reality, bolts into oxymoron and by way of self-expression bucks with hallucinating turgidity. It reminds one of sonal pools of insanity, bulging neatly but enormously with bat-wingéd words.

It is strange that Mr. Cummings does not go oftener into these tail-spins, since he has mastered their technique so thoroughly, and so much seems to enjoy them. He is also a master of conveying to you the essence of disagreeable smells, putrescences and vilenesses. I have nothing to say against anyone's describing a stinking French prison just as it is. But Mr. Cummings has a real flair and gusto for filth. Read his eager description of Ça Pue. Note how he happened upon "a smile which had something almost foetal about it." At such times one almost thinks he shares, with M. Le Directeur of the prison, to whom he imputes it, "an unobstreperous affinity for excrement."

But, upon laying down the book, one can almost say with him that "the stink was actually sublime." Again and again he touches off a phrase boiling hot with life. While most of the strange human wrecks and vermin he sees in the prison pour forth, under his attempts to describe them, a writhing fog of words, here and there a few quick touches reincarnate some face or gesture intensely felt or seen. For instance, of prisoners asleep: "on each paillasse . . . lay the headless body of a man smothered in his blanket, only the boots showing." Of the schoolmaster: "By some mistake he had three mustaches, two of them being eyebrows," or of Renée, a prostitute: "a perfectly toothless smile . . . ample and black . . . you saw through it into the back of her neck."

When Mr. Cummings untangles himself for a bit and stops

shaking up his favorite words as if in a dice box, and rolling them out anyhow upon the page, he can build up original and vivid portraits. For two chapters his verbal fogs clear up long enough to let you see full length mountains, rugged and real. Such are the portraits of Surplice, Jean Le Nègre and The Wanderer, though the latter is clouded by such expressions as "his deeply softnesses eyes."

Surplice is not easily forgotten. No mere quotations can rebuild for you his ridiculous, friendly and pitiable figure, a figure so abject that, "being unspeakably lonely," he "enjoyed any and all insults for the simple reason that they constituted or at least implied a recognition of his existence." Jean Le Nègre is even better—Jean whose eyes filled with tears when sixty francs were stolen from him, who kept repeating like a child, "Planton voleur—steal Jean munee." Only if you read Jean's story will you realize how good Mr. Cummings is at his best.

As a sample of *The Enormous Room* at this seldom-found best, here is a sketch of a new arrival at the prison. It is a rare flower lost in the patch where Mr. Cummings has willfully sowed hundreds of the wildest weeds.

An old man shabbily dressed in a shiny frock coat, upon whose peering and otherwise very aged face a pair of dirty spectacles rested. The first thing he did, upon securing a place, was to sit upon his mattress in a professorial manner, tremulously extract a journal from his left coat pocket, tremblingly produce a large magnifying glass from his upper right vest pocket, and forget everything. Subsequently, I discovered him promenading the room with an enormous expenditure of feeble energy, taking tiny steps flat-footedly and leaning in when he rounded a corner as if he were travelling at terrific speed.

Out of such pictures, no other quite so clear cut, and in spite of all his chasing after "mystic wrynesses," Mr. Cummings finally manages to fashion a picture of his prison which recalls not a little the morbid solidity of Piranesi. The book has few dead phrases in it—it lives, if somewhat with the horrible life of a centipede. It has fire, now smoldering, now for a bit blazing into unhealthy violet and mustard colored flame. There is precious metal in it, but Mr. Cummings has brought up from his agonized and subterranean digging along with some nuggets of character and description all manner of sweepings, cobwebs and twisted iron. I should however rather dig with him for his tarnished treasure than enjoy all the sane and competent enamel-ware which is the bulk of literature today.

Only for short spaces is the water clear. Mostly he is, with joy and a sort of agony, stirring up mud at the bottom which invades this clearness. He bears the scars—and loves to show them—of battle with the fiend, and has himself become "half serpent in the struggle."

A queer, strong, defeated book, all smeared and spattered with genius. A dark, bent tree, gnarled, hag ridden, gross and worm-bored, bearing few leaves, and whether it will outgrow its canker and live to be timber I cannot tell. But "there is no timber that has not strong roots among the clay and worms."

(1922)

ROBERT MORSS LOVETT

A Passage to India

Mr. Forster has made a contribution to the study of a great historical problem. It is such a contribution as only an artist and a novelist could make. He has brought the close observation of human relations, the delicate perception of character as it expresses itself in tones of feeling and shades of manner, which give to his *Howard's End* a quite unforgettable distinction, to a view of life in British India on the border line where British and Indians meet. The most obvious aspect of the situation in India is the presence in the midst of a vast native population, itself of extraordinary diversity, of an alien group, small in number but organized for power and prestige. This group justifies its presence by exercising the function of government in which it is supposed to be expert. In fact, however, its function is subordinate to its survival. The safety and comfort of the British officials and their families is the first charge upon the government of the Viceroy. Whatever happens to their wards, they must be protected. They are in the position which Ulster occupied in Ireland before the Irish Free State, with the difference that where the Scotch of Ulster were concentrated, the British in

India are scattered among a thousand stations, in contact with all manner of local complexities, united only in race loyalty and mutual dependence. The prestige of the British soldier, the honor of the British matron, the safety of the British child outweigh the lives of scores and hundreds of natives, today as in the time of the mutiny. Particularly the matron and the child. In one of Mr. Forster's revealing passages he refers to " 'women and children'—that phrase that exempts the male from sanity when it has been repeated a few times."

This is one phase of the situation—a tension that may at any moment break into tragedy. But this is not the phase which establishes the mood of Mr. Forster's novel. Rather it is the humor of infinitely incongruous relations. Misunderstanding is tragic; it is also comic; and there is abundant comedy in the association of the two races, in the amazing lapses in continuity of intercourse owing to difference of psychology, in the social inhibitions arising from different standards of behavior. "Tangles like this," he remarks with reference to his chief representatives of the Anglo-Indian entente, "still interrupted their intercourse. A pause in the wrong place, an intonation misunderstood, and a whole conversation went awry." And again: "Suspicion in the Oriental is a sort of malignant tumor, a mental malady, that makes him self-conscious and unfriendly suddenly; he trusts and mistrusts at the same time in a way the Westerner cannot comprehend. It is his demon as the Westerner's is hypocrisy."

All this Mr. Forster illustrates through the medium of his characters. He has developed a novel of manners against a background of conquest, a human comedy within the frame of the huge imperial joke. He has raised the racial question from the murky region of politics to the lighter air of social life. We have had before this pictures of Indian life and of British life in India. Mr. Forster has brought the two elements together into something indubitably new and strange in material and design. And the astonishing thing is that he seems to write of both worlds with equal understanding. It is his practiced skill in distinguishing the niceties of occidental character and conduct which gives him his clairvoyance, or is it sheer intuition like that of Mrs. Moore is his story? At all events his Indian life is as real to the senses and mind as Tagore's. Both worlds, again, he treats with the calm assurance and graceful poise of impartiality. His satire plays lambently upon both British and Indians. Hear the voice of Ronny Heaslop, agent of British justice:

"I am out here to work, mind, to hold this wretched country by force. I'm not a missionary or a Labor Member or a vague sentimental, sympathetic literary man. I'm just a servant of the Government.... We're not pleasant in India, and we don't intend to be pleasant. We've something more important to do." How Ronny revelled in the drawbacks of his situation! How he did rub it in that he was not in India to behave pleasantly, and derived positive satisfaction therefrom!

Playing about this rock of British deportment are the flames of Indian rivalry, jealousy, fear, pity, contempt, malice, in a multitude of scenes of which the pattern is sustained by gossamer threads of conversation amid the shifting light and shade of emotion. The story opens with a meeting of a group of Indians who are discussing the question whether or not it is possible to be friends with an Englishman, and this theme persists in an insistent minor key. Adroitly, by the way, appear the differences among the Indians themselves in their attitude toward the dominant race, in their attitude toward each other, especially the strange mixture of tolerance and unconcern, half-respectful, half-contemptuous, which marks the relation of Hindus and Mohammedans. The complication brings the story to the verge of the threatening racial tragedy; and then carries us blithely into the fantasy of a religious celebration in one of the native states which has the effect of broad farce out of the Arabian Nights.

The novel closes with the two chief characters as far apart as ever. The Englishman calmly scoffs at Indian nationalism. "India a nation! What an apotheosis! Last comer to the drab nineteenth century sisterhood! Waddling in at this hour of the world to take her seat." The Hindu cries: "Down with the English anyhow. That's certain. Clear out, you fellows, double quick I say. We may hate one another but we hate you most. . . . We shall get rid of you, yes, we shall drive every blasted Englishman into the sea, and then—and then" he concluded half kissing him, "you and I shall be friends."

Mr. Forster has given us a world of grotesque and maddening incongruities and absurdities, of humor and subtle meaning, of tragic suffering and patient striving, and unconquerable sympathy. From this omnivorous wine press he has drawn a stream of pure beauty—the beauty not of nature or of art but of humanity. This is the secret of India, of the East:

> Civilization strays about like a ghost here, revisiting the ruins of empires and is to be found not in great works of art or mighty deeds, but in the gestures well-bred Indians make when they sit or lie down. . . . The restfulness of the gesture—it is the peace that passeth understanding, after all, it is the social equivalent of Yoga. When the whirring of action ceases, it becomes visible, and reveals a civilization which the West can disturb but will never acquire. The hand stretches out for ever, the lifted knee has the eternity though not the sadness of the grave.

(1924)

ROBERT MORSS LOVETT

The Magic Mountain

Twenty-five years ago, Thomas Mann announced himself, through *Buddenbrooks*, as one of the first writers of fiction in Germany and of German prose. Today he belongs unquestionably among the writers whose art and significance are international—Gorky, Rolland, Wassermann, Hamsun, Shaw, to mention only enough to define the group. He is known to American readers through four of his works in translation, published by Mr. Knopf, in which can be clearly marked a movement, common to others of his generation, from realism through impressionism and symbolism to mysticism, from concentration on the objective environment to absorption in the personal life of the conscious and the subconscious. *Buddenbrooks* tells in masterly fashion the story of a commercial family of Lubeck, from the later Napoleonic period down through the nineteenth century. "Royal Highness" is a variation on the Cinderella theme; an American girl, beautiful and rich, but unclassed because of Negro blood, loves and marries the Grand Duke of Grimmburg, and restores the tottering fortunes of the reigning house. "A Death in Venice" is the title story of a volume consisting of three tales relating to the life of the artist. In all these forerunners are to be found anticipations of *The Magic Mountain*. In the midst of the detailed fortunes of the Buddenbrooks, commercial transactions, civic functions, family reunions, marriages, dowries, there is a passage in which Thomas, the captain of the slowly sinking ship, has a momentary vision of the meaning of life and the futility of his own experience of it. In "Royal Highness," the institution of the State and its interests is a background ironically treated. "A Death in Venice" is a *Liebestod,* the love of the great writer for a beautiful lad whom he scarcely approaches, mingling its passionate strains with the solemn burden of death. The second of the tales, "Tristan," brings us to the health establishment which is the scene of *The Magic Mountain,* and again the themes of love and death are mingled.

The Magic Mountain is the story of the experience of Hans Castorp of Hamburg, Before settling to his profession of ship-building, he goes to spend three weeks with his cousin, Joachim Ziemssen, who has been confined for months at the International Sanatorium Berghof, at Davos Platz. In the course of his visit he begins to have fever; a moist spot in the lung is discovered; he stays on and on with others whose will to action is broken, losing all desire to descend to the flat-lands below. His cousin breaks the cursed chain, and goes to join his regiment, to return the next year to die. Hans loves a beautiful Russian woman, but, caught by the spirit of the place, which destroys time, he delays to approach her, and possesses her only the night before her departure. She also returns to the establishment as the mistress of the Dutch magnate, Mynheer Peeperkorn, to leave again when the old man takes his life. Other figures recur, reflecting in their shadowy outline the ghostly character of this preliminary place of the departed. Two resolute antagonists, Signor Settembrini, who represents nineteenth century Liberalism, and its trust in enlightenment and progress, and Herr Naphta, a Jewish Jesuit, who upholds the cause of clerical reaction, appear again and again in wordy duels culminating in an actual encounter in which, true to type, Settembrini fires into the air and Naphta blows out his own brains. Slowly the truth dawns on us that, in the Berghof, Thomas Mann is presenting an allegory of a sick world. It is the "field full of folk" of Piers Plowman, the Heartbreak House of Shaw. It needs the catastrophe of the War to set the imprisoned souls free. Once Hans has a vision of the world of his idea, a youthful Arcadia, "full of beautiful, young creatures, so blithe, so good, so gay, so pleasing to see," all engaged in pleasurable tasks or serious pleasures. And this vision returns for a second, as we see Hans with three thousand other youths struggling forward through boggy ploughland, over human bodies trodden into the mud, amid the bursting of shells, the fire, the filth, the blood, the stench of war. It is the withdrawal from the world of faineant souls to enjoy the luxury of their decay which is paid for at the last.

But it would be a mistake to attribute to *The Magic Mountain* the crudeness of a social morality. Its significance is far wider and more subtle. Its themes enter far more deeply into the hidden places of the individual life. There is, for example, the mystery of time. The three weeks of Hans Castorp's original visit drag slowly by, day after day. He is unhappily conscious of every minute—and yet seven years pass as a tale that is told, or a watch in the night.

What was one day, taken, for instance, from the moment one sat down to the midday meal to the same moment four-and-twenty hours afterwards? It was, to be sure, four-and-twenty hours—but equally it was the simple sum of nothings. Or take an hour spent in the rest-cure, at the dinner-table, or on the daily walk—and these ways of employing the time-unit practically exhausted its possibilities—what was an hour? Again, nothing. And nothing were all these nothings, they were not serious in the nature of them, taken together. The only unit it was possible to regard with seriousness was the smallest one of all; those seven times sixty seconds during which one held the thermometer between one's lips and continued one's curve—they, indeed, were full of matter and tenacious of life; they could expand into a little eternity. . . .

The loudest challenge to modern art has been offered by science. In great ages of literature, the dominant conceptions of the time have furnished the natural, the unescapable material for expression; but science, which is unquestionably the leading aspect of modern thought, remains highly recalcitrant. A science of society, which is partly metaphoric, furnishes the background for serious fiction and drama, as history did in the earlier nineteenth century—but physical science in its more exact forms tends to elude the artist. Yet in the Berghof, where the physical conditions of life are a matter of daily scrutiny, such analysis seems natural. It is perhaps with a certain irony that Mann mingles scientific fact with emotion.

Then he, too, stood and wept, tears ran down his cheeks . . . those clear drops flowing in such bitter abundance every hour of our day all over our world, till in sheer poetic justice we have named the earth we live in after them; that alkaline, salty gland-secretion, which is pressed from our system by the nervous stress of acute pain, whether physical or mental. It contained, as Hans Castorp knew, a certain amount of mucin and albumen as well.

Music is the natural medium for the spiritual life in the modern world. It is again with a certain irony that the author, through the Herr Direktor of the Establishment, brings to the guests a gramophone. "Newest model, latest triumph of art, A-1, copper-bottomed, Polhymnia patent." To Hans Castorp the gramophone becomes a constant companion. And after all the passionate scenes of opera which he enjoys, it is Schubert's "Lindenbaum" which most closely searches and finds him. It is "Lindenbaum" which he is singing when we last see him in the hell of battle.

And music has a peculiar meaning in that world of decay which has slain action and slain time. "What was the world behind the song, which the motions of his conscience made to seem a world of forbidden love? It was death." Death is the great theme, which in this masterpiece replaces Love as the motive force of fiction. Death is the adversary which is fought with all the resources of science in the Establishment Berghof, and yet death is lord of the life which its inhabitants lead. The health-seekers lose all desire for health; their disease becomes their sin; they exemplify all the beauty of corruption and decay; they are death seekers. And the peculiar relation of death and life is symbolized by music, by the simplest *lied:*

> This was a fruit, sound and splendid enough for the instant or so, yet extraordinarily prone to decay; the purest refreshment of the spirit, if enjoyed at the right moment, but the next, capable of spreading decay and corruption among men. It was the fruit of life, conceived of death, pregnant of dissolution. . . . Ah, it was worth dying for, the enchanted *lied!* But he who died for it, died indeed no longer for it; was a hero only because he died for the new, the new word of love and the future that whispered in his heart.

The central theme of *The Magic Mountain* has been treated with the simplicity of earlier ages—from the Tännhäuser legend to De Quincey's *Confessions.* Here in the modern world in which it has social meaning it comes to a full symphonic utterance that is grandiose in its scope, tumultuous and overwhelming in intensity. It is a matter of gratitude that Mrs. Porter, in her translation, whatever the defects for which she apologizes, has caught in some measure these great qualities of a masterpiece.

(1927)

DONALD MALCOLM

The Outsider

It has occurred to Mr. Colin Wilson that what the world really needs just now is a new religion, preferably one based on the Will. The necessary raw materials are already at hand, he insists, in the person of the Outsider, whom he describes as a sort of prophet in embryonic form. Mr. Wilson's pursuit of this thesis is rather tortuous, and while attending to it, the reader is apt to find himself wishing, from time to time, that the author had followed instead the simple method prescribed by Voltaire for those who wish to start new religions: "First get yourself crucified: then rise from the dead."

But Mr. Wilson has chosen to do it the hard way and, in view of the enormous sensation his book has created in England, we must pay attention. So attend. The Outsider is a man who "sees too deep and too much," and "what he sees is essentially *chaos.*" He cannot accept the values of the "comfortable bourgeois world." Indeed, "he would like to escape triviality forever, and be 'possessed' by a Will to power, to more life." He "wants to be balanced," and he "wants to cease to be an Outsider." (I realize that the last two desires contradict each other, but you must take it up with Mr. Wilson, not with me. It is evident that he has only the vaguest notion of the meaning of his own term.) The Outsider's salvation "lies in extremes." And "the idea of a way out often comes in 'visions,' moments of intensity, etc." Hence the solution of the Outsider's problems and the accomplishment of the author's aim may be achieved at a single stroke by the Outsider's becoming a religious prophet and visionary.

Mr. Wilson's argument proceeds through what, in charity, we will term "analysis" of the lives and works of whole crowds of writers, artists, philosophers and saints, among whom we find Barbusse, Wells, Nijinsky, Sartre, Camus, Tolstoy, Rilke, Nietzsche, Blake, Dostoevsky, Hemingway, Yeats, Shaw, Ramakrishna, Hulme, Elio and Van Gogh. (No one can deny that Mr. Wilson has done a lot of reading, even if he *does* misquote the best-known lines from *Lear*.) It is probably not fair, even if space would permit it, to take the author to task for his frequent distortions of the writers he examines, since he has stated that his interest is not in literature but in tracing the Outsider theme. Still, one feels moved to protest when some of these writers are treated as mere porters for the Wilson luggage. "... *Crime and Punishment* is first and foremost a book about the Outsider's problems." "... *The Brothers Karamazov* is Dostoevsky's biggest attack on the Outsider theme." "Man can live on Ivan's level or Zossima's. Or he can do infinitely worse and live on the level of the common bourgeois." (Whenever, as frequently happens. Mr. Wilson speaks of the bourgeois, he means anyone who is not an Outsider. Thus not only does he lament "the fact that our language has become a tired and inefficient thing in the hands of journalists and writers who have nothing to say," but he is kind enough to illustrate the process himself. By defining "bourgeois" to include, among others, the Communist, he has brought this much-abused word to what must surely be its ultimate degradation.)

As Mr. Wilson scavenges the slopes of Parnassus, picking up a little nausea from Sartre, a "sense of unreality" from

Camus, pure Will from Nietzsche, and initiating all those gentlemen into the Outsiders Club by way of compensation, it grows painfully evident whither we are tending:

Then, as the Outsider's insight becomes deeper, so that he no longer sees men as a million million individuals but instead sees the world will that drives them all like ants in a formicary, he knows that they will never escape their stupidity and delusions, that no amount of logic and knowledge can make any more than an insect; the most irritating of the human lice is the humanist with his puffed-up pride in Reason and his ignorance of his own silliness.

And sure enough, we soon fetch up against William Blake, who "spent more time conversing with spirits than with human beings," and George Gurdjieff, who reports that a special commission of archangels once "implanted in man an organ, call *Kundabuffer*, whose special function was to make men perceive fantasy as reality." Needless to say, neither of them suffered from puffed-up pride in Reason.

Mr. Wilson appears to have it in not only for the humanist—"humanism is only another name for spiritual laziness"—but for humanity in general. "In most men, the instinct of brotherhood with other men is strongest—the herd instinct; in *me*, a sense of brotherhood with something other than man is strongest and demands priority." Thus, like certain other religious people and a good deal more snobbishly than most of them, he implies that all human beings would be saints and mystics if they could, but fail for want of Will. It has always been my opinion on the other hand, that a person of Mr. Wilson's saintly termperament has never felt any serious inclination to live as a human being at all. There is nothing to wonder at in the fact that he expresses dissatisfaction with the writers he examines, since a total disbelief in human dignity is not compatible with the tragic sense of life that is at the heart of all serious fiction. "The writer," he says patronizingly,

. . . has an instinct that makes him select the material that will make the best show on paper, and when that has . . . been carried to a limit from

which he finds it difficult to go forward, he selects a new approach . . . .
Unless a writer has unusual sincerity and unusual persistence, this is the
most certain to happen to him.

But the writer who goes "forward" in Mr. Wilson's sense,
goes forward into silence. Saints, visionaries and mystics do
not write tragedies.

In exchanging the above civilities with Mr. Wilson, I have
ascribed to him a remark about "brotherhood" which he
describes to the Outsider, but I think this is fair. This
Outsider is such a wildly variable and contradictory creature
that I can only assume he is intended to represent Mr. Wilson
himself; or rather, the moods he is thrown into by reading
snippets from authors who appeal to his imagination. At any
rate, if the Outsider *does* enjoy an independent existence, it
will have to be established by methods other than those the
author has chosen. Had he used physical qualities instead of
the subtler psychological ones, the fundamental fallacy of his
argument would have been immediately apparent. So
constituted, the argument would run something like this:

Let us first agree that all men with blues eyes are to be
called Outfielders. Very well, Bob has blue eyes so he
qualifies. Seymour has blue eyes too, keen blue eyes and a
motor scooter. Now we must expand our definition of the
Outfielder to include all men with motor scooters. But
Nathan *also* has a motor scooter; what's more, he wears
turtleneck sweaters, so a further expansion becomes
necessary. But, by a remarkable coincidence, Colin wears
turtleneck sweaters too, and sleeps on Hampstead Heath.
Clearly then, Colin, with his sleeping bag, is just like Bob,
who has blue eyes. And it should be obvious that they are all
Outfielders.

But it isn't. Nor is it obvious that Tolstoy is like Camus, or
Gurdjieff like Nietzsche. And when William Blake is made to
crawl into bed with Jean-Paul Sartre for the sake of the thesis,
the reader may be pardoned for suspecting that Mr. Wilson's
own *Kundabuffer* has been up to tricks.

Further reflection is apt to deepen this suspicion. Consider for a moment the inverted progression of the series. As Mr. Wilson broadens his study of the Outsider, he is borne back steadily into the past, from Sartre and Barbusse, through William James and Dostoevsky, to Blake and George Fox. In general, the farther back he goes, the closer his subjects came to understanding and resolving the "Outsider's dilemma." This is quite astonishing when you think about it. It implies, not only that Camus is incapable of reading Tolstoy for himself, but that the Outsider is living backwards in history, like Merlin in *The Sword in the Stone.* Restoring chronological sequence, we see that after all these years the Outsider has progressed, by painful degrees and sheer hard work, from a complete solution of his problems to a bare consciousness of their existence. Projecting this sequence into the future, we may even predict that the Outsider will soon lose sight of his dilemma altogether, thereby ceasing to exist, and all Mr. Wilson's work will have gone for nothing.

(1956)

T. S. MATTHEWS

A Farewell to Arms

The writings of Ernest Hemingway have very quickly put him in a prominent place among American writers, and his numerous admirers have looked forward with impatience and great expectations to his second novel. They should not be disappointed: *A Farewell to Arms* is worthy of their hopes and of its author's promise.

The book is cast in the form which Hemingway has apparently delimited for himself in the novel—a diary form. It is written in the first person, in that bare and unliterary style (unliterary except for echoes of Sherwood Anderson and Gertrude Stein), in that tone which suggests a roughly educated but sensitive poet who is prouder of his muscles than of his vocabulary, which we are now accustomed to associate with Hemingway's name. The conversation of the characters is as distinctly Hemingway conversation as the conversation in one of Shaw's plays is Shavian. But there are some marked differences between *A Farewell to Arms* and Hemingway's previous work.

For one thing, the design is more apparent, the material more solidly arranged. Perhaps the strongest criticism that

257

could be leveled against *The Sun Also Rises* was that its action was concerned with flotsam in the eddy of a backwater. It was apparently possible for some readers to appreciate the masculinity of Hemingway's "anti-literary" style, to admit the authenticity of his characters, and still to say, "What of it?" This criticism I do not consider valid—there has always been, it seems to me, in the implications of Hemingway's prose, and in his characters themselves, a kind of symbolic content that gives the least of his stories a wider range than it seems to cover—but such a criticism was certainly possible. It is not, however, a criticism that can possibly be directed against *A Farewell to Arms*. Fishing, drinking, and watching bullfights might be considered too superficial to be the stuff of tragedy, but love and death are not parochial themes.

The story begins in the summer of one of the middle years of World War I. The hero is an American, Frederick Henry, in the Italian army on the Isonzo, in charge of a section of ambulances. It is before America has declared war, and he is the only American in Gorizia. But an English hospital unit has been sent down: he meets one of the nurses, Catherine Barkley, and falls in love with her. In the Italian offensive, he is wounded, and taken back to the base hospital in Milan where she too manages to be transferred. He is ordered to the front again just in time to be caught in the Caporetto retreat. In the mad scramble across the plains he loses the main column, is almost cut off by the Germans, and then almost shot by the Italians for not being with his section. He escapes, makes up his mind to desert from the army, and gets to Milan, where he eventually finds Catherine again. He is in mufti, the police are suspicious, and with the connivance of a friendly barman they row across the border into Switzerland. Their passports are in order, so they escape being interned. Catherine is going to have a baby. They spend the winter in a little cottage in the mountains, and in the spring go down to Lausanne, where the baby is to be born. Everything goes well for a time; then the doctor advises a Caesarean operation: the baby is born dead, and Catherine has an unexpected hemorrhage and dies. Here the story ends. Or not quite here. Hemingway's characteristic last sentence is: "After a while I went out and left the hospital and walked back to the hotel in the rain."

The book has more in it than *The Sun Also Rises;* it is more of a story; and it is more carefully written. Sometimes this care is too evident.

I had gone to no such place but to the smoke of cafés and nights when the room whirled and you needed to look at the wall to make it stop, nights in bed, drunk, when you knew that this was all there was, and the strange excitement of waking and not knowing who it was with you, and the world all unreal in the dark and so exciting that you must resume again unknowing and not caring in the night, sure that this was all and all and all and not caring. Suddenly to care very much and to sleep to wake with it sometimes morning and all that had been there gone and everything sharp and hard and clear and sometimes a dispute about the cost.

This is a good description, but it is Hemingway gone temporarily Gertrude Stein. There is one other striking example of this manner, not new to Hemingway, but new to his serious vein:

"I love your beard," Catherine said. "It's a great success. It looks so stiff and fierce and it's very soft and a great pleasure."

This speech of Catherine's occurs toward the end of the book. When she is first introduced, she talks, plausibly enough, in a manner which, though distinctly Hemingway, might also pass as British. In the last half of the book (except for the Gertrude Stein lapse quoted above), she is pure Hemingway. The change that comes over her, the change that comes over both the main characters, is not, I think, due to the author's carelessness. Whether he deliberately planned this metamorphosis or half-consciously allowed it to take place is of minor interest. The interesting and the significant thing is the nature of the change. A typical Hemingway hero and a not-quite-so-typical Hemingway heroine are transformed, long before the end, into the figures of two ideal lovers.

Hemingway has been generally regarded as one of the most representative spokesmen of a lost generation—a generation remarkable chiefly for its cynicism, its godlessness, and its complete lack of faith. He can still, I think, be regarded as a representative spokesman, but the strictures generally implied against the generation will soon, perhaps, have to be modified or further refined. As far as Hemingway himself is concerned, it can certainly no longer be said that his characters do not embody a very definite faith.

"They won't get us," I said. "Because you're too brave. Nothing ever happens to the brave."

Rinaldi, the Italian surgeon who is the hero's roommate in the first part of the book, has what almost amounts to a breakdown because he can discover nothing in life outside his three anodynes of women, wine, and work. The note of hopelessness that dominated the whole of *The Sun Also Rises* is not absent in *A Farewell to Arms,* nor is it weaker, but it has been subtly modified, so that it is not the note of hopelessness we hear so much as the undertone of courage. Hemingway is now definitely on the side of the angels, fallen angels though they are. The principal instrument of this change is Catherine. Brett, the heroine of *The Sun Also Rises,* was really in a constant fever of despair; the selfless faith which Catherine gives her lover may seem to come from a knowledge very like despair, but it is not a fever. When we look back on the two women, it is much easier to believe in Brett's actual existence than in Catherine's—Brett was so imperfect, so unsatisfactory. And, like an old soldier, it would have been wrong for Brett to die. The Lady in *The Green Hat* died, but Brett must live. But Catherine is Brett—an ennobled, a purified Brett, who can show us how to live, who must die before she forgets how to show us—deified into that brave and lovely creature whom men, if they have never found her, will always invent.

This apotheosis of bravery in the person of a woman is the more striking because Hemingway is still the same apparently blunt-minded writer of two-fisted words. He still has a horror of expressing delicate or noble sentiments, except obliquely.

I did not say anything. I was always embarrassed by the words sacred, glorious, and sacrifice and the expression in vain. We had heard them . . . and had read them, on proclamations that were slapped up by billposters over other proclamations, now for a long time, and I had seen nothing sacred, and the things that were glorious had no glory and the sacrifices were like the stockyards at Chicago if nothing was done with the meat except to bury it. There were many words that you could not stand to hear and finally only the names of places had dignity.

And his prophecy of individual fate is, if anything, more brutally pessimistic than ever:

The world breaks every one and afterward many are strong at the broken places. But those that will not break it kills. It kills the very good and the very gentle and the very brave impartially. If you are none of these you can be sure it will kill you too but there will be no special hurry.

He will not even call Catherine brave, except through the lips of her lover. Here he is describing how she acted in the first stages of labor:

The pains came quite regularly, then slackened off. Catherine was very excited. When the pains were bad she called them good ones. When they started to fall off she was disappointed and ashamed.

Hemingway is not a realist. The billboards of the world, even as he writes about them, fade into something else: in place of the world to which we are accustomed, we see a land and a people of strong outlines, of conventionalized shadow; the people speak in a clipped and tacit language as stylized as their appearance. But Hemingway's report of reality is quite as valid as a realist's. The description of the war, in the first part of *A Farewell to Arms,* is perhaps as good a description of war just behind the front as has been written; and a fresh report from a point of view as original as Hemingway's is an addition to experience. But this book is not essentially a war story: it is a love story. If love stories mean nothing to you, gentle or hard-boiled reader, this is not your book.

The transition, indeed, from the comparative realism of the war scenes to the ideal reality of the idyll is not as effective as it might be. The meeting of the lovers after Henry's desertion from the army, and their escape into Switzerland, have not that ring of authenticity about them which from Hemingway we demand. We are accustomed to his apparent irrelevancies, which he knows how to use with such a strong and ironic effect, but the scene, for instance, between the lovers and Ferguson in the hotel at Stresa seems altogether too irrelevant, and has no ironic or dramatic value, but is merely an unwanted complication of the story. From this point until the time when the lovers are safely established in Switzerland, we feel a kind of uncertainty about everything that happens; we cannot quite believe in it. Why is it, then, that when our belief is reawakened, it grows with every page, until once more we are convinced, and passionately convinced, that we are hearing the truth?

I think it is because Hemingway, like every writer who has discovered in himself the secret of literature, has now invented the kind of ideal against which no man's heart is proof. In the conclusion of *A Farewell to Arms,* he has transferred his action to a stage very far from realism, and to a plane which may be criticized as the dramatics of a sentimental dream. And it is a dream. Catherine Barkley is one of the impossibly beautiful characters of modern tragedy—the Tesses, the Alyoshas, the Myshkins—who could never have existed, who could not live even in our minds if it were not for our hearts. In that sentimentalism, that intimation of impossible immortality, poets and those who hear them are alike guilty.

Hemingway himself is doubtless a very different sort of man from the people pictured in his books: he may well have very different ideas about the real nature of life; but as long as books remain a communication between us, we must take them as we understand them and feel them to be. "Nothing ever happens to the brave." It is an ambiguous statement of belief, and its implications are sufficiently sinister, but its meaning is as clear and as simple as the faith it voices. It is a man's faith; and men have lived and died by much worse.

(1929)

T. S. MATTHEWS

All Quiet on the Western Front

If a man has been in prison twenty years, and is then released, we should most of us agree that his life has been ruined. Not only have twenty years been taken away from him, but the bitterness of a special and futile knowledge will overshadow the rest of his days. But time, as we know (though none of us knows why), goes fast or slow according to what we are doing and where we find ourselves, and who shall say whether a few years in the trenches of the latest war might not have been the equivalent of at least twenty years in a peaceful jail?

In all the writing about World War I which has the stamp of truth on it we find this feeling of the ghastly slowness of time. In *All Quiet on the Western Front* it is the first thing that strikes us. It is as if the War had been going on forever, and was creeping forward into an endless succession of tomorrows. "We are at rest five miles behind the front. Yesterday we were relieved, and now our bellies are full of beef and haricot beans. We are satisfied and at peace." The present moment is all that can possibly exist. Neither the past nor the future will bear thinking about.

This is a book about something that nobody likes to talk of too much. It is about what happens to men in war. It has nothing whatever to do with the politenesses, the nobilities, or any of the sometimes pretty and sometimes ridiculous notions to which the world has once again settled down. The hero is a boy nineteen years old, a private in a German infantry regiment; his friends are mostly the same age. But it is hardly accurate to call them boys; as the author says of them: "We are forlorn like children, and experienced like old men, we are crude and sorrowful and superficial—I believe we are lost."

Some of them have volunteered; more have been drafted. The War, though they do not know it, has passed its peak: the slow decline of attrition has set in. The vague sense of fatality that we are made to feel in the opening pages gradually becomes a realization of approaching defeat. The new recruits come to the front younger and younger—so that even these boy-veterans of nineteen feel aged and protective. This is how the new recruits look when they are dead:

> Their sharp, downy faces have the awful expressionlessness of dead children.
> It brings a lump into the throat to see how they go over, and run and fall. A man would like to spank them, they are so stupid, and to take them by the arm and lead them away from here where they have no business to be. They wear grey coats and boots, but for most of them the uniform is far too big, it hangs on their limbs, their shoulders are too narrow, their bodies too slight; no uniform was ever made to these childish measurements.

The steady, unhurrying narrative picks its way from one desolation to another, following the fortunes of these precocious professionals, who have learned how to be soldiers and nothing else. They have their sprees and their moments of happiness, as when the indefatigable Tjaden spots an unlucky pig-pen or poultry-yard; they have their windfalls, of women and extra rations; they even have their vacations. But it was not always a pleasant change, in Germany of the last war years, to go from the comparative ease of a rest-camp to the evident starvation of home. And between the civilians and the soldiers returned from the front was a gulf impossible to bridge.

They talk to me too much. They have worries, aims, desires, that I cannot comprehend. I often am with one of them in the little beer-garden and try to explain to him that this is really the only thing, just to sit quietly, like this.

And behind all the momentary reprieves lies the inescapable reality of the life to which they are all doomed, "bombardments, barrage, curtain-fire, mines, gas, tanks, machine-guns, hand-grenades—words, words, but they held the horror of the world."

These youngsters whom the War is swiftly making unfit for civilian life (though many of them will not have to make the change) have cast aside, of necessity, all that they have been taught. They have had to become soldiers and they are nothing else. They believe in the present moment; it is not enough, but it is all they can be sure of. Love they have not known, patriotism and all the other abstract virtues and vices have vanished away in their first drum-fire; but something human they must cling to. They cling to their friends—not literally, and not even in words: when their friends are killed, there is nothing to be said. But what keeps them going in man's machine-made hell is the bodily presence of the friends around them.

They are more to me than life, these voices, they are more than motherliness and more than fear; they are the strongest, most comforting thing there is anywhere: they are the voices of my comrades.

I have said nothing in criticism of the book, and there is little I will say. It is written with simplicity and candor, and reads as if it had been well translated. There is nothing mawkish about it, and nothing "literary"—it is not the artful construction of fancy, but the sincere record of a man's suffering. Unlike the experimental artist, the author has nothing new to say; but he says it so honestly and so well that it is like news to us, though it is bad news.

I am young, I am twenty years old; yet I know nothing of life but despair, death, fear, and fatuous superficiality cast over an abyss of sorrow. I see how peoples are set against one another, and in silence, unknowingly, foolishly, obediently, innocently slay one another. I see that the keenest brains of the world invent weapons and words to make it yet more refined and enduring. And all men of my age, here and over there, throughout the whole world, see these things; all my generation is experiencing these things with me. What would our fathers do if we suddenly stood up and came before them and proffered our account? What do they expect of us if a time ever comes when the war is over? Through the years our business has been killing—it was our first calling in life. Our knowledge of life is limited to death. What will happen afterwards? And what shall come out of us?

Another country has been heard from. We know by now that the victor nations got nothing but evil from the War; had we expected, then, that the Germans had derived some virtue from defeat? No, the War did no good to anybody. Those of its generation whom it did not kill, it crippled, wasted, or used up. We hear hopes expressed that another generation may be wiser. Let us pray, rather, that it will not have to learn such costly wisdom.

(1929)

MALCOLM MUGGERIDGE

Corridors of Power

I first met C. P. Snow (later, Sir Charles Snow, and now Lord Snow of Leicester) some thirty-five years ago in Manchester when I was working on the *Guardian*. As I recall him in those days, he was a large, red-haired, rather wistful looking but still resolute man of about my own age. I was then twenty-seven. It emerged in the course of our conversation over tea that he was poised between being a writer and a scientist; had already written a thriller or so, but, I had the impression, leaned then in the direction of science. How good a scientist he was, I had, of course, no means of knowing. Nor, for that matter, have I now.

An impression that stayed with me was a worldly man. Worldliness is, by its nature, a highly romantic attitude; only mystics know how to be skeptical. Snow, I felt, was romantically worldly. Though, politically, he belonged to the Left (at that time, I should suppose, the fairly extreme Left), things like money and social eminence and success held great allure for him. My own romanticism (a late-Victorian throwback) was the converse of his. Success, I had convinced myself, was the hallmark of failure; the rich could only be contemptible, and, what was worse, bores. Thus, the idea of an ostensible intellectual like Snow wanting to be rich and successful struck me as bizarre, if not reprehensible.

Actually, as I see now, romantic worldliness like his is a great promoter of success in the field of action, though completely inimical to any other than the most mediocre achievement in the field of the imagination. The mists of desire obscure life's landscape, whether to portray, describe or understand it; they facilitate its conquest. Thus, Napoleon had so romantic a notion of the glories and delights of power that he was able to grab it, in the same way that a greedy child gets the best cakes. He took so glamorized a view of the thrones of Europe that he was able to overturn them, and then stand them up again to accommodate his repulsive Corsican relatives.

Similarly with a certain type of literature. For instance, Stendhal's novels derive much of their driving-force from his abject and ridiculous romanticism about being distinguished and important. One can trace the same thing in Evelyn Waugh, and, in a rather different way, in Proust. Snow is no Stendhal, certainly. Nor is he a Proust, or even a Waugh. One has, in fact, to agree with Dr. Leavis's preposterous and portentous tirade against him to the extent of agreeing that Snow is a negligible writer. All the same, his great popularity in England and America, and still more in Western Europe and the USSR derives from his already-mentioned romantic worldliness. He is the man rubbing his nose against the plate glass window of Vanity Fair, and telling the others who can't even get near the window what it is like inside. Pascal, a non-worldly man, said that judges and sovereigns had to be attired in elaborate regalia because otherwise the threadbare nature of their authority would be exposed. Snow, contrariwise, finds the regalia marvelous in itself, and deduces from it the reality of the authority beneath. His only authentic grouse was that he had no regalia to wear himself. Well, now, as a peer and member of Harold Wilson's Labour Government, he has.

Whatever may have been his inclination all those years ago when we met in Manchester, as things have turned out he has pursued neither science nor literature, but grazed in the limbo of no-man's-land between them. It is as an academic functionaire that he has made his mark, his novels being a by-product. They are narrated by Lewis Eliot, who is obviously himself; a fellow of Christ's College, Cambridge; an occasional civil servant and knighted; a scholar of sorts, and a lawyer—but he might just as well be a novelist.

The latest offering, *Corridors of Power,* is about a Tory politician, Roger Quaife, who undertakes a rather indeterminate political operation directed towards extricating the government from its nuclear commitments. Considered as an exercise in political strategy the whole thing is quite exceptionally silly and difficult to follow. There is no particular need to try. After a series of ups and downs, Quaife is worsted, and has to resign. His downfall is assisted by an affair he has with the wife of a fellow-Conservative M. P.; described by Snow with all the sensitivity and subtlety of an elephant pounding through a cornfield.

The dynamic of the novel, as of the series of which it is a part (there are, I gather, four more to come), lies in the lush descriptions of the alleged workings of power in England through the House of Commons and the Government, through high-born families and the civil service with money, patronage and influence as lubricants. There are the country house week-end gatherings at Basset, Diana Skidmore's house in Hampshire; the dinner parties at the Quaifes' house in Lord North Street, Westminster, presided over by Quaife's energetic wife, Lady Caroline, or Caro as she is known to her friends, and, of course, to Lewis Eliot; encounters with Lord Lufkin, an industrialist, and Lord Houghton, or Sammikins, who "had published a short book on Anglo-Indian relations ... it seemed anti-Churchill, pro-Nehru and passionately pro-Gandhi." Poor old Sammikins! He never should have come out in the open as an admirer of the Mahatma. It got him into trouble with his family and political associates. Words cannot convey the imbecility of this vision of power as conceived in Snow's ponderous, totally humorless and endearingly innocent, or at any rate naive, mind. To transubstantiate, as the dear old fellow has done, those moustached Westminster hostesses into divinities; to take Basset back to Trollope and Lord North Street back to Disraeli; to fabricate out of universal suffrage democracy in its, and England's, decrepitude a high drama of derring-do, a Church Lads Brigade Agincourt—this is something that only Snow could, or would, have attempted. Let me take, by way of illustration, a single sentence which caught my fancy. Snow mentions that "during the winter the gossip began to swirl out from the clubs and the Whitehall corridors." One imagines that so substantial figure; that huge moon face, unsmiling, portentous, looking across St. James's Park. Then, wetting a finger, holding it up to the wind, with an expression of great gravity: Yes (head on one side), yes, sure enough he can detect a decided current of gossip swirling past him from the clubs and Whitehall coridors.

But wait a minute—what clubs? What corridors? The Athenaeum, perhaps, where seedy clerics and atrocious dons desperately wash down bad food with bad wine. Or the Carlton, home of outmoded Conservative politicians in black coats hoping against hope for a telephone call that never comes to summon them to be under-under parliamentary secretary at the Ministry of Nothing. Or Whites whose red-faced members suck down their tenth Bloody Mary, still keeping a weather-eye open for Lord Boothby, or even Randolph Churchill. Or the Garrick, Dear God, the Garrick, frequented by noisy lawyers, moronic actors, and American newspaper and television correspondents who manage to persuade themselves that they are consorting with the mighty in their seats. Oh, Joe, oh Drew, come out from behind that decanter of port! I know you. As for Pratt—dear, gallant old Snow is on record as having reflected, while taking a drink in its dismal premises, how remarkable it was that he, a poor boy from a poor home, should even have found himself in this haunt of the smart and the great. Perhaps it is Pratts whence the rumors swirled. As it happens, it's the only club mentioned by name in *Corridors of Power,* and (the point has no particular relevance) the only London club I still belong to.

As for the corridors, we journalists who have paced them often and long enough in search of a story; who have visited those sad, sad knights in their ministries, looked at them across their desks; grey, listless men with black briefcases stamped with the Royal Arms (ministerial equivalent of the airline bag) which they take with them, to and fro, between Whitehall and their homes in Putney or Wimbledon—we just can't accept the swirling rumors. What wouldn't we have given for just one tiny swirl to take back to the office and knock out on a typewriter. The truth is that journalism unfits one for reading Snow. One's state of mind is all wrong. I give up. Sir Lewis Eliot, Lord Eliot, away! I want no more of you. Those last four volumes of yours, as far as I'm concerned, shall remain unread.

The rather amusing situation now is that Snow has been teamed up with Frank Cousins (about the nicest man, quite seriously, there is in England today; and hitherto head of the Transport and General Workers Union) to look after our technological development. Snow steps out of his novels into politics, and we shall all be watching closely to see how he fares. I have long held the view that power is to the collectivity what sex is to the individual. On this basis, writers like Snow obsessed with power may be compared, within their own terms of reference, with writers like D. H. Lawrence obsessed with sex; they display the same sort of seriousness; no more laughs in the corridors than in the woods when Lady Chatterley and Mellors were on the job there. They are, as it were, power-pornographers. For Snow to join a government is rather as though Lawrence had taken a job as a game-keeper. I am personally extremely grateful to Mr. Harold Wilson for having created this diverting situation, and only wish that he would cap it by taking Dr. Leavis into his government. What could Leavis be? The promised Ombudsman, perhaps. Or our first Minister of Culture.

(1964)

ROBERT PHELPS

The Genius of Colette—An Appreciation

I had just finished writing a review of this fascinating book when I learned that Colette had died. As it happended, I had been reading through her works all summer, slowly, and not without difficulty, in the original text (as Colette has remarked of her own reading in English), and I was so saturated in her vision, her genius, her personality, that her death seemed an intimate loss. I reread my review. It was impersonal and official. To do this to a writer who, like Colette, is so intensely given in her works, whose very syntax is warm with the ellipsis of spoken speech, whose "objective correlatives" are so close to her own secret self, who even uses her own name in many of her novels, and whose master-work will probably come to be the long series of meditative memoirs beginning with *La Maison de Claudine* and running through *Ces Plaisirs* and *L'Etoile Vesper* to *Le Fanal Bleu* seemed ungrateful, fatuous and wrong. I threw the review away. I should like, instead, to tell a little of what the art of Colette has taught me.

(1) Any writing is *live* if the writer is present. Colette wrote for over fifty years, and besides what offical referees

call creative writing, she also produced much of what they call hack writing. She described Queen Mary for the papers, *haute couture* for Vogue; she wrote the text for a book on butterflies; she reviewed plays; she was a war correspondent in Italy; she did a weekly cooking column. Yet she was never a hack. For a hack is someone who leaves himself out. In whatever Colette wrote, she was generously, necessarily personal. She never tried to be aloof. Young writers are frequently warned of the danger of "selling out." But refining themselves into anonymity, whether in *Time* magazine or their own novels, can be just as fatal. And no one can show them more aptly than Colette how to be gracefully, honestly present. The result, however slight, will never be neuter.

(2) A novelist writes primarily about people and their relationships. He may speak in either the first or the third person, subjectively or objectively, but he must always be looking at specific human beings, not myths, archetypes, psychological patterns. In American writing, we seem to have a strong bias toward the generalized. From Poe through Hawthorne, Melville, and James to Djuna Barnes, we tend toward the allegorical. We are north European, where the fairy tale and the parable prevail and in the past thirty years, as we have cross-fertilized ourselves for the first time with non-English writing, it is the German tradition of Thomas Mann, Kafka, Rilke and Brecht which has dominated. From the French, significantly, we have taken only the polemicists. We have worried over Malraux, Mauriac, Gide, Camus, Sartre, and have largely ignored Jouhandeau, Cocteau, Genet, Colette. Even with Proust, it is the philosopher, the artist with a notion about time and memory, whom we have preferred to the novelist *per se*.

As a result much of our young writing today is smothering. Our novels are airless and populated only by symbols. Kafka, Idea, and Myth-Over-All have shouldered out the world of particulars we all begin in. A novel like Colette's *Julie de*

Carneilhan—now available in English at twenty-five cents—can teach us as much that we need to learn at this juncture as *Finnegan's Wake*. Begin with people, with specific feelings, and keep your eye on them. The over-tones, the mythical parallels, the larger meanings, will speak for themselves.

(3) Is it only a coincidence that the American novelists who have in even a small degree been exposed to French literature, are our most satisfying as far as *making* is concerned? Look at *The Enormous Room, The Sun Also Rises, The Great Gatsby, The Pilgrim Hawk, The Wings of the Dove, Nightwood*. All by Americans who have known the French influence to temper, refine, and keep selection, in image and syntax, at a keen maximum.

Isn't it a mistake to go on assuming that because America is spatially vast and sprawling, her novels need necessarily be the same way? Isn't a work of art, anywhere, anytime, a harsh selection, an astringence, a deliberate forging? Because *Moby Dick* is improvisatorily made, need a young writer necessarily feel that his own genius will be betrayed unless he does the same? Certainly, before answerning this question, he should, in the privacy of his workroom, take *Chéri* apart—paragraph by paragraph, detail by detail. He should lift the book by its covers and shake it out over the floor. Nothing will fall out. Every word is essential. It is like a score by Stravinski. It is made to last.

(4) Major or minor, Proust or Forrest Reid, every true writer has a vision. It is by this that we finally judge him. No matter how imperfect his art, it is this figure in his carpet that counts, and no one can show us more clearly than Colette that a writer discovers his vision in only one way: by writing about whatever moves him most, no matter what it is. The first book Colette published under her own name was about animals. She loved them. ("You'll end up in the jungle," her husband once told her.) Her last published book was called *Cats*. And indeed, what her vision grows out of is

just this world which human beings have in common with creatures: the senses, the impulses, the pre-conscious virtues. But she also knew that to be human is to be self-conscious, and the basic relationship through her novels is the same; the lonely yearning of someone who is conscious and artful toward someone who is innocent, impulsive, and in the unpejorative sense, bestial. The former watches, loves, plans, gives. The latter stirs in self-absorption, accepts, and often without even knowing it, betrays and abandons.

(5) "Perfection of the life," warned Yeats, "or of the works." One must choose. Yet as Mrs. Crosland's biography shows, Colette proved that this is too great a simplification. Almost as amazing as her works is the resourcefulness with which the same passionate fantasy that begot them applied to her life. Like anyone who leaves over fifty books, she spent many hours at a desk: But she was no owl. Her extracurricular activities included professional acting, dancing, and miming, as well as homemaking, child-raising, and gardening. And lo! at fifty-nine, she opened a beauty salon.

(6) For me there are two classes of writers: those whose subject is the human heart, and those whose emphasis is upon all the other, perhaps more important possibilities in human experience. The latter include many of our most illustrious and bewitching contemporaries, from Valéry and Kafka, to Pirandello and Virginia Woolf. The former include all of my favorite writers, from Shakespeare to Jane Austen to Colette. Compare *All's Well That Ends Well, Persuasian,* and *Julie de Carneilhan.* Does one writer know any more about love than the other? Aren't they in this respect peers, all three of them, for all the ages?

(1954)

KATHERINE ANNE PORTER

Kay Boyle: Example to the Young

Miss Kay Boyle's way of thinking and writing stems from sources still new in the sense that they have not been supplanted. She is young enough to regard them as in the category of things past, a sign I suppose, that she is working in a tradition and not in a school. Gertrude Stein and James Joyce were and are the glories of their time and some very portentous talents have emerged from their shadows. Miss Boyle, one of the newest, I believe to be among the strongest. At present she is identified as one of the *Transition* group, but these two books just published should put an end to that. What is a group, anyhow? In this one were included—as associate editors and contributors to *Transition*—many Americans: Harry Crosby, William Carlos Williams, Hart Crane, Matthew Josephson, Isidor Schneider, Josephine Herbst, Murray Godwin, Malcolm Cowley, John Herrman, Laura Riding—how many others?—and Miss Boyle herself. They wrote in every style under heaven and they spent quite a lot of time fighting with each other. Not one but would have resented, and rightly, the notion of discipleship or of interdependence. They were all vigorous not so much in revolt as in assertion, and most of them had admirably subversive ideas. Three magazines sustained them and were sustained by them: *Transition,* Ernest Walsh's *This Quarter* and *Broom.* The tremendous presences of Gertrude Stein and James Joyce were everywhere about them, and so far as Miss Boyle is concerned, it comes to this: that she is a part of the most important literary movement of her time.

She sums up the salient qualities of that movement: a fighting spirit, freshness of feeling, curiosity, the courage of her own attitude and idiom, a violently dedicated search for the meanings and methods of art. In these short stories and this novel there are further positive virtues of the individual temperament: health of mind, wit and the sense of glory. All these are qualities in which the novel marks an advance over the stories, as it does, too, in command of method.

The stories have a range of motive and feeling as wide as the technical virtuosity employed to carry it. Not all of them are successful. In some of the shorter ones, a straining of the emotional situation leads to stridency and incoherence. In others, where this strain is employed as a deliberate device, it is sometimes very successful—as notably in "Vacation Time," an episode in which an obsessional grief distorts and makes tragic a present situation not tragic of itself; the reality is masked by drunkenness, evaded by hysteria, and it is all most beautifully done. "On the Run" is a bitter story of youth in literal flight from death, which gains on it steadily; but the theme deserved better treatment.

In such stories as "Episode in the Life of an Ancestor" and "Uncle Anne," there are the beginnings of objectiveness, a soberer, richer style; and the sense of comedy, which is like acid sometimes, is here gayer and more direct. In "Portrait" and "Polar Bears and Others," Miss Boyle writes of love not as if it were a disease, or a menace, or a soothing syrup to vanity, or something to be peered at through a microscope, or the fruit of original sin, or a battle between the sexes, or a bawdy pastime. She writes as one who believes in love and romance—not the "faded flower in a buttonhole," but love so fresh and clear it comes to the reader almost as a rediscovery in literature. It was high time someone rediscovered it. There are other stories, however—"Spring Morning," "Letters of a Lady," "Episode in the Life of an Ancestor"—in which an adult intelligence plays with destructive humor on the themes of sexual superstition and pretenses between men and women. "Madame Tout Petit," "Summer," "Theme" and "Bitte Nehmen Sie die Blumen" are entirely admirable, each one a subtle feat in unraveling a complicated predicament of the human heart. "Wedding Day," the title story, is the least satisfactory, displaying the weakness of Miss Boyle's strength in a lyricism that is not quite poetry.

The novel, *Plagued by the Nightingale,* has the same germinal intensity as the shorter works, but it is sustained from the first word to the last by a sure purpose and a steadier command of resources. The form, structure and theme are comfortably familiar. The freshness and brilliancy lie in the use of the words and the point of view.

It is the history of an American girl married to a young Frenchman, and living for a short period in the provinces with his wealthy bourgeois family. There is Papa, a blustering old fool, though Bridget never says it quite so plainly; Maman, a woman of energy, good will and appalling force of character; three unmarried sisters, Annick, Julie and Marthe; Charlotte the eldest sister, married to her cousin; Pierre the elder brother, a young doctor; and Nicholas, Bridget's husband. A taint in the blood causes eccentrics and paralytics to blossom like funeral wreaths in every generation. Nicholas is warned by his weakened legs that the family disease is likely to be the main portion of his inheritance. He is dependent on his people, his wife is dowerless. Charlotte's husband is little better than an imbecile, but he is wealthy. Uncle Robert, a perverse old maid of a man, is also wealthy, and he amuses himself by tampering with family affairs; the victims endure him in the hope that he may give someone money sometime. First and last it is the question of money that agitates the family bosom.

The three younger daughters are waiting, each in her own

way, for a proposal of marriage from Luc, an idolized young doctor, who nonchalantly enjoys the privilege of the devoted family without asking to become a member. Bridget is a vigorous personality, with powerful hates and loves, a merciless eye, and a range of prejudices which permits no offense against her secret faiths to be trivial. She has gayety and charm, and at first she is ingenuously fond of this household of persons so closely and tenderly bound, so united in their aims. Nicholas feels quite otherwise. He hates his dear good sweet people who are so warmly kind in small things, so hideously complacent and negligent in the larger essentials. He needs help, restitution really, from this family that has brought him disabled into the world. His father brutally—that is to say, with the utmost fatherly kindness—tells Nicholas that he will give him fifty thousand francs when Bridget has a child. Charlotte's five beautiful children are weak in the legs, but they are "the joy of existence" nonetheless. One's duty is to procreate for the family, however maimed the lives may be.

Bridget, caught in a whirling undercurrent of love and hatred and family intrigue, begins first to fear and then to despise these strangers as she realizes the ignoble motives back of all the family devotion. She sees her husband gradually growing hostile to her as he identifies her with his family, no longer with himself. She is confirmed in her instinctive distrust of situations and feelings sanctified by the rubber stamps of time and custom; she defends herself by mockery and the mental reservation against the blind cruelties and wrongs which are done under cover of love. Luc complicates matters by falling in love with her instead of asking for one of the sisters, but even so he does not speak until it is too late—until it is safe for him to speak, when marriage to one of the sisters is no longer the best investment he can make. And Bridget, who has wavered, been pulled almost to pieces by the tearing, gnawing, secretive antagonisms and separate aims of the family, comes to her conclusion—a rather bitter one, which in the end will solve very badly the problem. Of her own will she takes to herself the seed of decay.

This is no more than a bare and disfiguring outline of the plan of the novel. The whole manner of the telling is superb: there are long passages of prose which crackle and snap with electric energy, episodes in which inner drama and outward events occur against scenes bright with the vividness of things seen by the immediate eye: the bathing party on the beach, the fire in the village, the delicious all-day excursion to Castle Island, the scene in the market when Bridget and Nicholas quarrel, the death of Charlotte, the funeral. Nothing is misplaced or exaggerated, and the masterful use of symbol and allegory clarify and motivate the main great theme beneath the apparent one: the losing battle of youth and strength against the resistless army of age and death. This concept is implicit in the story itself, and it runs like music between the lines. The book is a magnificent performance; and as the short stories left the impression of reservoirs of power hardly tapped, so this novel, complete as it is, seems only a beginning.

(1931)

PHILIP RAHV

Henry James

Henry James is at once the most and least appreciated figure in American writing. His authority as a novelist of unique quality and as an archetypal American has grown immeasurably in the years since his death, and in some literary circles his name has of late been turned into the password of a cult. But at the same time he is still regarded, in those circles that exert the major influence on popular education and intelligence, with the coldness and even derision that he encountered in the most depressed period of his career, when his public deserted him and he found himself almost alone.

To illustrate the extent to which he is even now misunderstood, let me cite the opening gambit of the section on James in *The College Book of American Literature,* a text currently used in many schools. "It is not certain that Henry James really belongs to American literature, for he was critical of America and admired Europe." The attitude so automatically expressed by the editors of this academic volume obviously borders on caricature. The responsibility for it, however, must be laid at the door of all those critics and historians who, in response to a deep anti-intellectual compulsion or at the service of some blindly nationalistic or social creed, are not content merely to say no to the claims made in James's behalf but must ever try to despoil him utterly. The strategy is simple: James was nothing but a self-deluded expatriate snob, a concoctor of elegant if intricate trifles, a fugitive from "reality," etc., etc. Professor Pattee, a run-of-the-mill historian of American writing, permits himself the remark that James's novels "really accomplish nothing." Ludwig Lewisohn is likewise repelled by the novels—"cathedrals of frosted glass" he calls them; in his opinion only the shorter narratives are worth reading. In his *Main Currents* Parrington gives two pages to James as against eleven to James Branch Cabell, and he has the further temerity (and/or innocence) to round out his two pages by comparing James—much to his disadvantage, of course—to Sherwood Anderson. And Van Wyck Brooks does all he can, in *New England: Indian Summer,* to promote once more the notoriously low estimate of the later James to which he committed himself in *The Pilgrimage.* Brooks may well believe that the Jamesian attachment is to be counted among the fixed ideas of our native "coterie-writers"—and plainly the best cure for a fixed idea is to stamp on it.

This depreciation of James is prepared for by some of the leading assumptions of our culture. The attitude of Parrington, for example, is formed by the Populist spirit of the West and its open-air poetics, whereas that of Brooks is at bottom formed by the moralism of New England—a moralism to which he has reverted, even though in practice he applies it in a more or less impressionistic and sentimental manner, with all the vehemence of a penitent atoning for his backsliding in the past. And the difference between such typical attitudes is mainly this: that while Parrington—like Whitman and Mark Twain before him—rejects James entirely, Brooks at least recognizes the value and fidelity to life of his earlier novels. Yet if James can be named, in T. S. Eliot's phrase, "a positive continuator of the New England genius,"

283

then surely Brooks must be aware of it as well as any of us: for he is nothing if not a pious servitor of this genius; after all, he, too, is a paleface. But still he scoffs at the more complex and, so to speak, ultimate James. And this Brooks does essentially for the same reasons, I think, that the Boston public of the 1870s scoffed at the works he now admits into his canon. We know that when the first of James's books appeared in America, they were actively disliked in Boston: Mrs. Fields (the wife of the publisher) relates that they were thought "self-conscious, artificial and shallow." A like animus is now betrayed in Brooks's judgment of such novels as *The Spoils of Poynton, The Wings of the Dove* and *The Golden Bowl:*

> Magnificent pretensions, petty performances!—the fruits of an irresponsible imagination, of a deranged sense of values, of a mind working in a void, uncorrected by any clear consciousness of human cause and effect *(The Pilgrimage of Henry James)*.
>
> There was scarcely enough substance in these great ghosts of novels. . . .What concerned him now was form, almost regardless of content, the problems of calculation and construction . . . . His American characters might be nobler, but, if the old world was corrupt, its glamor outweighed its corruption in his mind . . . so that he later pictured people, actually base, as eminent, noble and great. *(New England: Indian Summer)*.

What are such extreme statements if not critical rationalizations of the original Boston prejudice? Brooks begins by magnifying the distinctions between James's early and late manner into an absolute contradiction, and ends by invoking the charge of degeneracy. But the fact is that the changes in James's work mark no such gap as Brooks supposes but are altogether inplicit in the quality of his vision, flowing from the combined release and elaboration of his basic tendency. Moreover, these changes, far from justifying the charge of degeneracy, define for a good many of his readers the one salient example in our literature of a novelist who, not exhausted by his initial assertion of power, learned how to nourish his gifts and grow to full maturity. To me he is the only really fine American writer of the nineteenth century who can truly be said to have mastered that "principle of growth," to the failure of which in our creative life Brooks has himself repeatedly called attention in his earlier preachments.

For what is to be admired in a late narrative like *The Wings of the Dove* is James's capacity to lift the nuclear theme of his first period—the theme of the American innocent's penetration into the "rich and deep and dark" hive of Europe—to a level of conscious experience and esthetic possession not previously attained. James orders his world with consummate awareness in this narrative, applying successfully his favorite rule of an "exquisite economy" in composition. There are brilliant scenes in it of London and Venice, and strongly contrasted symbols of social glamor and decay; it is invigorated, too, by an unflagging realism in the plotting of act and motive and by the large movement of the characters. No literary standpoint that allows for the dismissal of this creation as a "petty performance" can possibly be valid. Is its heroine, Milly Theale, a character without reality? She remains in our mind, writes Edmund Wilson, "as a personality independent of the novel, the kind of personality, deeply felt, invested with poetic beauty and unmistakably individualized, which only the creators of the first rank can give life to." James suffers from a certain one-sidedness, to be sure. This tends to throw off balance such readers as are unable to see it for what it is—the price he paid, given the circumstances of his career, for being faithful to his own genius. For James could continue to develop and sustain his "appeal to a high refinement and a handsome wholeness of effect" only through intensively exploiting his very limitations, through submitting himself to a process of creative yet cruel self-exaggeration. The strain shows in the stylization of his language, a stylization so rich that it turns into an intellectual quality of rare value, but which at times is apt to become overwrought and drop into unconscious parody. It is further shown in his obsessive refinement—a veritable delirium of refinement—which again serves at times to remove us from the actuality of the represented experience. This should be related to his all-too-persistent attempts, as Yvor Winters has observed, to make the sheer *tone* of speech and behavior "carry vastly more significance than is proper to it." It is true that, for instance, in novels like *The Sense of the Past* and *The Awkward Age,* he pushes his feelings for nuances and discriminations to an unworkable extreme. But such distortions, inflated into awful vices by his detractors, are of the kind which in one form or another not only James but most of the considerable modern artists are forced to cultivate as a means of coping with the negative environment that confines them. To regard such distortions as the traits of a willfull coterie is utterly naive. They are the traits, rather, of an art which, if it is to survive at all in a society inimical to all interests that are pure, gratuitous and without cash-value, has no other recourse save constantly to "refine its singularities" and expose itself more and more to the ravages of an unmitigated individualism.

But in all this I do not mean to imply that I agree with those enthusiasts who see no moral defects whatsoever in James. From the viewpoint of social criticism, there is a good deal of justice in Ferner Nuhn's mordant analysis of *The Golden Bowl* in his book, *The Wind Blows from the East.* Nuhn shows up one such defect in James's close identification with Adam and Maggie Verver's upper-class American illusions and self-righteousness. (One is persuaded of this view by the evidence of the tone and the inner manipulation of the scale of value, for here too the author makes the story "tell itself.") Nuhn fails to bring out, however, the enormous assets with which this novel is otherwise endowed. There is a use of symbols in it and a scenic and dramatic power scarcely equaled, to my mind, anywhere in American prose. Furthermore, whatever one may think of the millionaire self-indulgence of the Ververs, this is a far cry from the charge that his long exile put James into such a bad state that he could no longer distinguish between the noble and the base. This sort of charge is answered once and for all, it seems to me, by Stephen Spender in his study, *The Destructive Element:*

> The morality of the heroes and heroines [in the last great novels] is to "suffer generously." What they have to suffer from is being more intelligent than the other characters. Also, there are no villains. It is important to emphasize this, because in these really savage novels the behavior of some of the characters is exposed in its most brutal form. But the wickedness of the characters lies primarily in their situation. Once the situation is provided, the actors cannot act otherwise. Their only compensation is that by the use of their intelligence, by their ability to understand, to love and to suffer, they may to some extent atone for the evil which is simply the evil of the modern world.

As against the sundry moralizers and nationalists who belittle James, there are the cultists who go to the other extreme in presenting him as a kind of culture-hero, an ideal master whose perfection of form is equaled by his moral insight and stanch allegiance to "tradition." This image is no doubt of consolatory value to some high-minded literary men. It contributes, however, to the misunderstanding of James, in that it is so impeccable, one might say transcendent, that it all but eliminates the contradictions in him—and in modern literature, which bristles with anxieties and ideas of isolation, it is above all the creativity, the depth and quality of the contradictions that a writer unites within himself, that gives us the truest measure of his achievement. And this is not primarily a matter of the solutions, if any, provided by the writer—for it is hardly the writer's business to stand in for the scientist or philosopher—but of his force and integrity in reproducing these contradictions as felt experience. Very few of us would be able to appreciate Dostoevsky, for instance, if we first had to accept his answer to the problem of the Christian man, or Proust if we first had to accept his answer to the problem of the artist. We appreciate these novelists because they employ imaginative means that convince us of the reality of their problems, which are not *necessarily* ours.

T. S. Eliot was surely right in saying that the soil of James's origin imparted a "flavor" that was "precisely improved and given its chance, not worked off" by his living in Europe. Now James differs radically in his contradictions from European novelists—that is why readers lacking a background in American or at least Anglo-Saxon culture make so little of him. And the chief contradiction is that his work represents a positive and ardent search for "experience" and simultaneously a withdrawal from it, or rather, a dread of approaching it in its natural state. Breaking sharply with the then still dominant American morality of abstention, he pictures "experience" as the "real taste of life," as a longed-for "presence" at once "vast, vague, and dazzling—an irradiation of light from objects undefined, mixed with the atmosphere of Paris and Venice." Nevertheless, to prove truly acceptable, it must first be Americanized as it were, that is to say, penetrated by the new-world conscience and cleansed of its taint of "evil." This tension between the impulse to plunge into "experience" and the impulse to renounce it is the chief source of the internal yet astonishingly abundant Jamesian emotion; and because the tension is not always adequately resolved, we sometimes get that effect, so well described by Glenway Wescott, of "embarrassed passion and hinted meaning in excess of the narrated facts; the psychic content is too great for its container of elegantly forged happenings; it all overflows and slops about and is magnificently wasted." On this side of James we touch upon his relationship to Hawthorne, whose characters, likewise tempted by "experience," are held back by the fear of sin. And Hawthorne's ancestral idea of sin survives in James, though in a secularized form. It has entered the sensibility and been translated into a revulsion, an exasperated feeling, almost morbid in its sensitiveness, against any conceivable crudity of scene or crudity of conduct. (The trouble with American life, he wrote, is not that it is "ugly"—the ugly can be strange and grotesque—but that it is "plain"; "even nature, in the western world, has the peculiarity of seeming rather crude and immature.") Any failure of discrimination is sin, whereas virtue is a compound of intelligence, moral delicacy and the sense of the past.

And Hawthorne's remembrance of the religious mythology of New England and his fanciful concern with it is replaced in James—and this too is a kind of transmutation—by the remembrance and fanciful concern with history. It was for the sake of Europe's historical "opulence" that he left his native land. Yet this idea is also managed by him in a contradictory fashion, and for this reason W. C. Brownell was able to say that he showed no real interest in the "course of history." Now as a critic Brownell had no eye for James's historical picture of the American experience in Europe; but it is true that on the whole James's sense of history is restricted by the point of view of the "passionate pilgrim" who comes to rest in the shade of civilization. Above all, he comes to enrich his personality. Thus there is produced the Jamesian conception of history as a static yet irreproachable standard, a beautiful display, a treasured background, whose function is at once to adorn and lend perspective to his well nigh metaphysical probing of personal relations, of the private life. There never was a writer so immersed in personal relations, and his consistency in this respect implies an anti-historical attitude. This helps to explain the peculiarities of his consciousness, which is intellectual yet at the same time indifferent to general ideas, deeply comprehensive yet unattached to any open philosophical motive.

These contradictions in James—and there are others besides those I have mentioned—are chiefly to be accounted for in terms of his situation as an American writer who experienced his nationality and the social class to which he belonged at once as an ordeal and as an inspiration. His characteristic themes all express this doubleness. The "great world" is corrupt, yet it represents an irresistible goal. Innocence points to all the wanted things one has been deprived of, yet it is profound in its good faith and not to be tampered with without loss. History and culture are the supreme ideal, but why not make of them a strictly private possession? Europe is romance and reality and civilization, but the spirit resides in America. James never faltered in the maze of these contraries; he knew how to take hold of them creatively and weave them into the web of his art. And the secret of their combination is the secret of his irony and of his humor.

(1943)

CHARLES THOMAS SAMUELS

The Fixer

When Bernard Malamud's first novel appeared in 1952, it was infrequently reviewed and poorly comprehended. With condescension it reserves for experiments neither European nor chic, *The New Yorker* described *The Natural* as "book about a baseball player, related in a thin and ingenuous voice that seems to indicate that the writer would like to have us search beneath the surface for the meaning he has hidden there." Even so perceptive an early advocate as Norman Podhoretz found the search difficult: though the novel's team, the Knights, is presided over by a manager named Fisher who has bandaged hands and prays for rain, Podhoretz discovered Homeric parallels. Somehow, its initial reception earned *The Natural* a reputation for obscurity that has not been successfully challenged.

Instead, like most of Malamud's work, *The Natural* is rather too obvious. Yet it is first-rate, criticizing with wit and wild invention those American cults of youth, success, and unlimited fulfillment which find their popular apotheosis in baseball. An improbable combination of *Mad* magazine and T. S. Eliot, its humor enriched by tenderness, Malamud's first novel has been unjustly neglected.

Not so his second book. *The Assistant* is such a full
realization of Malamud's talent that it has threatened to
freeze his reputation and bind him to a formula. This tale of
a young Italian's moral apprenticeship to an anguished but
charitable Jew contains *the* Malamud situation and theme
(*The Natural* is about a failed apprenticeship, an education
missed through proud reliance on natural gifts). Well received
and now part of the post-war fictional canon, *The Assistant*
has been celebrated too often for its ideas. Yet Malamud is
not a probing thinker, as his new novel makes clear, but
rather a master of plotting and effect. One moment in *The
Assistant* will suggest what I mean.

Though Frank Alpine has begged a job in Morris Bober's
grocery to expiate his sins, he is constantly backsliding. In
petty theft, gluttonous raids on the stock, and peeping at the
interdicted Jewish daughter, Frank remains a natural man.
Yet Helen comes to believe that he will reform. Religious
differences and sexual inhibitions yield to a seriousness
symbolized by his gift of a complete Shakespeare, the perfect
token for a girl whose dearest wish is to attend NYU nights.
Frank woos Helen with his suffering, his desire for
regeneration, his respect for her chastity and high purpose.

But the past is implacable. One night while waiting for him
on a secluded park bench, Helen is attacked by his former
confederate but saved when Frank appears. In the passionate
moment which follows, Frank's natural self is stirred to take
the girl he had won through abstinence and education.
Afterwards, Helen curses him, screaming "Dog—uncircumcised
dog" to remind him that he is, after all, an ignorant goy.
Ironically, the terms of her curse come from the very symbol
of Frank's urge for self-transcendence: the words recall those
spoken in self-loating by Shakespeare's Othello. This moment
contains within itself all the heartbreak of Frank's situation.
It is a masterpiece of plotting which one reads with a gasp,
and it is typical of the skill that makes its author the most
moving of our recent novelists. Yet so far as I know it has
never been analyzed while critics spend their wit chewing

over those easily digested pieces of Malamud's conservative ethics. No admirer neglects his humor or irony (for which the names Chagall and Dostoevsky have become inevitable emblems), but the emphasis is usually placed on Malamud's affirmation and morality, an emphasis which, in too many interviews that make him seem a Yiddish Vincent Peale, the author supports.

That this emphasis is misplaced *The Magic Barrel* should have shown. Its title story, as good as anything he has written, proves Malamud a virtuoso of the heart. With few exceptions, the other stories are second-rate: thin little exempla in which the characters' sufferings become as predictable and thus as ineffective as the calls for love and charity with which they conclude.

Despite its success, this book did alert critics to Malamud's limitations. Doubts about narrowness of range began to be heard, and Alfred Kazin mounted his hobbyhorse Reality to charge Malamud's neglect of a commodity "too precious to turn into symbols." Together with the adulation for ethics, this attack constitutes a dismissal of the very gifts which make Malamud unique. *A New Life,* Malamud's third novel, gives unfortunate signs that this author often heeds his worst critcs.

In that uneven book, Malamud makes a transparent attempt to answer the objection about lack of specificity and novelistic scope. Having spent over ten years in the university, however, he had available only the most intractable of *moeurs* to make a *roman* out of. As a result, the book's satire is by turns implausible, irrelevant, and peevish, while its redeeming feature is yet another version of the education of strength in the school of adversity. Attempting to extend his range, Malamud merely proved how very good he is at what he is good at.

The second story collection, *Idiots First,* shows a further misuse of talent. Having failed to become a conventional novelist of manners, Malamud tries in this book to be an entertainer (there is, for example, a marked increase and new candor in his treatment of sex). Again we have one fine tale: "The Maid's Shoes." But the inferior stories are as thin and predictable as those in *The Magic Barrel* and also trivial and cozy in a way Malamud had never before been. In *Idiots First* Malamud reminds one of a very sophisticated O. Henry. The story "Still Life," about a Jewish painter's attempt to seduce his guilt-ridden Catholic landlady, concludes by locking its irony within a splendid euphemism for intercourse ("Pumping slowly he nailed her to her cross"), but this is very much a case of the tail wagging the dog. "Black is My Favorite Color" is a contrived and embarrassing anecdote about race prejudice, the shorter tales are like standup jokes, and the title story virtually parodies Malamud's affirmation—portraying a distraught father vanquishing the angel of death with only the anguish reflected in his eyes.

By exhorting him to greater displays of meanings—never to firmer arabesques, sharper images of souls in progress—Malamud's critics have encouraged him to subvert his best talents. His new novel shows how fully he has taken their bad advice, reaching as it does for effects of verisimilitude and social-consciousness which have little to do with his fabulous and feeling art.

In *The Assistant* Frank Alpine ultimately learns:

"Suffering . . . is like a piece of goods. I bet the Jews could make a suit of clothes out of it. The other funny thing is that there are more of them around than anybody knows."

Malamud himself has suffered from readers who fail to take this statement metaphorically. By Jewishness, Malamud means that moral fervor dormant in all men which creates, when disciplined by suffering, a necessary refusal to make others suffer. The hero of *The Fixer,* a Russian Jew wrongly accused of murder, comes to a very different definition of Judaism:

One thing I've learned, he thought, there's no such thing as an un-political man, especially a Jew. You can't be one without the other, that's clear enough.

This too is metaphoric ("Jew" now means victim of society), but the word "political" is stretched so far that the statement constitutes a quality already symbolizing something else defined by a word which doesn't mean what it says. Many men are unpolitical so that "politics" has a very special meaning in the quoted statement; worse, the statement concludes a story which fails to provide adequate illustration.

The novel's opening works. Recounting the hero's journey to Kiev where he hopes to forget inborn squalor and old troubles (his wife has just left him), Malamud is very good at depicting the Jew's imagination of disaster as he makes his way to the typically ironic new life. But things soon go wrong. After he arrives in Kiev, Yakov Bok chances upon a drunken man lying in the snow. Though the drunkard wears in his lapel the emblem of a notorious anti-Semitic legion, Yakov rescues him, accepts his offer of a job, and becomes an intimate of his household. That a Jew who is literally frightened by his shadow should involve himself with his worst enemy is implausible, though perhaps Malamud wished to symbolize a putative Jewish masochism or an ironic affinity for the feared gentile. Neither suggestion is developed. The implausibility in plotting is never redeemed; Malamud cares only for his main episodes, and perfunctory plotting serves because it is expeditious.

The first seventy pages are like an old movie so familiar that we can predict each consequence. Surely Malamud wanted an effect of irreversible fate, but he obtains only an air of secondhand contrivance. When Yakov spurns the attentions of the anti-Semite's daughter, we know she will later turn on him in injured vanity, just as we know his zealous scrutiny of the workers over whom he is made foreman can only result in dangerous resentment. Everything we are told about his first weeks in Kiev falls into place when he is finally charged with murder. He rescues an old Jew from some rock-throwing boys; the old Jew is later said to have been in league with him. He chases such boys himself; one of them turns out to be the murderer's victim.

In jail, the novel's main stage, the plotting becomes neither fresher nor more instructive. Evidence is brought against him by corrupt priests and a theatrically grieving mother who is really a prostitute and probably an accomplice in the crime. Most of the Russians are in cahoots to wring false testimony of a conspiracy so that they can start a pogrom; with obvious irony, Yakov's most strenuous persecutors are the devoutest Christians.

Malamud has never been interested in analyzing character, only in displaying it. Since Yakov's ordeal is so clichéd, his growing heroism can only seem synthetic. Moreover, it is unattached to larger issues. The passage I cited alludes to the political basis for Russian anti-Semitism, but politics has no demonstrated bearing on the action and is not even discussed until page 300. At that point in Yakov's long incarceration, a lawyer enters to rationalize Bok's experience. This speech reminded me of the psychiatrist's summing up in Hitchcock's "Psycho": a professionally lucid though intellectually predictable excuse for a sadistic debauch.

The main action of *The Fixer* is intricate not in political analysis, character development, twist of plot, but in physical torment. Where Malamud's heroes formerly suffered the pain of being locked in selfhood, Yakov suffers only the pains of being locked in jail. For the harpy Harriet Bird of *The Natural,* the demons which well up in Frank Alpine's soul, the dead spirits who torment Sy Levin a *A New Life,* Malamud substitutes a dead mouse in a can of soup, physical humiliations by the prison guards, gratuitous beatings by the inmates.

And after 150 pages of this politically inflated theatre of cruelty, Malamud concludes with sentimental uplift. In the last moments, one of Yakov's Russian guards is shot for trying to protect him, Yakov forgives his erring wife by heroically accepting her bastard son in the same pencil stroke with which he denies a Jewish plan to murder the other child, and Yakov goes to trial, thinking rousing thoughts, amidst prefigurements of the Russian Revolution:

Where there's no fight for it there's no freedom. What is it Spinoza says? If the state acts in ways that are abhorrent to human nature it's the lesser evil to destroy it. Death to the anti-Semites! Long live revolution! Long live liberty!

One can guess why Malamud chose this subject. It contains precisely those opportunities for a large social canvas and engagement with important issues which his critics have been urging. Moreover, with its Jewish *schlemiel* who becomes a hero it employs the sort of inner drama which Malamud stages so well, but the outer drama is unsuited to Malamud's gifts, so he falls back on a dreary round of inquisitions and tortures which is meant to represent it but which rather measures his unfitness for these materials.

Such a novel cries out for a character in whom the conflict between justice and political barbarism might find a reflection. *The Fixer* has one such character: the Investigating Magistrate, Bibkov. But after forcing him to orate embarrassingly on Spinoza and showing how unhappy he is in his official role, Malamud kills him off. Lacking an intellectual center for his theme, Malamud can only have recourse to blocks of rhetoric which alternate with torture.

At last, the plot defeats the theme in the most fundamental way. Malamud needs the torture to further the process of Bok's heroism, but that the Russians need to spend such time torturing a confession out of him before they can authorize his destruction comes ironically to affirm the very restraints of justice and order the absence of which was to give the book its power. *The Fixer* is not powerful, merely repelling. It should not have been a novel. With prose so flat, exposition so contrived and speedy, a dramatic center so dependent on visual action and rhetoric, and a denouement so theatrical, *The Fixer* should have been a play (the most recent of the author's projects, since abandoned, was a play). Unfortunately, if it were, it would probably resemble not those great dramatizations of single souls tried by the massed power of bigotry and reaction, like Shaw's *Saint Joan* or Brecht's *Galileo,* but the perfect example of liberal evasion:

Arthur Miller's *The Crucible.* As in Miller's play, Malamud shows that bigots are mean, hysterical, and venal, that simple folk caught up in their midst can show inspiring apostasy, and that complex political abominations can be defeated by private gestures of quixotic integrity. This sort of wish-fulfillment is all that Malamud can come up with by way of political comprehension. One wonders whether to lament his innocence or the fact that the world is more brutal.

The career of Bernard Malamud seems to me exemplary. There can be no doubt that his first books revealed a distinguished and original art. But we live in a time and place where art's illuminations and delights have come to seem peripheral, even timid, in the face of the great social problems crowding our attention. Artists are being pressed into uniform. What difference does it make if James Baldwin is a poor writer; he is a vivid spokesman. What difference does it make if the *aperçus* which glitter through Herzog are frequently embarrassments; Bellow is engaged. It is a bad time for skill, perhaps because we have so little of it. But because we have so little of it, writers like Malamud constitute a precious national resource: an image of discipline and craft without which, ironically, even the problems they are said to neglect can never be solved. It is a small but real defeat for us all that Malamud has traded this dark place so lighted by crazy sparks for a soapbox in the public arena.

(1966)

MARK SCHORER

The World of Sinclair Lewis

Sinclair Lewis' first and last novels neither of them among his
happiest efforts and enclosing within their ragged brackets
twenty other novels most of which are better, are curiously
alike; indeed, toward the end of the first novel we find the
phrase, echoed from Kipling, that supplies the title of the
last, in which Kipling is acknowledged: "the world so wide."
Both novels take as their theme that theme traditionally
favored by our novelists, of the American innocent abroad,
and while the two heroes are in some ways very different
(one a nearly illiterate clerk, the other a successful architect),
they are in some more basic ways than these, alike, and
therefore the pattern of their experience is almost identical.
There is something compulsive in this theme for Sinclair
Lewis as for our other novelists, and the pattern, which is
resolved by a vindication of our innocence, is no doubt now,
as it was a hundred years ago, a portion of our folklore.

In each case, an accident frees the hero from the routines
that give structure to his life, and he eagerly seeks the
long-desired European experience. Each, without the
embracing clichés of "the job," finds himself freed only to

his own lonely emptiness. " . . . he was desolatingly free to wander in a world too bleakly, too intimidatingly wide. . . ." "In Newlife [Colorado] . . . I was as lonely as I am here [Firenze] —only busier there." So for the later hero. The earlier, more desperately, "had no friend in all the hostile world" of London. However, each encounters a girl who seems at home in this hostile world, an American sophisticate, the first a bohemian painter, the second a scholar of the Renaissance; these women, familiar with Europe, are also half-corrupted by it, easily seduced by the false values that they associate with it. After a period in which the innocence of these heroes has been exposed to the dubious experience of these heroines, each hero turns to a sounder heroine, the undiluted American Miss with no intellectual or artistic nonsense about her. These fresher ladies are, again, basically alike, in spite of the superficial differences between the incredibly modest, hard-working girl of 1914 (employed by "Wanamacy"), and the incredibly brash career woman of 1950 who has a heart of modest gold under the lavers of professional lacquer, a seeing eye under the mascara.

These novels are vastly imperfect, but it would be a mistake to call them simple. Each contains unresolved complexities that are not so peculiar to Lewis as they are to the American imagination itself. Europe is as fascinating to these heroes as it must be proved to be false. The yearning for a deeper experience than America offers is as strong in them as the loneliness that overcomes them when they are freed to that experience which they are then unable, in their wholesome naiveté, to utilize. There is in these novels an undercurrent of fear, fear of Europe itself: in *World So Wide,* Sam Dodsworth lectures the young hero at some length on the importance of not staying abroad too long lest he succumb to Europe; and in both novels Lewis, like Henry James, has his Osmonds and his Madame Merles, those Americans who have yielded up their native inheritance only to be vitiated by an alien tradition that they can not make their own. Yet, curiously, it is the "Europeanized" women—silly Istra Nash of *Our Mr. Wrenn* and cool Dr. Olivia Lomond of *World So Wide*—the women whom the heroes must reject, who, nevertheless, communicate such higher values, intellectual and spiritual, as are implied by the total situation in each novel. The result is that when Mr. Wrenn turns to his simple American, Nelly Croubel, Lewis must necessarily write a satire on the limits of suburbia; and when Hayden Chart, in the last novel, turns to Roxanna Eldritch, Lewis must force his plot into sentimental melodrama to bring about the turn at all. These endings are hardly what one could call clear vindications of American values. We are left with the large, staring question: what *was* America to Sinclair Lewis? It is perhaps too early to expect a complete answer to this question, but the happy publication of *The Man From Main Street* goes far in providing one. As the first and last novels, with the stretch of nearly forty years between them, reveal what is apparently a central concern over all those years, an imaginative coherence compelled by the primary importance of a single question; so this new book, a collection of non-fiction writing executed over an even longer period, almost fifty years, provides a bright and vigorous documentation to that central concern, shows it to us in all its modulations and varieties.

While writing novels, more often in the periods between writing novels, Sinclair Lewis wrote a vast amount of non-fiction. Most of this material was published in periodicals of all kinds except the seriously literary, and most it would be difficult to find today except by an intimate of Lewis' or an enthusiastic bibliographer. The editors of the present volume form a perfect combination: Melville H. Cane, poet, old friend, and executor of the Lewis Estate; Harry E. Maule, old friend and Lewis' editor; Philip Allan Friedman, graduate student in Columbia University who is interested in the Lewis bibliography.

From the whole spread of possible materials, Mr. Cane and Mr. Maule have selected what appears to be an admirable and representative sampling; Mr. Maule has provided useful as well as sympathetic biographical headnotes to the several sections and to the individual pieces within each section; Mr. Friedman has assisted in bibliographical research; other authorities, like Joseph Henry Jackson of the *San Francisco Chronicle,* were invited to participate when special bio-bibliographical information seemed to be necessary. Altogether, in its care and thoughtfulness, the book is really a unique tribute to a distinguished contemporary name.

And what, these selections continuously make us ask ourselves, what was America to Sinclair Lewis? It was, in the first place, as the novels tell us, too, an entity vast and formless that must be scolded into sense. Assuming this stance, Lewis needs the European reference, as the characters in his novels need it; and thus we have the famous Nobel Prize Address, delivered of course in Stockholm, called "The American Fear of Literature," and the almost equally famous letter to a purely native institution, declining the Pulitzer Prize on the ground that no institutionalized body could, without danger to the republic of letters, arrogate to itself the assumption of good judgment that such a reward implies. The Nobel speech is an impassioned diatribe against gentility in American literature (but made long after the victory was already won, as Lewis' own public reputation in 1930 demonstrates) and a plea for "a literature worthy of her vastness." The letter to the Pulitzer Committee, is a rejection of any official body that might threaten to restrict such a literature.

This is the heart of the matter. What Lewis loved so passionately about America was its potentiality for and constant expression of a wide, casually human freedom, the individual life lived in honest and perhaps eccentric effort (all the better), the social life lived in a spirit that first of all tolerates variety. And what he hated about America, what made him scold it, sometimes so shrilly, was everything that militated against such a free life: social timidity, economic system, intellectual rigidity, theological dogma, legal repression, class convention. These two, the individual impulse to freedom and the social impulse to restrict it, provide the bases of his plots. "If I seem to have criticized prairie villages, I have certainly criticized them no more than New York, or Paris, or the great universities." The point perhaps, is that in his novels it was easier for him to dramatize the repressions than it was to dramatically affirm the freedoms, and therefore, even in such a character as Carol Kennicott of *Main Street,* there is a considerable ambiguity, as there is in the endings of the novels I have here discussed. The conflict is not so much between America and Europe as between the true America as Lewis saw it—that is, Americans true to themselves, and the false America, or Americans who submit to values not their own, not free. The result in the novels is often an apparent praise of provincialism, but the praise, in its impulse, is of something much larger.

In the non-fiction here collected, a more positive view emerges, and in the best pieces, where the invective grows hottest, the active bias of Lewis' satirical imagination becomes quite clear. The piece called "Cheap and Contented Labor," a diatribe against the brutalities of life in the company town of Marion, North Carolina, has exactly the same motive as "Fools, Liars, and Mr. DeVoto," a diatribe against a restrictively nationalistic critical dogma. Lewis' literary judgments, like his social judgments, rest on the same large assumption about the potentialities of American life. The judgments are not always sure, and the ironic tone often shifts to a sneer, but at his best, as in his self-judgments, the nobility of his motives carries directly over into his prose. In page after page of this book, we read an expository prose of the most remarkable authority, a prose that, in the syntax alone, reminds us that we are reading the product of an educated mind for which the dialect, the cracker barrel, and the whiskers were only a counterpose to the stuffed shirt. The high anger with others find its balance in Lewis' persistent humility toward himself and his own reputation, in the poise of his self-criticism, in his capacity for doing a thing superbly and then throwing it away. This humility is without self-consciousness, as we are reminded many times in this book by the easy way in which he incorporates the famous symbols of his own life and work—Main Street, Sauk Centre, Zenith, Babbitt, Minnesota, Hobohemia—into his discussion of the life and work of others. His own best qualities as a writer are shown in high relief in many of these pieces: the swift talent for classification and characterization of surface ("the traditional pedagogues—the long-faced and dry and disapproving, the bushy and hearty, or the dapper and cynical," and "women in business—developing narrow white tearooms into millionaire candy companies"); the capacity to summon up, as from an endless reservoir, a brilliant, flashing parade of solid detail, no single item ever lingered over, (as in that remarkable piece, "Is America A Paradise for Women?"); the true sense of craft that lies behind his highly judicious and lucidly intelligent contrast of the novel *Dodsworth* and its dramatized version.

There were grave defects in this imagination. Lewis himself reminds us, again and again, of his primary sentimentality. There are lapses in taste as in judgment. There is a deep pit of naiveté about human nature. There is that curious gift for seeming always a little old-fashioned that comes with the determination to be only bright and new. These are defects not unfamiliar in Americans in general. But above all there is another quality that we have almost forgotten to look for in him: there is a high and dedicated sense of justice that also has much to do with the making of Americans.

(1953)

JAMES THURBER

Voices of Revolution

The old bitter challenges to the bourgeois as critic, writer and human being (in answer to the old bitter challenges of the bourgeois to the proletarian as critic, writer and human being) ring out right at the start in Joseph Freeman's introduction to *Proletarian Literature in the United States.* Nothing, I am afraid, will ever change this. We shall all meet at the barricades shouting, or writing, invective at the top of our voices. Interspersed, of course, with sound arguments (to which the other side will not listen). The bourgeois writer and critic and the proletarian writer and critic do not seem to be able to meet, sanely, on a forum. Their meeting place is the battlefield. They are cat and dog, Smith and Roosevelt. This cannot, I suppose, be changed and it is a rather melancholy reflection. Out of it are bound to come distortion, exaggeration and, what is probably worse, triviality. But it presents a colorful, if meaningless, free-for-all, which members of both armies, being human beings born of war, are bound to find rather more pleasurable than deplorable.

Mr. Freeman sets himself a large and important task in his

introduction and, in great part, he discharges it well, the great part being an explanation of, and argument for, the values of revolutionary art. But here and there the old urge springs up, the old bitter desire to take irrelevant cracks at bourgeois literature (without specific instances) and at the more intimate emotions of the bourgeoisie, all the more intimate emotions of all the bourgeoisie. He hates to use the word "love" in relation to them. Thus he speaks of "lechery" and of "flirtations"; when he does use the word "lovers" he joins it up with "loafers." This petty bitterness—it seems almost a neurosis—disfigures his arguments. He writes:

> Every writer creates not only out of his feelings, but out of his knowledge and his concepts and his will .... The feelings of the proletarian writer are molded by his experience and by the science which explains that experience, just as the bourgeois writer's feelings are molded by his experiences and the class theories which rationalize them. Out of the experiences and the science of the proletariat the revolutionary poets, playwrights and novelists are developing an art which reveals more forces in the world than the love of the lecher and the pride of the Narcissist.

Well, there you are: the old slipping out of a sonorous and imposing argument into what is nothing more than a hot-tempered jibe, a silly sweeping insinuation. It is odd how that kind of thing has somehow or other become one of the major points in the literary battle. Studies of the effects of class backgrounds and social concepts upon the emotions belong in such works as *Middletown,* or in articles by themselves, but they should scarcely be flung helter-skelter into an analysis of the kind Mr. Freeman sets out to write, particularly if they degenerate into what has the thin ring of an absurd personal insult. So much of the critical writing of both proletarians and bourgeoisie sounds as if the writer were striking back at some individual who has been striking at him. I am afraid that is too often the case. Schoolgirls; boys behind the barn. And literature can go die, on the barricades, or behind the barn.

But this is not getting into the book, which is divided into

Fiction, Poetry, Reportage (that's what they call it, don't look at me), Drama and Literary Criticism. It contains selections from the work of proletarian writers in the past five or six years. I have read it with great interest and I believe anybody with any sense of what is going on, would also. I was mainly interested in the fiction; first, because it takes up more than a third of the volume; second, because, of the five divisions, I care most for fiction.

The fiction here I found uneven: sincere generally, sometimes groping, often hysterical or overwrought, now and then distinctly moving. The only thing in this section that I think can last is John Dos Passos' "The Body of an American" from *1919*. Many of the other authors have the fault of whipping themselves up to a lather, or whipping their characters up to a lather, whereas Dos Passos whips his reader up to a lather. Somewhere in this book there should be a critical piece on his method. It might well have been put in, under Literary Criticism, in place of Mr. Gold's famous attack on Thornton Wilder, which seems as dated as the Dempsey-Carpenter fight, or in place of Phillips' and Rahv's "Recent Problems of Revolutionary Literature," which loses its points in a mass of heavy, difficult and pedantic writing. For what some of these proletarian writers need to learn is simply how to write, not only with intensity, but with conviction, not only with a feeling for the worker but a feeling for literary effects. Even the Erskins Caldwell of "Daughter" (by which flabby story he is unfortunately represented here) might learn from Dos Passos. Compare (and you'll have to read both pieces to see the really important difference) Caldwell's refrain: "Daughter oike up hungry again . . . I just couldn't stand it" with Dos Passos': "Say buddy can't you tell me how I can get back to my outfit?" The first flops, the second gets you.

Many of the stories are simply not convincing. I have read several two or three times to see if I could discover why. I think I found a few reasons. You don't always believe that these authors *were there*, ever had been there; that they ever saw and heard these people they write about. They give you the feeling that they are writing what they want these people to have said. This seems to me an important point. It is not the subject matter, but the method of presentation, I believe, which has raised the bourgeois cry of "propaganda." Proletarian literature must be written by men and women with a keen ear and eye for gestures and for words, for mannerisms and for idioms, or it fails. Jack Conroy catches perfectly the words of the Negro in his "A Coal Miner's Widow" (particularly in the fine paragraph beginning " 'Scuse me!"); but I don't feel reality—I vaguely feel some literary influence—in most of Ben Field's "Cow." And he should be forever ashamed of having written this sentence: "He said something about her being without either and without clothes, but for the sake of somebody who liked him, as he had been unable to get her off, he had had all added." But then read his "The Cock's Funeral" in the first issue of *Partisan Review* and *Anvil;* it is fine, and it has what nothing in this anthology has: humor. Some of the richest humor in the world is the humor of the American proletariat.

I think Albert Halper fails to make his scab taxi-driver come to life. I did not believe the driver and I did not believe his fares; I believed Mr. Halper's sincerity; and that is not enough. More care and hard work, in watching and listening and writing, is what was needed here. The driver is not nearly so good as Joseph North's driver in his reporter piece called "Taxi Strike," and Mr. North's study is far from excellent. I believe both Halper and North might profit by an examination into the way Robert Coates or St. Clair McKelway handles such pieces. I can tell you that their observation and their writing is hard, painstaking, and long. Nobody, however greatly aroused, can successfully bat off anything.

Now I *did* believe Albert Maltz's "Man on a Road" (minor note: I am told that no user of "you-all" ever addresses a solitary person as "you-all"). This story is written with sympathy and understanding but also with detachment (and oh, my friends, and oh, my foes, in detachment there is strength, not weakness). Mr. Maltz leaves the clear plight of his victim undefiled by exaggeration, anger and what I can only call the "editorial comment" which seeps into some of the other pieces. You remember the man on the road after you have forgotten most of the figures in the book. Mr. Maltz knows how to make his reader angry without demanding that he be angry. And if this is not the procedure of class, it will forever remain the dictate of art.

I thought that the dialogue in Grace Lumpkin's "John Stevens" had an artificial sound—one gets to thinking more about the writer than about her people, more about her faults than about what is troubling her characters. I can understand why the Communist literati bewail the loss to the cause of Ring Lardner—as they should also bewail the straying of John O'Hara. In this kind of story an ear like theirs is worth more than rubies. To go on: there is too obvious strain and effort in Tillie Lerner; she grabs tremendously at the reader and at life and fails to fetch the reader and fails to capture life. William Rollins Jr. has a deplorable affection for typographical pyrotechnics: caps, italics, dashes. It makes his story almost impossible to read. I was reminded, in trying to read it, of what an old English professor of mine, the late Joseph Russell Taylor, used to say: you can't get passion into a story with exclamation points. But Mr. Rollins deserves credit for one thing, at least: he is the only writer in this book who uses "God damn" in place of "goddam." Josephine Herbst, so often authentic, writes: "A newsboy sang out, 'Big Strike at Cumley's, night crew walk out, big strike threatened, mayor urges arbitration." That is what she wanted to hear a newsboy sing out but it is not what any newsboy in this country ever sang out. I grant the importance of the scenes on which all these stories are based, but they cannot have reality, they cannot be literature, if they are slovenly done—merely because there is a rush for the barricades and proletarian writers are in a hurry. Art does not rush to the barricades. Nobody wants to believe that these authors sat in warm surroundings hurriedly writing of things they had never seen, or had merely glimpsed, yet that is often the impression they give.

At the end of the fiction section is the worst example of failure in method and effect, Philip Stevenson's "Death of a Century." What might have been sharp satire is a badly done, overwrought and merely gross burlesque. Even burlesque must keep one foot on verisimilitude. It grows better out of healthy ridicule than wild-eyed hate. In the poetry and drama departments there are fine things ("Waiting for Lefty" among them). The reportage section is, in some instances, excellent and it should have been widely expanded, preferably at the expense of the literary criticism, almost all of which could have been left out. There is, as I have said, not a note of humor in the anthology, not even in Robert Forsythe's piece on the Yale Bowl.

(1936)

JAMES THURBER

The Last Tycoon

The novel F. Scott Fitzgerald was working on when he died in December, 1940, has been on the counters for three months now. His publishers tell me that it has sold only about 3,500 copies. This indicates, I think, that it has fallen, and will continue to fall, into the right hands. In its unfinished state, *The Last Tycoon* is for the writer, the critic, the sensitive appreciator of literature. The book, I have discovered, can be found in very few Womrath stores or other lending libraries. This, one feels sure, would have pleased Scott Fitzgerald. The book would have fared badly in the minds and discussions of readers who read books simply to finish them.

Fitzgerald's work in progress was to have told the life story of a big Hollywood producer. In the form in which the author left it, it runs to six chapters, the last one unfinished. There follows a synopsis of what was to have come, and then there are twenty-eight pages of notes, comments, descriptive sentences, and paragraphs, jotted down by the author, and a complete letter he wrote outlining his story idea. All these were carefully selected and arranged by Edmund Wilson (who

311

also contributes a preface) and anyone interested in the ideas and craftsmanship of one of America's foremost fiction writers will find them exciting reading. Mr. Wilson has also included *The Great Gatsby* in the volume, and the five short stories which he considers likely to be of permanent interest. His choices are "The Rich Boy," "The Diamond as Big as the Ritz," "May Day," "Absolution," and "Crazy Sunday." This collection belongs on a shelf of every proud library.

No book published here in a long time has created more discussion and argument among writers and lovers of writing them *The Last Tycoon*. Had it been completed, would it have been Fitzgerald's best book? Should it, in a draft which surely represented only the middle stages of rewriting, have been published alongside the flawless final writing of *The Great Gatsby?* In the larger view, it is sentimental nonsense to argue against the book's publication. It was the last work of a first-rate novelist; it shows his development, it rounds out his all too brief career; it gives us what he had done and indicates what he was going to do on the largest canvas of his life; it is filled with a great many excellent things as it stands. It is good to be acquainted with all these things. In the smaller, the personal view, there is a valid argument, however. Writers who rewrite and rewrite until they reach the perfection they are after consider anything less than that perfection nothing at all. They would not, as a rule, show it to their wives or to their most valued friends. Fitzgerald's perfection of style and form as in *The Great Gatsby* has a way of making something that lies between your stomach and your heart quiver a little.

The Last Tycoon is the story of Monroe Stahr, one of the founders of Hollywood, the builder of a movie empire. We see him in his relation to the hundreds of human parts of the vast machine he has constructed, and in his relation to the woman he loves, and to a Communist Party organizer (their first contact is one of the best and most promising parts of the book). We were to have seen him on an even larger scale, ending in a tremendous upheaval and disintegration of his work and his world and a final tragedy. Fitzgerald would have brought it off brilliantly in the end. This would have been another book in the fine one-color mood of *The Great Gatsby,* with that book's sure form and sure direction. He had got away from what he calls the "deterioration novel" that he wrote in *Tender Is the Night.* He had a long way yet to go in *The Last Tycoon* and his notes show that he realized this.

In one of these notes he tells himself that his first chapter is "stilted from rewriting" and he instructs himself to rewrite it, not from the last draft, but from mood. It is good as it stands, but he knew it wasn't right. In the last of the notes, Fitzgerald had written, with all the letters in capitals: "ACTION IS CHARACTER." A brilliant perfectionist in the managing of his ultimate effects, Fitzgerald knew that Stahr had been too boldly blocked out in the draft which has come to us. There was too much direct description of the great man. He fails to live up to it all. Such a passage as this would surely have been done over: "He had flown up very high to see, on strong wings, when he was young. And while he was up there he had looked on all the kingdoms, with the kind of eyes that can stare straight into the sun. Beating his wings tenaciously—finally frantically—and keeping on beating them, he had stayed up there longer than most of us, and then, remembering all he had seen from his great height of how things were, he had settled gradually to earth." There are other large, unhewn lines which would have given place to something else, such as the speech by one of his worshipers: "So I came to you, Monroe. I never saw a situation where you didn't know a way out. I said to myself: even if he advises me to kill myself, I'll ask Monroe." The Monroe Stahr we see is not yet the man this speaker is talking about. I would like to see him as he would have emerged from one or two more rewrites of what is here, excellent, sharp, witty and moving as a great deal of it is.

It must inevitably seem to some of us that Fitzgerald could not have set himself a harder task than that of whipping up a real and moving interest in Hollywood and its great and little men. Although the movie empire constitutes one of the largest and therefore one of the most important industries in the world, it is a genuine feat, at least for me, to pull this appreciation of Bel-Air and Beverly Hills from the mind down into the emotions, where, for complete and satisfying surrender to a novel and its people, it properly belongs. It is a high tribute to Scott Fitzgerald to say that he would have accomplished this. I know of no one else who could.

Everyone will be glad to find "The Rich Boy" and "Absolution" included among the short stories in the volume. "Crazy Sunday" is perhaps of value to the student of Fitzgerald because it contains the germ of *The Last Tycoon*, but I find it impossible to sustain a permanent, or even a passing, interest in the personalities and problems of the Hollywood persons it is concerned with. A lot of us will always be interested in "Babylon Revisited," even though it is the pet of the professors of English who compile anthologies; and I mourn the absence of "A Short Trip Home" whether you do or not.

(1942)

HONOR TRACY

Graham Greene

To entertain his fellow men in one of the kindest things an author can do: and as an entertainer Mr. Graham Greene has few rivals in the English field. For sheer readability—a mysterious attribute having no connection with either beauty or truth and indeed wellnigh absent from some of the world's greatest literature—he comes perhaps second only to Mr. Somerset Maugham. From the fact that he divides his work into Novels and Entertainments, however, it may be doubted if he is content with this. In the distinction there is something self-conscious, even something arbitary: we cannot but wonder what Mr. Greene has in mind. Although he might not thank us for a suggestion that the Novels are not entertaining, or that the Entertainments are not novels, the implication of a difference in genre is clear. It would make quite a sticky last point for a radio quiz:

Which is *The Quiet American?*
—Novel.
Which is *Our Man in Havana?*
—Entertainment.
Quite right! (studio applause)

And thousands and thousands of dollars would change hands.

We live in a popular age, and the first care in arranging literary quizzes must be to avoid deleterious strains to the mind, and excessive claims on the knowledge, of competitor and audience. The prize might be less easily won if the aspirant had to explain the reasons of the author. What has that quiet American specifically got that our man in Havana hasn't, it might be asked, to justify his place in the higher category? The honest fellow does not even offer us a message, except Mr. Green's personal one as to the futility of messages. Pyle is young and earnest, "impregnably amoured by his good intentions and his ignorance": in the name of what he calls democracy he brings suffering and death to the Indochinese people he assumes he is helping: when the bomb laid by his democratic Third Force explodes in the Place Garnier "a man without his legs lay twitching at the edge of the ornamental gardens," saved from Communism and French Imperialism alike. Wormold in Havana is middle-aged, disillusioned and frivolous except in what concerns his daughter: to get money for her finishing school and her dowry he accepts the post of British secret agent, writing imaginary reports, cooking expense sheets and recruiting a phantom staff among names haphazardly picked out, which in the police state of Cuba inevitably leads to the death of their flesh and blood owners.

Evil results arising from intentions not in themselves blameworthy, held by people neither good nor bad, are the theme in both cases. Why then is the greater weight given in the first? Certainly, the author has taken more pains with it, it is better worked out and written, the story is more probable, the characters less mechanical; but there is no essential difference. Indeed, the implied deprecation of the second sounds like an appeal to the public. "Don't be hard on me," Mr. Greene seems to say, "I wasn't really trying." Or can it be that, because Pyle is American, because Pyle stands for wealth and material power, because there are so many Pyles, because anti-imperialist Pyle is not yet hep to the fact of his own imperialism, he ranks by sheer portentousness? Has Mr. Greene succumbed so far to the present-day fallacy of mass, of quantity, to the notion that ten Pyles are worse, a hundred deaths more terrible, than one?

The question is interesting because of a widespread belief that Mr. Greene, when not deliberately playing down to us, is a very serious and, above all, a very Catholic writer: a puzzling belief, since the mental climate of his books is so unmistakably, so fashionably pagan. Obsession with aspects of the doctrine and practice, an artful decoration of text with the vocabulary, does not make a "Catholic" novel any more than does a quotation from Péguy, placed with a flourish at the head of chapter one. Undoubtedly one of the themes in *The Power and the Glory,* that the sacraments are valid even though the priest administering them is a coward and a soak, may be described; but we do not read and re-read the novel for the sake of this simple, and to many of us familiar, truth but for the terror of it, the suspense, the heat, dust and smell of Mexican town and village, the flight through the rain, the deliberate rejection of safety by the hunted priest; in a word, for the story. Even less does *The Heart of the Matter* grip us by the force of Scobie's religious dilemma, if that is the word for presumption so enormous. It is by the sense, wonderfully conveyed, of empire in decay, of the seediness of colonial life delivered up to suburbia, to the Bungaloids, of the despair in loveless, childless marriage, of the terrible African heat that smothers the good impulses and brings on the rest like weeds; and, Heaven forgive us, we may be more anxious to know if Scobie was promoted after all, or how he got the money for his wife's passage to South Africa, than whether he damned his immortal soul.

It is, then, the story-teller and not the thinker or moralist who compels our admiration. Mr. Greene is a dazzling showman who functions on different levels with, we cannot help thinking, a similar fundamental purpose at each. Like the Fat Boy, he wants to make our flesh creep: he wants to make us sit up and cry *Oh!* The dictionary says that to "entertain" is to "amuse, agreeably hold the attention of" and it is perhaps worth noting that our author's ingredients for achieving this are murder, lust, lunacy, failure, poverty, disgrace. Even *Loser Takes All,* his one attempt at pure comedy, has to be brightened up with a broken marriage. This does not deter him from offering any number of rueful asides on the degenerate times in which we are fated to live: having created his joyless world Mr. Greene thoroughly disapproves of it, having looked upon his work and seen that it was bad he reviles it like any puritan. The aging Fowler speaks to his native mistress: " 'Phuong,' I said—which means Phoenix, but nothing nowadays is fabulous and nothing rises from its ashes," a remark meaningless enough to satisfy the most incorrigibly middlebrow reader and one of a kind that runs unabashed through all the books, whether Novel or Entertainment. Again, "A picture postcard is a symptom of loneliness," Mr. Wormold somewhere avers: statements of this sort encourage the library reader to think that he or she is getting value for money, and rather recall Mr. Thurber's Dr. Bisch, who together with his large following believed that an automobile bearing down on him was a symbol of sex. It took, we may remember, the luminous mind of a Thurber to perceive that in fact it was an automobile. The flow of Mr. Greene's wry, facile comment helps to establish him as a philosopher among the unphilosophical without interrupting the fun: fresh or difficult truths would stand up from it like rocks, demanding respect and attention.

But if Mr. Greene is not a philosopher, he is a psychologist: he knows just what, deplorably enough, we all like. A mere list of his villains will show how aware he is of the vestigial Neanderthaler lying doggo in the bosoms of the readership. And how full-blooded the villians of the earlier period were! Dr. Forester, the fiendish German spy and psychoanalyst of *The Ministry of Fear* into whose "nursing-home" prominent anti-Nazis vanish for "treatment" might well have come from "Sapper": so might the harelipped Simon Raven in *A Gun for Sale,* estranged from humanity by his disfigurement, ready for murder at a glance; and Mr. Cholmondley too, fat, white, smooth and unctuous, with his great emerald ring and his passion for sweet things, who paid the assassin with stolen banknotes.

A cut above them is Acky, the unfrocked clergyman, endlessly overflowing in letters of remonstrance to the Bishop and in Latin obscenities, with his slut of a wife, his murderousness: a truly sinister creation that might have figured in a prize-winning French film, or even in a novel by Wilkie Collins. And with the Boy in *Brighton Rock* Mr. Greene hits the jackpot in repulsiveness. It is not that this little monster is more depraved or more sadistic than so many luminaries of the "tough" American novels that were poured out at the time, to which indeed—since it is unrelated to English life—*Brighton Rock* may well have been a spirited English reply. It is the fact of his being an adolescent, almost a child. When the book appeared baby gangsters and murderers were less familiar in both life and literature than they afterwards became, and Mr. Greene scores heavily with this device; and not content with that he gives an occasional turn to the screw by emphasizing the traits of immaturity in the creature, such as the dread of sexual failure and of the girl's possible contempt or ridicule, or the lack of ease vis-à-vis his middle-aged gangster rival. This destroys of course any belief we may have had in him as the leader of grown, hard men, but Mr. Greene is always willing to sacrifice the general effect for a particular one. And finally there is the knock-out when the Boy's widow, the depressed little slavey whom he married to prevent her being called to give evidence against him, goes to play over the message he had recorded for her one day on the pier. She expects words of tenderness, uttered in a beloved voice she will never hear again; but we know she is going to receive the coarsest, most cruel abuse. Strange to say, this piece of brilliant Grand Guignol is included among the Novels.

It is no great wonder if the children of Adam find their

attention agreeably held by such matters: they interest us more than any others, as every news editor will confirm. Where Mr. Greene excels, where indeed he approaches wizardry, is in the power of holding it also by descriptions of the most squalid of people, the drabbest of milieux. Grey little commercial travelers, bad journalists, private detectives, slatternly waitresses, priests without a vocation, humbugs of every sort, suffering from indigestion, body odor, decayed teeth or sheer chronic futility, bob up in their seedy environments, the seaside promenade or boarding-house, the colonial Nissen hut, the genteel villa or the dusty office, and keep us as enthralled as would the most glittering assembly in the land. No English novelist but Dickens has written as vividly of the failed, the come down, of all that in life we incline to turn away from; but where Dickens transfigures it by the warmth of his humanity and the magic of his genius, Mr. Greene simply treats it as exotic. His eye is original, if his mind is not: the masterly, film director's eye that in Africa, Indochina, Mexico picks out infallibly the one detail to bring the character, the landscape, before the reader's own, achieves, in playing on the familiar and the dreary, an even greater triumph.

With this eye, and an ear no less acute, with a prodigious knack of description, dialogue and narrative, Mr. Greene is incapable of being dull; and only the most ungrateful wretch alive would harp on the fact that the verities of God and man ask for something more.

(1959)

JOHN UPDIKE

The Loneliness of the Long-Distance Runner

On a British-owned island in the West Indies recently, I read through an anthology of "schoolboy" stories—a genre special to the English, who take their schoolboys with a strange, hovering high seriousness. Some of the stories were jolly spoofs, but the most exciting and convincing were those nakedly concerned with inculcating the social virtues of endeavor, pluck, and fair play. The plot was always the same: a young lad, named Pip or Snip or Fudge or Pudge, by a mighty effort succeeded, though half-blinded by the flapping flags of School and Nation, in kicking the winning goal or bowling the innings that turned the tide. The title story of Alan Sillitoe's collection, "The Loneliness of the Long-distance Runner," is squarely in this tradition, nonetheless squarely for being an inversion of it. The school is not Eton or Willows-in-the-Dale but an Essex Borstal; the hero, Smith, makes his mighty effort not to win the race but to lose it; the nation for whom he strives is not Green England but the black kingdom of Downtroddendom; and the vision with which he gives himself strength is that of his father's prolonged death of throat cancer.

Now Mr. Sillitoe is a writer of great gifts, and Smith's inner stream of invective is often very beautiful: "They're training me up fine for the big sports day when all the pig-faced snotty-nosed dukes and ladies—who can't add two and two together and would mess themselves like loonies if they didn't have slavies to beck-and-call—come and make speeches to us about sports being just the thing to get us leading an honest life and keep our itching finger-ends off them shop locks and safe-handles and hairgrips to open gas meters ... The pop-eyed potbellied governor said to a pop-eyed potbellied Member of Parliament who sat next to his pop-eyed pot-bellied whore of a wife ..."

But it raises the question: Is a literature in which all the Haves are pop-eyed potbellies an improvement over one in which the Havenots are docile animals in livery or comic grotesques pottering around the street? The question would be irrelevant if the author did not go out of his way, in an unexpectedly awkward bit at the end, to associate himself with his anti-social hero: "And if I don't get caught the bloke I give this story to will never give me away; he's lived in our terrace for as long as I can remember, and he's my pal. That I do know."

It is not for me to doubt the hard lot of the English working class. It was the Industrial Revolution's first child, and took the worst she had to give. A visitor to England, especially to London or Oxford, seems to see two different races of men: the one pink and smooth, and gay; the other dwarfish, dark, and sullen. Yet on the evidence of the other stories in this book, one is lead to wonder if a sense of alienation as logical and systematic as Smith's is not so exceptional as to be unreal. Elsewhere, there is this glimpse: "On the Sunday morning that my mother and father shook their heads over Chamberlain's melancholy voice issuing from the webbed heart-shaped speaker of our wireless set, I met Frankie in the street." This rings truer; Chamberlain's voice, remote and webbed, still has the power to sadden. For surely the discouraging thing, from the Marxist's point of view, about the English lower class is that they persist in believing they posses a share, a miserable, bitter share, in the nation. Throughout these stories, for that matter, the revolutionary spirit, where it is articulated, is done so by adolescents, and merges indistinguishably with the revolt against the Grown-ups. And the acquiescent state of old men is portrayed with a genius that cuts through categories of class.

It has taken an uncomfortable amount of space to get this worry off my chest, the worry, that is, that Mr. Sillitoe sometimes plays "tails" to Nancy Mitford's "heads." The comfortable duty remains of praising the author's artistry. It is great. The least of his nine stories is better than fair; the best are splendid. Monologues like "On Saturday Afternoon" and "The Disgrace of Jim Scarfedale" have a rasp, a comedy, a casually callous acceptance of misery that would be remarkable even without the poetic swing, snap, and surprise. They have a wonderful way of going on, of not stopping short (for instance, Mrs. Scarfedale's maternal tirade when her son threatens marriage) that lifts us twice, and shows enviable assurance and abundance in the writer. Now and then he fusses too much with *why* his narrators are telling the story, and occasionally, (as in "The Fishing-Boat Picture") seems embarrassed for an ending. To write endings worthy of these beginnings and middles must have been a technical challenge: the "turn" is too complacently bourgeois and the "dying fall" too languidly aristocratic. I liked best those endings in which the boy-narrator stood right up in his shabby shoes and explained what lesson he had learned, as if he were assembling a personal Bible out of scraps of sadness and folly blowing in the gutters.

In the third-person stories, the language is not always appropriate to the subject. "Mr. Raynor the School-teacher" is a sequence of words in perfect adjustment. The futile confusion within a classroom and the brutal fate of a pretty

323

girl—*"timide et libertine et fragile et robuste"*—glimpsed from the window work in effortless parallel to convey the brooding over-presence of a slum. I was grateful, too, for "The Match," a piece of Saturday afternoon fog bottled for keeps. But in "Noah's Ark," the incident is smothered under rather aloof phrase-making, and "Uncle Ernest" is marred by intermittent niceties.

The dust-jacket mentions hundreds of poems and a hundred-thousand-word novel that Mr. Sillitoe has destroyed; and in the last story, "The Decline and Fall of Frankie Buller," we discover the author himself, wearing his own name of Alan, glumly contemplating the books he has read (or not read):

And so on and so on, items that have become part of me, foliage that has grown to conceal the bare stem of my real personality, what I was like before I ever saw these books, or any book at all, come to that. Often I would like to rip them away from me one by one, extract their shadows out of my mouth and heart . . .

So would we all. The lack of connection between the experiences, usually accumulated by the age of twenty, that seem worth telling about, and the sophistication needed to render them in writing, is the Unmentionable at the root of the mysterious Fall of so many auspicious writers. For a moment, the two intersect; the memories are fresh, the new tools are sharp, and a vivid imitation of life is produced. Then the memories recede, and the writer is left holding the tools. It may be merely distance, simplifying distance, that makes the long-distance runner seem a little too pure to be true. But Mr. Sillitoe's achievement is the measure of his shortcomings, and in his battle with his books he is well-armed with intelligence, humor, and life.

(1960)

JOHN UPDIKE

The Defense

One hesitates to call him an "American writer"; the phrase fetches to mind Norman Mailer and James Jones and other homegrown cabbages loyally mistaken for roses. Say, rather, that Vladimir Nabokov distinctly seems to be the best writer of English prose at present holding American citizenship, the only writer, with the possible exception of the long-silent Thornton Wilder, whose books, considered as a whole, give the happy impression of an *oeuvre*, of a continuous task carried forward variously, of a solid personality, of a plenitude of gifts exploited knowingly. His works are an edifice whose every corner rewards inspection. Each book, including the super-slim *Poems* and the uproariously pedantic and copious commentaries to his translation of *Eugene Onegin*, yields delight and presents to the aesthetic sense the peculiar hardness of a finished, fully meant thing. His sentences are beautiful out of context and doubly beautiful in it. He writes prose the only way it should be written—that is, ecstatically. In the intensity of its intelligence and reflective joy, his fiction is unique in this decade and scarcely precedented in American literature. Melville and James do not, oddly, offer themselves for comparison. Yet our literature, that scraggly association of hermits, cranks, and exiles, is strange enough to include this arrogant immigrant; as an expatriate Nabokov is squarely in the native tradition.

Very curiously, his *oeuvre* is growing at both ends. At one end, the end pointed toward the future, are the works composed in English, beinning with the gentlest of his novels, *The Real Life of Sebastian Knight,* and terminating, for the time being, in his—the word must be—monumental translation of *Onegin,* a physically gorgeous, sumptuously erudite gift from one language to another; it is pleasant to think of Nabokov laboring in the libraries of his adopted land, the libraries fondly described in *Pnin,* laboring with Janus-faced patriotism on the filigreed guy-wires and piled buttresses of this bridge whereby the genius of Pushkin is to cross after him into America. The translation itself, so laconic compared to the footnotes, with its breathtaking gaps, pages long, of omitted stanzas whose lines are eerily numbered as if they were there, ranks with Horace Gregory's Catullus and Richmond Lattimore's *Iliad* as superb, quirky, and definitive: a permanent contribution to the demi-art of "Englishing" and a final refutation, let's hope, of the fallacy of equivalent rhyme. In retrospect, Nabokov's more recent novels— obviously *Pale Fire* but there are also Humbert Humbert's mysterious "scholarly exertions" on a "manual of French literature for English-speaking students"—transparently reveal glimpses of the Pushkinian travail begun in 1950.

At the other end (an end, as in earthworms, not immediately distinguishable), Nabokov's *oeuvre* is growing backwards, into the past, as English versions appear of those novels he wrote in Russian, for a post-Revolutionary émigré audience concentrated in Paris and Berlin, during his twenty years of European residence (1919-1940), under the pen name of "V. Sirin." *The Defense,* originally *Zashchita Luzhina,* is the latest of these to be translated. In the chronology of his eight Russian novels, *The Luzhin Defense* (this literal title was used by *The New Yorker* and seems better, in clearly suggesting a chess ploy, though the ghosts of "illusion" and "losin' " fluttering around the proper name perhaps were worth exorcising) comes third, after two untranslated ones and just before *Laughter in the Dark*. It is thus the earliest Nabokov work now available in English. An author's foreword states that it was written in 1929—that is, when Nabokov was thirty, which is the age of Luzhin, an ex-chess prodigy and international grandmaster. Like his hero, the author seems older; few Americans so young could write a novel wherein the autobiographical elements are so cunningly rearranged and transmuted by a fictional design, and the emotional content so obedient to such cruelly ingenious commands, and the characterization so little colored by indignation or the shock of discovery. On this last point, it needs to be said—so much has been pointlessly said about Nabokov's "virtuosity," as if he is a verbal magician working with stuffed rabbits and hats nobody could wear—that Nabokov's characters live. They "read" as art students say; their frames are loaded with bright color and twisted to fit abstract schemes but remain anatomically credible. The humanity that has come within Nabokov's rather narrow field of vision has been illuminated by a guarded but genuine compassion. Two characters occur to me, randomly and vividly: Charlotte Haze of *Lolita,* with her blatant bourgeois Bohemianism, her cigarettes, her Mexican doodads, her touchingly clumsy sexuality, her utterly savage and believable war with her daughter; and Albinus Kretschmar of *Laughter in the Dark,* with his doll-like dignity, his bestial softness, his hobbies, his family feelings, his craven romanticism, his quaint competence. An American housewife and a German businessman, both observed, certainly, from well on the outside, yet animated from well within. How much more, then, can Nabokov do with characters who are Russian, and whose concerns circle close to his own aloof passions!

His forword, shameless and disdainful in his usual

first-person style, specifies, for "hack reviewers" and "persons who move their lips when reading," the forked appeal of "this attractive novel"—the intricate immanence in plot and imagery of chess as a prevailing metaphor, and the weird lovableness of the virtually inert hero.

Of all my Russian books, *The Defense* contains and diffuses the greatest "warmth"—which may seem odd seeing how supremely abstract chess is supposed to be. In point of fact, Luzhin has been found lovable even by those who understand nothing about chess and/or detest all my other books. He is uncouth, unwashed, uncomely—but as my gentle young lady (a dear girl in her own right) so quickly notices, there is something in him that transcends...the coarseness of his gray flesh and the sterility of his recondite genius.

What makes characters endearing does not admit of such analysis: I would divide Luzhin's charm into *(a)* the delineation of his childhood *(b)* the evocation of his chess prowess. As to *(a)*, Nabokov has always warmed to the subject of children, precocious children—David Krug, Victor Wind, the all-seeing "I" of *Conclusive Evidence*, and, most precocious and achingly childlike of all, Dolores Haze. The four chapters devoted to little Luzhin are pure gold, a fascinating extraction of the thread of genius from the tangle of a lonely boy's existence. The child's ominous lethargy: his father's brooding ambitiousness for him; the hints of talent in his heredity; the first gropings, through mathematical and jigsaw puzzles, of his peculiar aptitude toward the light; the bizarre introduction, at the hands of a nameless violinist who tinges the game forever with a somehow cursed musicality, to the bare pieces; his instruction in the rules, ironically counterpointed against an amorous intrigue of which he is oblivious; his rapid climb through a hierarchy of adult opponents—all this is witty, tender, delicate, resonant. By abruptly switching to Luzhin as a chess-sodden adult, Nabokov island the childhood, frames its naive brightness so that, superimposed upon the grown figure, it operates as a kind of heart, as an abruptly doused light reddens the subsequent darkness.

As to *(b)* Nabokov has never shied from characters who excel. In *Pale Fire* he presumed to give us a long poem by an American poet second only to Frost; Adam Krug in *Bend Sinister* is the leading intellectual of his nation; no doubt is left that Fyodor Godunov-Cherdyntsev of *The Gift* is truly gifted. Luzhin's "recondite genius" is delineated as if by one who knows—though we know, from chapter XIV of his autobiography, that Nabokov's forte was not tournament play but the "beautiful, complex and sterile art" of composing chess problems of a "poetico-mathematical type." On its level as a work-epic of chess (as *Moby Dick* is a work-epic of whaling) *The Defense* is splendidly shaped toward Luzhin's match with Turati, the dashing Italian grandmaster against whose unorthodox attack, "leaving the middle of the board unoccupied by Pawns but exercising a most dangerous influence on the center from the sides," Luzhin's defense is devised. Of Turati physically we are given the briefest glimpses, "rubbing his hands and deeply clearing his throat like a bass singer," but his chess presence is surpassingly vivid, and during the tournament in which Luzhin thinks himself into a nervous breakdown suspense mounts as to whether "the limpidity and lightness of Luzhin's thought would prevail over the Italian's tumultuous fantasy." Their game, a potential draw which is never completed, draws forth a display of metaphorical brilliance that turns pure thought heroic. Beneath the singing, quivering, trumpeting, humming battlefield of the chessboard, Turati and Luzhin become fabulous monsters groping through unthinkable tunnels:

Lushin's thought, roamed through entrancing and terrible labyrinths, meeting there now and then the anxious thought of Turati, who sought the same thing as he. . . . Luzhin, preparing an attack for which it was first necessary to explore a maze of variations, where his every step aroused a perilous echo, began a long meditation. . . .Suddenly, something occurred outside his being, a scorching pain—and he let out a loud cry, shaking his hand stung by the flame of a match, which he had lit and forgotten to apply to his cigarette. The pain immediately passed, but in the fiery gap he had seen something unbearably awesome, the full horror of the abysmal depths of chess.

The game is adjourned, and after such evocation we have no difficulty in feeling with Luzhin how the chess-images that have haunted the fringes of his existence now move into the center and render the real world phantasmal. The metaphors have reversed the terms.

Chess imagery has infiltrated the book from all sides. Nabokov in his foreword preens perhaps unduly on the tiled and parqueted floors, the Knight-like leaps of the plot. His hero's monomania plays tricks with the objective world: "The urns that stood on stone pedestals at the four corners of the terrace threatened one another across their diagonals." He sat thinking . . . that with a Knight's move of this lime tree standing on a sunlit slope one could take that telegraph pole over there . . ." ". . . Luzhin involuntarily put out a hand to remove shadow's King from the threat of light's Pawn." He warily watches the floor, "where a slight movement was taking place perceptible to him alone, an evil differentiation of shadows." Throughout the book, glimpses of black and white abound—tuxedos, raspberries and milk, "the white boat on the lake, black with the reflected conifers." Many lamps are lit against the night; Luzhin's father thinks it "strange and awesome . . . to sit on this bright veranda amid the black summer night, across from this boy whose tensed forehead seemed to expand and swell as soon as he bent over the pieces," this boy for whom "the whole world suddenly went dark" when he learned chess and who is to glide, across the alternation of many nights and days, from the oblivion of breakdown into the whiteness of a hospital where the psychiatrist wears "a black Assyrian beard."

The squares on the board can also be construed as chess vs. sex. The child maneuvers his own initiation on the blind board of an illicit affair. His father, while he is poring over chess diagrams in the attic, fears that "his son might have been looking for pictures of naked women." Valentinov (!), his sinister "chess father," part manager and part pimp, "fearing lest Luzhin should squander his precious power in releasing by natural means the beneficial inner tension . . . kept him at a distance from women and rejoiced over his chaste moroseness." His marriage, then, is a kind of defensive castling undertaken too late, for the black forces that have put him in check press on irresistibly, past his impotent Queen, toward certain mate. The Luzhin defense becomes abandonment of play—suicide. Such a design eminently satisfies Nabokov's exacting criteria of artistic performance, which, in a memorable section in *Conclusive Evidence* concerning butterflies, he relates to the "mysteries of mimicry": "I discovered in nature the non-utilitarian delights that I sought in art. Both were a form of magic, both were a game of intricate enchantment and deception."

However, I am not sure it perfectly works, this chess puzzle pieced out with human characters. In the last third of the book, the author's youth may begin to show; émigré parties, arranged by Mrs. Luzhin, are introduced for no apparent better reason than that Nabokov was going to such parties at this time. A "mercilessly stupid" Leningrad visitor pops up irrelevantly, as a naked index of editorial distaste for the Soviet regime. It is as if pawns were proliferating to plug a leaky problem. The reintroduction of Valentinov, though well-prepared, does not function smoothly; if the plot were scored like a game, this move would receive a (?). One becomes conscious of rather aimless intricacies: the chronic mention of a one-armed schoolmate (Nabokov's teasing of cripples, not the most sympathetic of his fads, deserves a monograph to itself), and the somewhat mannered withholding of the hero's first name and patronymic until the last sentences, which then link up with the first. In short, the novel loses inevitability as it needs it most. Suicide, being one experience no writer or reader has undergone, requires extra credentials to pass into belief. I can believe in the suicides of Anna Karenina and Emma Bovary as terrible but just—in the sense of fitting—events within the worlds the authors have evolved. I am even more willing to believe in Kirillov's suicide in *The Possessed* as the outcome of a philosophic-psychotic mental state explored with frightening empathy. But I am unable to feel Luzhin's descent into an eternity of "dark and pale square" as anything but the foreordained outcome of a scheme that, however pretty, is less weighty than the human fictions it has conjured up.

Early in *The Defense* Nabokov describes an obtuse chess spectator who, exasperated by what seems to him a premature concession, itches to pick up the pieces and play the game out. So too, I cannot see why, now that Luzhin is equipped with a willing if not enthusiastic female caretaker and furthermore a wealthy father-in-law, the grandmaster is hopelessly blocked from pursuing, this side of madness, his vocation. He is lovable, this child within a monster, this "chess moron," and we want him to go on, to finish his classic game with Turati, and, win or lose, to play other games, to warm and dazzle the exquisite twilit world of his preoccupation with the "limpidity and lightness" of his thought. He seems blocked by something outside the novel, perhaps by the lepidopterist's habit of killing what it loves; how remarkably few, after all, of Nabokov's characters do evade the mounting pin. But in asking (irrationally, he has been dead for over thirty years) that Luzhin survive and be fruitful, we are asking no more than his creator, no pet of fate, has asked of himself and has, to his great honor, done.

(1964)

JOHN UPDIKE

Swans on an Autumn River

The stories of Sylvia Townsend Warner stick up from *The New Yorker*'s fluent fiction-stream with a certain stony air of mastery. They are granular and adamant and irregular in shape. The prose has a much-worked yet abrasive texture of minute juxtaposition and compounded accuracies. Candles are lit in an antique shop, and "The polished surfaces reflected the little flames with an intensification of their various colors—amber in satinwood, audit ale in mahogany, dragon's blood in tortoise shell." Two old ladies reminisce: "They talked untiringly about their girlhood—about the winters when they went skating, the summers when they went boating, the period when they were so very pious, the period when they were pious no longer and sent a valentine to the curate: the curate blushed, a crack rang out like a pistol shot and Hector Gillespie went through the ice, the fox terriers fought under old Mrs. Bulliver's chair, the laundry ruined the blue voile, the dentist cut his throat in Century Wood, Claude Hopkins came back from Cambridge with a motorcar and drove it at thirty miles an hour with flames shooting out behind, Addie Carew was married with a wasp under her veil." How particular, yet how inclusive and shapely in this catalogue! Though Miss Warner can be trivial in her effects and vague in her intentions, she rarely lacks concreteness. On every page there is something to be seen or smelled or felt.

In *Repetition,* Kierkegaard, who had considerable fabling powers, interrupted his narrative to write: "If I were to pursue in detail the moods of the young man as I learned to know them, not to speak of including in a poetical manner a multitude of irrelevant matters—salons, wearing apparel, beautiful scenery, relatives and friends—this story might be drawn out to yard lengths. That, however, I have no inclination to do. I eat lettuce, it is true, but I eat only the heart; the leaves, in my opinion, are fit for swine." Contrariwise, Miss Warner's appetite for the leaves of circumstance is excellent. One story in this collection ("An Act of Reparation") is basically a recipe for oxtail stew; several others ("Happiness," "The View of Rome") are like architectural drawings of houses with people sketched in for scale. The furniture in her fiction is always vivacious and in her stories about Mr. Edom's antique shop, not included in this collection, *objets* dominate. The grit of factuality scintillates for her and she inhales the world's rank melancholy as if it were ambrosial perfume. Churches especially arouse her olfactory relish:

Candles were burning, some before this image, some before that. They gave a sort of top-dressing of warmth to the building, but basically it was as cold as river mud, and under a glazing of incense it smelt of poverty.

In another church, the preserved corpse of a local saint is wonderingly detailed:

What extraordinary gloves—so thin that the nails, long and rather dirty, showed through. . . . She looked at the face. It had blue glass eyes, to match the blue dress. One of them projected from the face, squeezed out by the shrivelling socket into which it had been fitted. It seemed to stare at her with alarm. The other eye was still in place, and placid.

The story containing the placid glass eye, "Fenella," and others such as "Healthy Landscape with Dormouse" and "Total Loss" pursue a steadily deepening drabness with a remorseless exhilaration. The septuagenarian Miss Warner's continued health as a writer of fiction is a testimonial to her iron diet. She has the spiritual digestion of a goat, and a ravenous eye for unpleasantness.

Between her firm particulars and the overbrooding Olympian forbearance of tone there is, sometimes, an unexpected vacuum. Her sense of form, of direction, is erratic, which is to say she has no prejudices about her material. Her endings are often weak—abrupt and enigmatic ("A Stranger with a Bag," "Their Quiet Lives"), sentimental ("Happiness"), crowded and vague ("Johnnie Brewer"). Here, where an author normally gathers his matter to a point in a final phrase or word, a dominant that will reverberate backward through the fabric of imagery, Miss Warner wanders off in the middle of the measure, or goes on a measure too long, or comes down hard on a note so wrong we doubt our ears. As I read these bound stories I had the impression that some were better when I first read them in *The New Yorker*. A little research proved it to be so.

"The View of Rome" is a generally charming story about an old engraver recovering from a nearly fatal illness. He is very anxious to return to his home and in order to secure early release from the hospital pretends that his cat, Hattie, is a stepniece coming from the Isle of Wight to nurse him. Though rather lightweight, the story gathers substance from the many sharp small touches ("The clock, with its light hopping gait, like a robin's, ticked on"), the persuasive limning of a gentle old bachelor (Miss Warner makes herself quite at home in male minds), and its articulation of a kind of joy, the joy of domestic possession, not often dramatized. I enjoyed rereading it until the last sentences, which went: "God is an Oriental potentate, unaffectedly lavish and sumptuous. He would not think it extravagant to heap up all these apples into a cenotaph for a Rural Dean. Here was no need for jam pots. They could stay in the attic." The apples, we know, are lying all about, and making jam of them has preoccupied the hero in the hospital, and we have been told of the Dean who died of a wasp sting incurred at a Harvest Festival. But those last two sentences, besides choppily cutting across the preceding grand strophes about God as an Oriental potentate, bring some unlooked-for words to the fore. Jam pots? Attic? The house's attic has not been previously mentioned, and abruptly occupies the position of a keystone. It is bewildering, and dulling. *The New Yorker* version, in place of these last two sentences, has: "There was no call for jam pots here." Surely this is better: "call" for "need," "here" for "attic," and the simpler phrasing permits the potentate-lavish-extravagant-cenotaph conceit to sound the conclusive chord in this wry fugue of mortality and gratitude.

Miss Warner thought well enough of "Swans on an Autumn River" to name her collection after it. It tells of Norman Repton, overweight and sixty-nine, attending a congress of sanitary engineers in Dublin. He has never been in Ireland, though when he was young it had represented romance to him. He sightsees confusedly, overeats in a restaurant, and, while feeding bread to some swans on a river and angrily fending off hungry seagulls, dies of a heart attack. Some women waiting for a bus and a *garda* directing traffic witness his death. The book version ends with the paragraph:

The *garda* who had left his place amid the traffic, now came up to where Norman Repton lay motionless. After a momentary hesitation, as though he were hastily summoning up something he had learned, he knelt beside him. The women drew closer together, and one of them pulled her coat about her, as though she had suddenly became conscious of the cold. Presently the *garda* looked up. "Will one of you ladies go across to the hotel," he said, "and ask them to telephone for the ambulance?" Two women detached themselves from the group and hurried across the road, arguing in whisper.

The New Yorker version is the same, until:

Presently, the *garda* got up from his knees. Looking gravely down at the figure on the pavement, he pulled off his cap and crossed himself. The action unloosed a flutter of hands, a murmur of sound, among those waiting for the bus, as though it had stirred a dovecote.

Now, this at least gives us a vivid image in which Ireland, an exotic Catholic land, and birds, whose aloof beauty and sordid hunger have lured the hero to his death, intersect. The ending Miss Warner has chosen to preserve in her book is totally centrifugal, a burst of irrelevancies. Of what significance is the mechanical request for an ambulance? Who are the two women who go to telephone, and what if they argue "in whispers"? Whispers have nothing to do with Norman Repton, and though neither ending is quite satisfactory, it is Miss Warner's that confirms our suspicion that this story is aimless. It is an insistently ugly story whose ugliness has not been shaped to any purpose. We do not know enough about Repton to feel his terminal fight with the seagulls as anything more than the irritable fit of a choleric man. The editorial process that brought two endings into being is not at issue; either *The New Yorker* version is the original one, later revised, or it is a revision prompted by the magazine and finally discarded. In either case, Miss Warner has expressed her old-fashioned preference for events over gestures. The two women walking across the road to the telephone, however flat and irrelevant as an image, are, as an event, more world-engaging and, as it were, negotiable. In an artistic age of credit manipulation, Miss Warner deals in quaintly hard cash.

Her stories tend to convince us in process and baffle us in conclusion; they are not rounded with meaning but lift jaggedly toward new, unseen, developments. "Healthy Landscape with Dormouse" presents with unblinking clairvoyance a miserably married and (therefore) unrepentantly mischievous young woman, Belinda. The story's locale is Belinda's consciousness, but instead of ending there the story leaps out of her head and concludes on a village street. Some suddenly introduced bus passengers have seen Belinda and her husband fight and jump into a car: "They ran to the car, leaped in, drove away. Several quick-witted voices exclaimed, 'Take the number! Take the number!' But the car went so fast, there wasn't time." It suggests a Mack Sennett comedy; it suggests furthermore an almost compulsive need, in Miss Warner's work, for witnesses. Her world is thoroughly social, like those rings of Hades where the sinners, frozen into eternal postures, must stare at each other. "A Stranger with a Bag" and "A Long Night" make the act of onlooking centrally dramatic; and the excellent "A Jump Ahead" ends with the narrator understanding what he has seen: his ex-wife preparing to die of leukemia.

The very best story in the book, and a masterpiece, is "A Love Match." It too is a story of witnessing: a brother and sister, Justin and Celia, love incestuously in a small English town and finally, killed by a stray bomb while in bed together, are discovered. The witnesses, the men who find their bodies, agree upon a fiction:

Then young Foe spoke out. "He must have come in to comfort her. That's my opinion." The others concurred.

The tale, with its congenial mixture of the Gothic and the pedestrian, excites her prose to a fine vividness:

The rescue workers. . .followed the trail of bricks and rubble upstairs and into a bedroom whose door slanted from its hinges. A cold air met them; looking up, they saw the sky. The floor was deep in rubble; bits of broken masonry, clots of brickwork, stood up from it like rocks on a beach. A dark bulk crouched on the hearth, and was part of the chimney stack, and a torrent of slates had fallen on the bed, crushing the two bodies that lay there.

The first act of love, the initial violation of this most sacred taboo, is beautifully described and justified as an incident within the horror and fatalism and hysteria of the First World War. Their quiet life and smoldering secret allegorize England between the wars. Framed by monstrous cataclysms, the diffident gallantry and fuddling ordinariness of the nation, personified by an incestuous couple, are seen as somehow monstrous—the cozy sibling idyll of Victorian mythology gone mad. The historical context is indicated; twenty years of truce pass in terms of private social strategies and public social movements. Justin arranges the dusty items of a dead eccentric's military collection; Celia interests herself in the poor, in Communism. They make a few friends and sometimes attend church.

There was a nice, stuffy pitch-pine St. Cuthbert's near by, and at judicious intervals they went there for evensong—thereby renewing another bond of childhood: the pleasure of hurrying home on a cold evening to eat baked potatoes hot from the oven.

The odors and occupations of *inter-bella* England, evoking Miss Warner's full vocabulary of flowers and foods and architectures, are suffused with the blameless decadence of the central situation. The story moves with unforced symbolism to the level of epic statement. Incest is civilization's ultimate recourse:

Loving each other criminally and sincerely, they took pains to live together and to safeguard their happiness from injuries of their own infliction or from outside.

Of course, no touch of implied condemnation, or of undue compassion, intrudes upon the perfect sympathy with which this scandalous marriage is chronicled. Miss Warner's genius is an uncannily equable openness to human data, and beneath her refined witchery lies a strange freshness one can only call, in praise, primitive.

(1966)

CARL VAN DOREN

Barren Ground

No contemporary American novelist is more intelligent then Ellen Glasgow. If she has latterly been somewhat overlooked in the press of other novelists, she owes it to a fact for which she is not to blame: the fact that early in her career she was popularly assigned to a school of fiction in which she belongs by geography but not by temperament. Even when she has touched the traditional Virginia in her stories, she has touched it, any critical eye should see, with a difference. Leaving others to be nostalgic for the lost cause, she has been the realist, the one important realist, of the new dominion. In particular, she has distanced all her rivals in her portraits of Southern women, who with her assistance have escaped from the sweet shadows thrown over them by chivalry, and have been permitted to amount to something in their own right.

Like Virginia and Gabriella, the most striking heroines hitherto created by Miss Glasgow, Dorinda in *Barren Ground* goes through love and beyond it before her story ends. Love takes her like a flame and burns her; love takes her like a whirlwind and drives her far outside her expected path. Then for three-fifths of her chronicle she builds herself up on what seemed the ruin of her life. Though she has thought she lived for love alone, she find she has in her a certain yeomanly endurance which sends her back to become a farmer on the scene of her defeat by love. That part of her which has been consumed by her tragedy leaves her, because she lacks it, all the freer to bend her energies to the work she has chosen. Among the heroes of fiction this circumstance is common enough; among the heroines it is so rare that Dorinda stands like a tower. She never for a moment ceases to be a woman; her ambiguous costumes hide tender flesh. But she is the husband of her farm, working her creative will upon it, mastering it and cherishing it till it responds with the harvests she has desired. The process is as dramatic as a marriage.

Old Farm, to which Dorinda is thus wedded, becomes in Miss Glasgow's handling a symbol of fate and victory. At the same time, the symbolism is not carried, as it might easily have been, to the point of poetic fallacy. What this farm is, any farm in any average neightborhood might be. The region is without splendor and without miracles. No great plantation varies the monotony of plain existence. No shining adventures light up the dusty roads. The conflict is between mankind, toiling with little hope, and nature, resisting with a bored inertia. In the record of the conflict Miss Glasgow has gone so thoroughly into detail that she furnishes a valuable document upon a typical Virginia. Life there has, of course, its poetic elements. Storms descend upon it with the roar of thunder and the fury of lightning. The sun strikes across wide fields and colors gray mists. The seasons march by in diverse moods, the flowers spring in their places, the grasshoppers chant through the hot days. Some of Dorinda's neighbors are quaint and some are horrible. But on the whole the picture is drawn in the kind of honest white and black which perhaps most nearly reproduces the color of life for most men and women.

The narrative, kept so constantly in hand by a realistic conscience, recalls Miss Glasgow's admirable novel *The Miller of Old Church*, which has much the same setting as *Barren*

Ground. The new book, however, in denying itself the softness which imparted to the older its special charm, is thereby made more true. Yet it must be admitted that the truthfulness of *Barren Ground* is bought at a price. Now and then the story lags under the weight of its materials. It would have been better if it had been shorter. As it stands, it tends to obscure a trait which is no less characteristic of Miss Glasgow than her austere fidelity. That trait is her dramatic passion. For all she has continued the story of Dorinda after her civil war through her reconstruction, and that without any effect of anti-climax, the chapters dealing with the unhappy love affair are the best in the book. Not only is there more heat in the subject itself, but there is more ease and flexibility in the representation of it. The end of the act seems somehow always in sight, even though surprises may be looked for. Reading these ardent chapters, a critic who has read all Miss Glasgow's novels with genuine admiration for their rounded substances may nevertheless venture the hope that she will some time give another of her qualities the rein and try a sparer plot of the difficult but rewarding length of *Ethan Frome, Miss Lulu Bett,* or *A Lost Lady.*

(1925)

JOHN WAIN

Ben Hecht

One can't help speaking of Mr. Hecht as a "case," if only because that is how he presents himself. He is one of those writers who step between the printed page and the reader, exploiting their own personalities, coaxing us to be interested in this or that because of our undoubted interest in *them*. The advent of television has put this kind of writer in a stronger position—as a "personality," that is; as an artist, I am not sure that it has not weakened him still further.

With those three sentences I leave the public Mr. Hecht; and I feel justified in doing so, because as a literary critic I am concerned with the private Mr. Hecht, the one who communicates with me in the quietness of my armchair. The exploitation of the personality is still there, but it recedes into the perspective of a literary device. If a man writing a story decides to bring himself in as a character, there is no reason why he shouldn't. If he puts a certain amount of energy into implying that he, the story-teller, is a man of the world, moves in circles unknown to his desk-bound brethren, gets around and meets people generally, that is simply one more ingredient in the flavoring of the story.

Mr. Hecht generally manages to give his stories a top-dressing of this kind, and usually it doesn't come amiss, especially when he is in his O. Henry vein, writing about the teeming and shifting world of Manhattan. O. Henry is the basis here, with flecks of Hemingway in the constant reminders that the writer is a man of action and no mere word-merchant. But neither of these two influences goes at all deep. Mr. Hecht's heart is elsewhere. His eyes, for all their shrewd Manhattan glitter, are in reality fixed far away, on a vision he had once and has never ceased to stare after.

In a word, Mr. Hecht is a romantic. Not just any kind of romantic, but a Wildean romantic, a man of the nineties. If, instead of being a mid-twentieth century New Yorker, he had been a *fin de siècle* Londoner, he would have been faithfully present, week in and week out, at the Cheshire Cheese. His figure would have been a familiar one in the bars of Fleet Street, where he would have made an attentive listener to the monologues of Lionel Johnson. Possibly Mr. Hecht's would be the hands that raised Johnson's lifeless body after his last fatal fall from a stool in one of these same bars. He would have known Yeats, Beardsley and Richard le Gallienne.

That is Mr. Hecht's misfortune. Owing to an unaccountable kink in the time-corridor, he slipped sixty-five years and landed on the wrong side of the Atlantic into the bargain. As a man of the nineties, he has never been very comfortable in the surroundings that Fate wrongly issued him with. For all his talk of prize-fighters and night-clubs, for all his Runyonesque familiarity with the sidewalks of little old N.Y., his heart is back there with the aesthetes carrying lilies down the Strand and the *poets maudits* dying young for the sake of an adjective. Take a sample:

The story of Marcia's nine years of stardom is a tale that wants a longer telling than this. It was the corner of a high heart in a higher mind. To those who kept pace with her or contributed to her life she seemed as complicated as music by Stravinsky, as troublesome as a handful of fine but broken glass. She owned an acidulous mind and a schoolgirl's heart.

She was ironic and disillusioned, yet ineptly romantic. She was always beautiful. Her hair shone as if a light were concealed in her coiffure. Her green eyes were never without comment—amusement, derision. Her skin was pale, her mouth wide and mobile, with restless lips. And, as in women of personality, her face seemed bolder, more strongly modelled than suited her taut, slender body. Her crisp voice was an instrument for wit rather than sights, and her beauty, despite her reputation, was a thing of which men seldom thought lightly. There was too much character and epigram behind it. Clever people have a way of seeming always gay and this was Marcia's manner—to jest at scars, her own or others'. Her sprightliness, however, was disconcerting, not only because of the cruelty it contained but for the fact that in her very laughter lurked always the antonym of weariness. She was like one of those fragile chemicals that burn too sharply, giving off a curious and vicious light. (*Actor's Blood*)

Where have we read this kind of description before? *Dorian Gray,* answers the reader dutifully. There's no surprise. The resemblance is there, on the surface, from the minute we begin to read. Admittedly it takes Mr. Hecht till the end of the paragraph to get really into his Wildean stride and begin rolling off the cadencess. "In her very laughter lurked always the antonym of weariness." And that bit about the "curious and vicious" light.

Marcia's weariness was an "antonym." It had, that is to say, an existence and an authority that were contradictory of anything she did with the other parts of her being. Like the weariness of Des Esseintes, Dorian Gray, and the figures in Beardsley's drawings. And any reader who tackles Mr. Hecht's work in bulk soon learns that this is the kind of figure he most enjoys writing about. At the center of his imagination lurks the romantic sardonic dandy, like a carp in a pool; and one cannot watch for long without seeing him rise.

Like his fellow aesthetes, Mr. Hecht is a good deal preoccupied with "the artist" as a human type. To the nineties it seemed that the artist was the only survivor from the wreck of their century: the decay of religious belief, and a growing sense of the futility of well-meaning social engineering, left the artist as the one significant figure but also doomed him to discontent. As Yeats asked,

> . . . What portion in the world can the artist have
> That has awakened from the common dream.
> But dissipation and despair?

During the last fifty years, this idea has come in for a good deal of stringent criticism. Both in the occasional masterpieces like *Tonio Kroeger* and in the broad day-to-day stream of literature and criticism, the notion of the absinthe-drinking *poet maudit* has been not so much attacked as quietly superseded. Mr. Hecht, however, still holds to it loyally. We get a clue to this when he tells us, in the preface to his new collection, that the play *Winkelberg* "is one of the best of my work." *Winkelberg* is, indeed, no mean theatrical performance. It is irreproachable as regards stagecraft and dialogue, and must be an enjoyable play to act in and to watch. But the interesting thing about it from my present point of view is that it shows the extraordinarily intact survival of "aesthetic" notions of the artist and the artistic life.

Winkelberg is a poet. As such, he will sign no truce with society, which to him is so many hogs wallowing in a trough. He spends his life sitting about on benches, sleeping in dime flop-houses and railway waiting-rooms and naturally he never has the price of a drink in his pocket. Women generally love him and want to protect him, but men are harder to please, and in fact before the curtain opens Winkelberg has been clubbed to death by an irate sailor: the play is a series of retrospective scenes from his life.

Mr. Hecht has worked hard over Winkelberg. He has even made up quite a lot of verse for him to utter. It is free verse of the Greenwich Village twenties, picturesque and evidently quite content to go on being picturesque. For the thing that Winkelberg avoids from start to finish is involvement. When, during a law hearing, the attorney asks him if he is married, he replies, "I have not yet achieved that moral eminence."

Neither has he achieved the moral eminence of earning a living, or indeed of doing anything about life except make up bar-room epigrams about it.

I don't want to be ponderously disapproving about Winkelberg. He is an amiable enough fellow, with his epigrams that limp somewhere in the rear of Wilde and his poems that reach out towards a faded picturesqueness. Here he is in action, making a big impression on a girl he meets at a C.P. meeting:

Ellen (shyly): Do you believe in Communism, Mr. Winkelberg?
Poet: Belief is the noisy partner of hope. (He smiles at her). Your hair is like a friendly smile.
Ellen: I like to hear you talk.
Poet: Why?
Ellen: Because you are very kind—and you wrote me a poem. Tell it to me again.
Poet:
Her eyes are bright as petals after rain,
Her lips tiptoe towards a smile
That only virgins know—
Ellen (repeating slowly):
Her lips tiptoe towards a smile
That only virgins know—

The play ends with a speech in which Winkelberg defends himself against the hostile jury of posterity:

I agree with the verdict. I was a dirty drunk. I robbed myself and blamed others. I wanted to be distinguished, and I wooed fame out of a booze bottle. I fouled myself. But that wasn't all! There was something more to me. I was a poet who tried to paint the color of the wind. I was a little kite of words in an enormous sky. I was a poet who sang of streets where poverty and despair perform their microscopic somersaults. I danced with rebellious elves in empty rooms. When I was hungry, I licked the moon and dined on the dawn. And I am a poet still. I need no other dream but the one I gave myself. You in Charge—whatever your debatable name is—you have your heaven of petulant cliches. And I have mine of words. I want no more. Let me stretch out in some celestial alley with hungry cats for angels—and my poems around me.

Now, all this rhetoric is demonstrably *about* something. It represents a view of art, and of life, in which Mr. Hecht genuinely believes: indeed, it is the genuineness of his belief that gives *Winkelberg* its undeniable dabs and flashes of dramatic power. And yet, of course it won't do. Winkelberg and his like can no more stand as types of the imaginative artist than children playing with mud-pies can stand as types of the architect. Winkelberg is serious in his devotion to art, but he is insufficiently serious about art itself. To him, it is little more than a decoration; something fragile and destructible, affording a contrast to the sombre selfishness of "practical" life. These are the faults of better men than Winkelberg; of Wilde, for example. If one compares Wilde with the really great artists who were working at about that time—with Chekhov, say—one sees that his weakness is precisely a lack of that sense of common humanity, that tough and persistent involvement with human concerns, that insatiable curiosity about people, which we look for in art that is likely to hold any durable interest for us. Winkelberg has no curiosity about people, no sense of a shared fate; he has his "bright words." In the end, it is the alley cats who will provide his true audience, because his involvement with humanity is as shallow as theirs.

The trouble, in short, with this disengaged "aesthetic" attitude is simply that is is not sufficiently interesting. There are too many important areas of human experience which it does not touch upon. It was justifiable for Wilde to say, cooly, that "all art is completely useless," because he came at the tail-end of a long period during which art had been insistently urged, by every kind of public spokesman, to be instructive and profitable in the crudest way. Nevertheless, as we well know, art is *not* "useless." Only Mr. Hecht's dream-people, they of the brittle epigrams and the eternally tired souls, think it is, and both art and life have a way of revenging themselves on such people.

This whole problem comes out very clearly in Mr. Hecht's new novel *The Sensualists*. Without giving away the plot details, the story tells of a worldly-wise publisher named Henry, much given to epigrams of the sort Mr. Hecht enjoys making up, married for eight years to Ann, a woman evidently much younger than himself, and whom he has rescued from frigidity. In the opening chapter, Ann has just discovered that Henry is carrying on with one Liza King, a night-club singer; the rest of the plot involves detectives, drug addicts, a sadistic murder, an errant husband who tries to get at Ann while Henry, by a pardonable error of the Police Department, is spending a few days in the local hoosegow, and, to top off, some incidental lesbianism. The book is constructed with all the skill we expect from Mr. Hecht, and the ingenuity with which he has worked in so many kinds of sexual episode, while stopping short before the point of actual farce, is impressive indeed. But we have to come back, finally, to this one obstinately troubling objection. It isn't interesting enough. Henry is a sensualist, and he has taught Ann to be one; their marriage (which, by his wish, is childless) is simply an association for pleasure; there is no reason why they should stay together once the pleasure has slackened. Such marriages do exist, and there is no reason why a novelist should not write about them. But the thinness of purpose, the wearily selective nature of the feelings the characters can permit themselves, are so boring that after about half-way point the book becomes a positive effort to read. It no longer seems, in spite of the proliferation of incident, to be *about* anything.

In the closing pages, Henry, like any other peccant husband, "repents." He "confesses," not only to Liza, but to a whole string of what he calls "paraffined tarts." Reading this scene, one feels impelled to pause and ask why it is so radically unsatisfactory. The reasons, I think, are two. In the first place, one simply doesn't care whether Henry gets Ann back or not. She can get straight up out of her twin bed and walk out on him, for all it seems to matter, in a genuine human way, to anybody. Secondly, Henry's return to Ann is still on the old shallow level. It is concerned with pleasure.

He repents because he has discovered, or says he has discovered, that the extramarital pleasure was an illusion.

Ann, it seems, has kept her shape. "You're very good sexually," Henry tells Ann. "A fine lubricity and tender lewdness. Not to mention a beautiful skin and a superb shape." But why go on? The real deficiency of this book is that it doesn't, in fact, take up the challenge of its own implications. Wilde's remark that he found pleasure a more interesting study than happiness, because of its tragic possibilities, indicates the only way of extracting significant art out of this kind of theme. At the moment, Ann still has her shape and her skin and Henry can still divert her. What we need is a sequel, ten years further on, when the real problems have caught up with them. *That* might be interesting.

(1959)

JOHN WAIN

Naked Lunch

Naked Lunch belongs to that very large category of books, from Macpherson's *Ossian* to *Peyton Place,* whose interest lies not in their own qualities but in the reception given to them in their own time. In itself, *Naked Lunch* is of very small significance. It consists of a prolonged scream of hatred and disgust, an effort to keep the reader's nose down in the mud for 250 pages. Before reading it I had heard it described as pornography, but this is not the case. The object of pornographic writing is to flood the reader's mind with lust, and lust is at any rate a positive thing to the extent that none of us would exist without it. A pornographic novel is, in however backhanded a way, on the side of something describable as life.

Naked Lunch, by contrast, is unreservedly on the side of death. It seeks to flood the reader's mind not with images of sexual desire but with images of pain, illness, cruelty and corruption.

This is not in fact a very difficult thing to do, since all that is necessary is to brood on everything capable of arousing disgust and revulsion, let the images well up, and dash them down onto the paper. A book like *Naked Lunch* requires far less talent in the writer, and for that matter less intelligence in the reader than the humblest magazine story or circulating-library novel. From the literary point of view, it is the merest trash, not worth a second glance.

What is worth a glance, however, is the respectful attitude that some well-known writers and critics have shown towards it. Some of the tributes on the wrapper are entirely routine and unsurprising; to find Norman Mailer, for instance, solemnly declaring that this is "a book of beauty, great difficulty, and maniacally exquisite insight," will startle no one, since Mailer has in recent years worked himself round to a position which makes it impossible for him to apply normal values to literature. Kerouac's confident invoking of Swift, Rabelais and Sterne will also pass without comment, since he has given no indication that he knows these writers except as names to be bandied about. E. S. Seldon, on the other hand, a name not previously known to me but evidently well-known enough to be quoted in a blurb, seems to write like a literate man, and his verdict that "Burroughs is a superb writer, and *Naked Lunch* a novel of revolt in the best late-modern sense," pulls one up. It sounds, on the surface at any rate, as if it ought to mean something.

What in fact do we understand by a "novel of revolt" in "the best late-modern sense"? To begin with, such a book would have to belong to the anti-art movement. Secondly, it would have to deal with characters whose lives are largely devoted to escaping from normal day-to-day living, with its pleasures and responsibilities, and achieving, with the aid of drugs and other stimuli, a more or less permanent state of abnormality, where the monstrous becomes the habitual. Thirdly, it would have to be written out of a mood of disgust and hostility. Fourthly, it would have to be urban in atmosphere, saturated with the details of megalopolis.

All these tendencies can be found in writers who were well under way by 1910—in Alfred Jarry, for example. After 1918 the method was very quickly brought to full development, and the only way of carrying it any further was to increase the element of nausea. The impulse behind anti-art, from Dada manifestos to Action Painting, has always been two-fold. Part of the thrust was towards truthfulness and a closer grip on reality. Conventional art, which always admitted a degree of stylization, tended to put reality at a distance, whereas (it was claimed) anti-art had the immediacy of something actually happening; it was not "culture." Naturally this was closely allied with the second objective, which was to shock and startle, to insult, to open people's eyes by affronting them. What Mr. Seldon would call "late-modern" is characterized by nothing new except that it digs deeper for its mud, and crushes out more ruthlessly any spark of lyricism or positiveness. Where genuine imaginative writing increases the sensitiveness of the minds exposed to it, leading them on to a wider and deeper range of feelings, writing of this kind makes the mind blunt and callow. Anyone who really accepted its values, as opposed to pretending to accept them as part of some modish parade, would be the enemy not only of art but of the human race.

The idea seems to have got about that Burroughs is the same kind of writer as Henry Miller; indeed, I have seen it stated several times that *Naked Lunch* is, so to speak, Miller's *Tropics* carried a stage further. In fact, they are writers of entirely opposite tendency. Miller is an affirmative writer. He preaches incessantly, and his "message," boiled down to its essentials, is that happiness is attainable by anyone who sheds his responsibilities and lives by impulse, never doing anything that he doesn't feel exactly like doing at that moment. The "I" of Henry Miller's writings, who may or may not bear any close relationship to the author, is a figure who has achieved complete liberation from the hampering ties of daily life, and as a result has broken through into a dimension where existence seems to comprise nothing but epiphanies. "This is the first day of my life. . . . I bless the world, every inch of it, every living atom, and it is all alive." And so forth. Just how sound this is, as a guide to the seeker after happiness, is open to question. There are so many things you can't do without accepting responsibility; an acceptance like that made by the "I" of Miller's fantasies is based on an enormous refusal—a refusal of family relationships, a refusal of anything stable and fixed, and even—since it prevents one from holding down a job—a refusal of skill. What Miller offers is attractive and interesting on a superficial level; as soon as one begins to think seriously about it, the emptiness and weariness come into focus. At a certain stage of adolescence, no doubt, it is pleasant for a boy to picture himself as having endlessly to do with women yet always successfully refusing to take emotional responsibility for any particular one. But to remain in that state is to remain in adolescence, a prey to the melancholy and instability of adolescence as well as a beneficiary of its energy and heightened emotions.

Still, if we take him on the half-serious level on which he deserves to be taken, Miller has something to offer, and that something is an affirmation. He is a great celebrator. *The Air-Conditioned Nightmare*, for instance, is full of abuse of American life, but its final effect, when you have shut the book and allowed it to sink in a day or two, is one of praise. Miller is an enjoyer; wherever he goes he finds something to enjoy, even if it is only the pleasure of hurling insults at things he finds hateful. He isn't depressed; he hurls the insults with the abandon of a schoolboy shying at coconuts. America threatened him, to begin with, because it was home, and home meant (however distantly) responsibility and authority:

When I came up on deck to catch my first glimpse of the shore line I was disappointed. Not only disappointed, I might say, but actually saddened. The American coast looked bleak and uninviting to me. I didn't like the look of the American house; there is something cold, austere, something barren and chill, about the architecture of the American home. It was *home,* with all the ugly, evil, sinister connotations which the word contains for a restless soul. There was a frigid, moral aspect to it which chilled me to the bone.

After this unpromising start, however, America swallows him

up in her vast landscape, and he begins to enjoy himself. With time off every now and then for howls of execration, the rest of the book is a celebration. It isn't as good as *The Colossus of Maroussi,* but it's good, because Miller is always good when he can praise anything. In however addlepated a way, he loves life. Though his recipe for happiness is one that for any thoughtful person just wouldn't work, nevertheless happiness is what he wants.

What is more, Miller has developed a style that is very well fitted for this continual act of celebration. He writes a hurrying, turbulent prose that gives the impression of complete spontaneity, but only the most naive reader will imagine that such prose can be produced without a great deal of hard work. The rhythms never get out of hand, the pauses are varied with considerable skill, and the words are chosen with great effectiveness. If this is anti-art, it is at least not anti-craft. George Orwell, in his classic essay on Miller ("Inside the Whale," 1940) declared that Miller's books "give you an idea of what can still be done, even at this late date, with English prose. In them, English is treated as a spoken language, but spoken *without fear,* i.e. without fear of rhetoric or of the unusual or poetical word. The adjective has come back, after its ten years' exile. It is a flowing, swelling prose, a prose with rhythms in it, something quite different from the flat cautious statements and snack bar dialects that are now in fashion."

Like most English people of my generation, I first heard of Miller through Orwell's essay, and when, some years later, I at last got hold of his books, I found that whereas Orwell had completely misled me about the scope and nature of Miller's work, he had prepared me very well for the style. Miller is a very contagious writer: after reading him for an hour or so, you find that if you sit down to write it is difficult not to produce something that sounds like an imitation of him. Orwell, in that same essay, has some amusing examples, passages where he has quite unconsciously deserted his own steel-gray, incisive prose for something rather like pastiche of Miller. For instance: "What is he accepting? In the first place,

355

not America, but the ancient bone-heap of Europe, where every grain of soil has passed through innumerable human bodies." That sentence is not in Orwell's idiom but in Miller's—though, it is fair to add, Miller would have put it rather better. Orwell has been drawn into rhetoric against his better judgment, because Miller makes rhetoric seem easy and attractive. Likewise when he writes, a few pages later, "He is fiddling while Rome is burning, and, unlike the enormous majority of people who do this, fiddling with his face towards the flames," we recognize once again the pull towards rhetoric—a much stronger tribute to Miller's gifts than the rather guarded, give-and-take-away praise which he accords him.

Miller, then, is contagious because he is an enjoyer. The "freedom" he proclaims would in practice turn out to be self-defeating, but at least it is a freedom to enjoy life. Burroughts, by contrast, belongs more to the tradition of Céline. He doesn't want to enjoy himself and he doesn't want us to, either. Imagine him looking at a landscape and getting anything out of it! The nearest he gets to a description of pleasure, of anybody doing anything because they *liked* it, is (at the worst) in his obsessive descriptions of fearful sadistic violence and (at the best) in a passage like:

Iris—half Chinese and half Negro—addicted to dihy-dro-oxy-heroin—takes a shot every fifteen minutes to which end she leaves droppers and needles sticking out all over her. The needles rust in her flesh, which, here and there, has grown completely over a joint to form a smooth green brown wen. On the table in front of her is a samovar of tea and a twenty-pound hamper of brown sugar. No one has ever seen her eat anything else. It is only just before a shot that she hears what anyone says or talks herself.

The only writer of any talent of whom Burroughs occasionally manages to remind one is the Marquis de Sade; but if one turns to the pages of Sade after *Naked Lunch* the resemblance soon fades, since Sade, however degenerate he can be at times, has always some saving wit and irony. Burroughs takes himself with a complete, owlish seriousness;

indeed, in his opening section he seems, as far as one can make out through the pea-soup fog of his prose, to be offering the book as some kind of tract against drug addiction. *"The junk virus is public health problem number one of the world to-day.* Since *Naked Lunch* treats this health problem, it is necessarily brutal, obscene and disgusting. Sickness is often repulsive details not for weak stomachs." The claim is, of course, balderdash, since the only effect of the flood of writing which takes the junkie or hipster as its central theme is to romanticize those unfortunates, as Byron and the "Byronists" romanticized a certain kind of romantic self-pity and caused it to spread throughout the world.

Altogether, *Naked Lunch* offers a very interesting field for speculation, both pathological and sociological. No lover of medical text-books on deformity should miss it. The rest of us, however, can afford to spend our six dollars on something else.

(1962)

ROBERT PENN WARREN

The Portable Faulkner

I

Malcolm Cowley's editing of *The Portable Faulkner* is remarkable on two counts. First, the selection from Faulkner's work is made not merely to give a cross section or a group of good examples but to demonstrate one of the principles of integration in the work. Second, the essay is one of the few things ever written on Faulkner which is not hag-ridden by prejudice or preconception and which really sheds some light on the subject.

The selections here are made to describe the place, Yoknapatawpha County, Mississippi, which is, as Cowley puts it, "Faulkner's mythical kingdom," and to give the history of that kingdom. The place is the locale of most of Faulkner's work. Its 2,400 square miles lie between the hills of North Mississippi and the rich, black bottom lands. It has a population of 15,611 persons, composing a society with characters as different as the Bundrens, the Snopeses, Ike McCaslin, Percy Grimm, Temple Drake, the Compsons, Christmas, Dilsey and the tall convict of *The Wild Palms*. No land in all fiction lives more vividly in its physical presence than this mythical county—the "pine-winey" afternoons, the nights with "a thin sickle of moon like the heel print of a boot in wet sand," the tremendous reach of the big river in flood, "yellow and sleepy in the afternoon," and the "little" piddling creeks, that run backward one day and forward the next and come busting down on a man full of dead mules and hen houses," the ruined plantation which was Popeye's hangout, the swamps and fields and hot, dusty roads of the Frenchman's Bend section, and the remnants of the great original forests, "green with gloom" in summer, "if anything actually dimmer than they had been in November's gray dissolution, where even at noon the sun fell only in windless dappling upon the earth which never completely dried." And no land in all fiction is more painstakingly analyzed from the sociological standpoint. The descendants of the old families, the descendants of bushwhackers and carpetbaggers, the swamp rats, the Negro cooks and farm hands, bootleggers and gangsters, peddlers, college boys, tenant farmers, country store-keepers, county-seat lawyers are all here. The marks of class, occupation and history are fully rendered and we know completely their speech, dress, food, houses, manners and attitudes. Nature and sociology, geography and human geography, are scrupulously though effortlessly presented in Faulkner's work, and their significance for his work is very great; but the significance is of a conditioning order. They are, as it were, aspects of man's "doom"—a word of which Faulkner is very fond—but his manhood in the face of that doom is what is important.

Cowley's selections are made to give the description of the mythical kingdom, but more important, they are made to give its history. Most critics, even those who have most naively or deliberately misread the meaning of the fact, have been aware that the sense of the past is crucial in Faulkner's work. Cowley has here set up selections running in date of action from 1820 to 1940. The first, "A Justice," is a story about Ikkemotubbe, the nephew of a Chickasaw chief who went to New Orleans, where he received the name of *l'Homme*, which became Doom; who came back to the tribe to poison his way to the Man-ship; and who, in the end (in Faulkner's "history" though not in "A Justice" itself), swaps a mile square of "virgin north Mississippi dirt" for a racing mare owned by Jason Lycurgus Compson, the founder of the Compson family in Mississippi. The last selection, "Delta Autumn," shows us Isaac McCaslin, the man who brings the best of the old order, philosopher, aristocrat, woodsman, into the modern world and who gives the silver-mounted horn which General Compson had left him to a mulatto woman for her bastard son by a relative of McCaslin's. In between "A Justice" and "Delta Autumn" fall such pieces as the magnificent "Red Leaves," the profoundly symbolic story called "The Bear," the Civil War and Reconstruction stories, "Rain" (from *The Unvanquished)* and "Wash," "Old Man" (the story of the tall convict from *The Wild Palms),* and the often anthologized "That Evening Sun" and "A Rose for Emily," and the brilliant episode of "Percy Grimm" (from *Light in August).* There are other pieces included, but these are the best, and the best for showing the high points in the history of Yoknapatawpha County.

Cowley's introduction undertakes to define the significance of place and history in Faulkner's work, that "labor of imagination that has not been equaled in our time." That labor is, as he points out, a double labor: "first, to invent a Mississippi county that was like a mythical kingdom, but was complete and living in all its details; second, to make his story of Yoknapatawpha County stand as a parable or legend of all the Deep South." The legend—called a legend "because it is obviously no more intended as a historical account of the country south of the Ohio than *The Scarlet Letter* was intended as a history of Massachusetts"—is, as Cowley defines it, this:

The South was settled by Sartorises (aristocrats) and Sutpens (nameless, ambitious men) who, seizing the land from the Indians, were determined to found an enduring and stable order. But despite their strength and integrity their project was, to use Faulkner's word, "accursed" by slavery, which, with the Civil War as instrument, frustrated their design. Their attempt to rebuild according to the old plan and old values was defeated by a combination of forces—the carpetbaggers and Snopeses ("a new exploiting class descended from the landless whites"). Most of the descendants of the old order are in various ways incompetent: they are prevented by their code from competing with the codeless Snopeses, they cling to the letter and forget the spirit of their tradition, they lose contact with the realities of the present and escape into a dream world of alcohol or rhetoric or gentility or madness, they fall in love with defeat or death, they lose nerve and become cowards or they, like the last Jason in *The Sound and the Fury,* adopt Snopesism and become worse than any Snopes. Figures like Popeye (eyes like "rubber knobs," a creature having "that vicious depthless quality of stamped tin," the man "who made money and had nothing he could do with it, spend it for, since he knew that alcohol would kill him like poison, who had no friends and had never known a woman") are in their dehumanized quality symbols of modernism, for the society of finance capitalism. The violence of some of Faulkner's work is, according to Cowley, "an example of the Freudian method turned backward, being full of sexual nightmares that are in reality social symbols. It is somehow connected in the author's mind with what he regards as the rape and corruption of the South."

This is, in brief, Cowley's interpretation of the legend, and it provides an excellent way into Faulkner; it exactly serves the purpose which an introduction should serve. The interpretation is indebted, no doubt, to that of George Marion O'Donnell (the first and still an indispensable study of Faulkner's theme), but it modifies O'Donnell's tendency to read Faulkner with an allegorical rigidity and with a kind of doctrinal single-mindedness.

It is possible that the present view, however, should be somewhat modified, at least in emphasis. Although no writer is more deeply committed to a locality than Faulkner, the emphasis on the Southern elements may blind us to other elements, or at least other applications, of deep significance. And this is especially true in so far as the work is interpreted merely as Southern apologetics or, as it is by Maxwell Geismar, as the "extreme hallucinations" of a "cultural psychosis."

It is important, I think, that Faulkner's work be regarded not in terms of the South against the North, but in terms of issues which are common to our modern world. The legend is not merely a legend of the South, but is also a legend of our general plight and problem. The modern world is in moral confusion. It does suffer from a lack of discipline, of sanctions, of community of values, of a sense of a mission. It is a world in which self-interest, workableness, success, provide the standards. It is a world which is the victim of abstraction and of mechanism, or at least, at moments, feels itself to be. It can look back nostalgically upon the old world of traditional values and feel loss and perhaps despair—upon the world in which, as one of Faulkner's characters puts it, men "had the gift of living once or dying once instead of being diffused and scattered creatures drawn blindly from a grab bag and assembled"—a world in which men were, "integer for integer," more simple and complete. If it be objected that Faulkner's view is unrealistic, that had the old order satisfied human needs it would have survived, and that it is sentimental to hold that it was killed from the outside, the answer is clear in the work: the old order did not satisfy human needs—the Southern old order or any other—for it, not being founded on justice, was "accursed" and held the seeds of its own ruin in itself. But even in terms of the curse the old order, as opposed to the new order (in so far as the new is to be equated with Snopesism) allowed the traditional man to define himself as human by setting up codes, concepts of virtue, obligations, and by accepting the risks of his humanity. Within the traditional order was a notion of truth, even if man in the flow of things did not succeed in realizing that truth. Take, for instance, the passage from "The Bear":

"All right," he said. "Listen," and read again, but only one stanza this time and closed the book and laid it on the table. "She cannot fade, though thou hast not thy bliss," McCaslin said: "Forever wilt thou love, she be fair."

"He's talking about a girl," he said.

"He had to talk about something," McCaslin said. Then he said, "He was talking about truth. Truth is one. It doesn't change. It covers all things which touch the heart—honor and pride and pity and justice and courage and love. Do you see now?"

The human effort is what is important, the capacity to make the effort to rise above the mechanical process of life, the pride to endure, for in endurance there is a kind of self-conquest.

When it is said, as it is often said, that Faulkner's work is "backward-looking," the answer is that the constant ethical center is to be found in the glorification of the human effort and of human endurance, which are not in time, even though in modernity they seem to persist most surely among the despised and rejected. It is true that Faulkner's work contains a savage attack on modernity, but it is to be remembered that Elizabethan tragedy, for instance, contained just such an attack on its own special "modernity." (Ambition is the most constant tragic crime, and ambition is the attitude special to an opening society; all villains are rationalists and appeal to "nature" beyond traditional morality for justification, and rationalism is, in the sense implied here, the attitude special to the rise of a secular and scientific order before a new morality can be formulated.)

It is not ultimately important whether the traditional order (Southern or other) as depicted by Faulkner fits exactly the picture which critical historical method provides. Let it be granted, for the sake of discussion, that Faulkner does oversimplify the matter. What is ultimately important, both ethically and artistically, is the symbolic function of

that order in relation to the world which is set in opposition
to it. The oppositon between the old order and the new does
not, however, exhaust the picture. What of the order to
come? "We will have to wait," old Ike McCaslin says to the
mulatto girl who is in love with a white man. A curse may
work itself out in time; and in such glimpses, which occur
now and then, we get the notion of a grudging meliorism, a
practical supplement to the idealism, like Ike McCaslin's,
which finds compensation in the human effort and the
contemplation of "truth."

The discussion, even at a large scope and with more
satisfactory analysis, of the central theme of Faulkner would
not exhaust the interest of this work. In fact, the discussion
of this question always runs the risk of making his work
appear too schematic, too dry and too complacent when in
actual fact it is full of rich detail, of shadings and
complexities of attitude, or ironies and ambivalences.
Cowley's introduction cautions the reader on this point and
suggests various fruitful topics for investigation and thought.
But I shall make bold—and in the general barrenness of
criticism of Faulkner it does not require excessive
boldness—to list and comment on certain topics which seem
to me to demand further critical study.

Nature—The vividness of the natural background is one of
the impressive features of Faulkner's work. It is accurately
observed, but observation only provides the stuff from which
the characteristic effects are gained. It is the atmosphere
which counts, the poetry, the infusion of feeling, the
symbolic weight. Nature provides a backdrop—of lyric beauty
(the meadow in the cow episode of *The Hamlet*), of homely
charm (the trial scene of the "Spotted Horses" story from
the same book), of sinister, brooding force (the river in "Old
Man" from *The Wild Palms)*, of massive dignity (the forest in
"The Bear")—for the human action and passion. The in-
destructible beauty is there: "God created man," Ike
McCaslin says in "Delta Autumn," "and He created the world

for him to live in and I reckon He created the kind of world He would have wanted to live in if He had been a man."

Ideally, if man were like God, as Ike McCaslin puts it, man's attitude toward nature would be one of pure contemplation, pure participation in its great forms and appearances; the appropriate attitude is love, for with Ike McCaslin the moment of love is equated with Godhood. But since man "wasn't quite God himself," since he lives in the world of flesh, he must be a hunter, user and violator. To return to McCaslin: God "put them both here: man and the game he would follow and kill, foreknowing it. I believe He said, 'So be it.' I reckon He even foreknew the end. But He said, 'I will give him his chance. I will give him warning and foreknowledge too, along with the desire to follow and the power to slay. The woods and the fields he ravages and the game he devastates will be the consequence and signature of his crime and guilt, and his punishment."

There is, then, a contamination implicit in the human condition—a kind of Original Sin, as it were—but it is possible, even in the contaminating act, the violation, for man to achieve some measure of redemption, a redemption through love. For instance, in "The Bear," the great legendary beast which is pursued for eyars to the death is also an object of love and veneration, and the symbol of virtue, and the deer hunt of "Delta Autumn" is for Ike McCaslin a ritual of renewal. Those who have learned the right relationship to nature—"the pride and humility" which young Ike McCaslin learns from the half-Negro, half-Indian Sam Fathers—are set over against those who have not. In "The Bear," General Compson speaks up to Cass McCaslin to defend the wish of the boy Ike McCaslin to stay an extra week in the woods:

"You got one foot straddled into a farm and the other foot straddled into a bank; you ain't even got a good hand-hold where this boy was already an old man long before you damned Sartorises and Edmondses invented farms and banks to keep yourselves from having to find out what this boy was born knowing and fearing too maybe, but without being afraid, that could go ten miles on a compass because he wanted to look at a bear none of us had ever got near enough to put a bullet in and looked at the bear and came the ten miles back on the compass in the dark; maybe by God that's the why and the wherefore of farms and banks."

Those who have the wrong attitude toward nature are the pure exploiters, the apostles of abstractionism, the truly evil men. For instance, the very opening of Sanctuary presents a distinction on this ground between Benbow and Popeye. While the threat of Popeye keeps Benbow crouching by the spring, he hears a Carolina wren sing, and even under these circumstances tries to recall the local name for it. And he says to Popeye: "And of course you don't know the name of it. I don't suppose you'd know a bird at all, without it was singing in a cage in a hotel lounge, or cost four dollars on a plate." Popeye, as we may remember, spits in the spring (he hates nature and must foul it), is afraid to go through the woods ("Through all them trees?" he demands when Benhow points out the short cut), and when an owl whisks past them in the twilight, claws at Benhow's coat with almost hysterical fear (" 'It's just an owl,' Benhow said, 'It's nothing but an owl.' ").

The pure exploiters, though they may gain ownership and use of a thing, never really have it; like Popeye, they are impotent. For instance, Flem Snopes, the central character and villain of *The Hamlet,* who brings the exploiter's mentality to Frenchman's Bend, finally marries Eula Varner, a kind of fertility goddess or earth goddess; but his ownership is meaningless, for she always refers to him as "that man" (she does not even have a name for him), and he has only got her after she has given herself willingly to one of the bold, hot-blooded boys of the neighborhood. In fact, nature can't in one sense, be "owned." Ike McCaslin, in "The Bear," says of the land which has some down to him:

It was never Father's and Uncle Buddy's to bequeath me to repudiate, because it was never Grandfather's to bequeath them to bequeath me to repudiate, because it was never old Ikkemotubbe's to sell to

Grandfather for bequeathment and repudiation. Because it was never Ikkemotubbe's fathers' father's to bequeath Ikkemotubbe to sell to Grandfather or any man because on the instant when Ikkemotubbe discovered, realized, that he could sell it for money, on that instant it ceased ever to have been his forever, father to father, to father, and the man who bought it bought nothing.

The right attitude toward nature is, as a matter of fact, associated with the right attitude toward man, and the mere lust for power over nature is associated with the lust for power over other men, for God gave the earth to man, we read in "The Bear," not "to hold for himself and his descendants inviolable title forever, generation after generation, to the oblongs and squares of the earth, but to hold the earth mutual and intact in the communal anonymity of brotherhood, and all the fee He asked was pity and humility and sufferance and endurance and the sweat of his face for bread." It is the failure of this pity which curses the earth (the land in Faulkner's particular country is "accursed" by chattel slavery, but slavery is simply one of the possible forms of the failure). But the rape of nature and the crime against man are always avenged. The rape of nature, the mere exploitation of it without love, is always avenged because the attitude which commits that crime also commits the crime against men which in turn exacts vengeance, so that man finally punishes himself. It is only by this line of reasoning that one can, I think, read the last page of "Delta Autumn":

This land which man has deswamped and denuded and deriverered in two generations so that white men can own plantations and commute every night to Memphis and black men own plantations and ride in Jim Crow cars to Chicago to live in millionaires' mansions on Lake Shore Drive; where white men rent farms and live like niggers and niggers crop on shares and live like animals; where cotton is planted and grows man-tall in the very cracks of the sidewalks, and usury and mortgage and bankruptcy and measureless wealth, Chinese and African and Aryan and Jew, all breed and spawn together until no man has time to say which one is which nor cares. . . .No wonder the ruined woods I used to know don't cry for retribution! he thought: The people who have destroyed it will accomplish its revenge.

The attitude toward nature in Faulkner's work, however, does not involve a sinking into nature. In Faulkner's mythology man has "suzerainty over the earth," he is not of the earth, and it is the human virtues which count—"pity and humility and sufference and endurance." If we take even the extreme case of the idiot Snopes and his fixation on the cow in *The Hamlet* (a scene whose function in the total order of the book is to show that even the idiot pervert is superior to Flem), a scene which shows the human being as close as possible to the "natural" level, we find that the scene is the most lyrical in Faulkner's work: even the idiot is human and not animal, for only human desires, not animal, clothe themselves in poetry. I think that George Marion O'Donnell is right in pointing to the humanism-naturalism opposition in Faulkner's work, and over and over again we find that the point of some novel or story has to do with the human effort to find or create values in the mechanical round of experience—"not just to eat and evacuate and sleep warm," as Charlotte Rittenmeyer says in *The Wild Palms*, "so we can get up and eat and evacuate in order to sleep warm again," or not just to raise cotton to buy niggers to raise cotton to buy niggers, as it is put in another place. Even when a character seems to be caught in the iron ring of some compulsion, of some mechanical process (the hunted Negro of "Red Leaves," the tall convict of *The Wild Palms*, Christmas of *Light in August)*, the effort may be discernible. And in Quentin's attempt, in *The Sound and the Fury*, to persuade his sister Caddy, who is pregnant by one of the boys of Jefferson, to confess that she has committed incest with him, we find among other things the idea that "the horror" and "the clean flame" would be preferable to the meaninglessness of the "loud world."

II

One of the most important remarks in Cowley's introduction is that concerning humor. There is, especially in the later books, "a sort of homely and sober-sided frontier humor that is seldom achieved in contemporary writing." Cowley continues: "In a curious way, Faulkner combines two of the principal traditions in American letters: the tradition of psychological horror, often close to symbolism, that begins with Charles Brockden Brown, our first professional novelist, and extends through Poe, Melville, Henry James (in his later stories), Stephen Crane and Hemingway; and the other tradition of frontier humor and realism, beginning with Augustus Longstreet's *Georgia Scenes* and having Mark Twain as its best example." The observation is an acute one, for the distortions of humor and the distortions of horror in Faulkner's work are closely akin and frequently, in a given instance, can scarcely be disentangled.

It is true that the most important strain of humor in Faulkner's work is derived from the tradition of frontier humor (though it is probable that he got it from the porches of country stores and the court-house yards of county-seat towns and not from any book), and it is true that the most spectacular displays of Faulkner's humor are of this order—for example, the "Spotted Horses" episode from *The Hamlet* or the story "Was." But there are other strains which might be distinguished and investigated. For example, there is a kind of Dickensian humor; the scene in the Memphis brothel from *Sanctuary,* which is reprinted here under the title "Uncle Bud and the Three Madams," is certainly more Dickensian than frontier. There is a subdued humor, sometimes shading into pathos, in the treatment of some of the Negro characters and in their dialogue. And there is an irony ranging from that in the scene in *Sanctuary* where Miss Reba, the madam, in offended decency keeps telling Temple, "Lie down and cover up your nekkidness," while the girl talks with Benbow, to that in the magnificently sustained monologue of Jason at the end of *The Sound and the Fury.*

In any case, humor in Faulkner's work is never exploited for its own sake. It is regularly used as an index, as a lead, to other effects. The humor in itself may be striking, but Faulkner is not a humorist in the sense, say, that Mark Twain is. His humor is but one perspective on the material and it is never a final perspective, as we can see from such an example as the episode of "Spotted Horses." Nothing could be more wide of the point than the remark in Maxwell Geismar's essay on Faulkner to the effect that Faulkner in *The Hamlet* "seems now to accept the antics of his provincial morons, to enjoy the chronicle of their low-grade behavior; he submerges himself in their clownish degradation." All the critic seems to find in Mink Snopes' victim with his life-long devotion to the memory of his dead wife, and in Ratliff with his good heart and ironical mind and quiet wisdom, comic "descendants of the gangling and giggling Wash Jones."

The Poor White—The above remark leads us to the not uncommon misconception about the role of the poor white in Faulkner's work. It is true that the Snopeses are poor whites, descendants of bushwhackers (and therefore outside society, as the bushwhacker was outside society, had no "side" in the Civil War but tried to make a good thing of it), and it is true that Snopesism represents a special kind of villainy and degradation the form that the pure doctrine of exploitation and degradation takes in the society of which Faulkner writes, but any careful reader realizes that a Snopes is not to be equated with a poor white. For instance the book most fully about the poor white, *As I Lay Dying,* is full of sympathy and poetry. There are a hundred touches like that in Cash's soliloquy about the phonograph: "I reckon it's a good thing we aint got ere a one of them. I reckon I wouldn't never get no work done a-tall for listening to it. I dont know if a little music aint about the nicest thing a fellow can have. Seems like when he comes in tired of a night, it aint nothing could rest him like having a little music played and him resting." Or like the long section toward the middle of the book devoted to Addie Bundren, a section which is full of eloquence like that of this paragraph: "And then he died. He did not know he was dead. I would lie by him in the dark, hearing the dark land talking of God's love and His beauty and His sin; hearing the dark voicelessness in which the words are the deeds, and the other words that are not deeds, that are just the gaps in peoples' lacks, coming down like the cries of geese out of the wild darkness in the old terrible nights, fumbling at the deeds like orphans to whom are pointed out in a crowd two faces and told, That is your father, your mother." Do these passages indicate a relish in the "antics of his provincial morons"?

The whole of *As I Lay Dying* is based on the heroic effort of the Bundren family to fulfill the promise to the dead mother, to take her body to Jefferson; and the fact that Anse Bundren, after the heroic effort has been completed, immediately gets him a new wife, the "duck-shaped woman" with the "hard-looking pop-eyes," does not negate the heroism of the effort nor the poetry and feeling which give flesh to the book. We are told by one critic that "what should have been the drama of the Bundrens thus becomes in the end a sort of brutal farce," and that we are "unable to feel the tragedy because the author has refused to accept the Bundrens, as he did accept the Compsons, as tragic." Rather, I should say, the Bundrens may come off a little better than the latter-day Compsons, the whining mother, the promiscuous Caddy, the ineffectual Quentin and the rest. The Bundrens, at least, are capable of the heroic effort, and the promise is fulfilled. What the conclusion indicates is that even such a fellow as Anse Bundren (who is not typical of his family, by the way), in the grip of an idea, in terms of promise or code, is capable of rising out of his ordinary level; Anse falls back at the end, but only after the prop of the idea and obligation have been removed. And we may recall that even the "gangling and giggling Wash Jones" has always been capable of some kind of obscure dream and aspiration (his very attachment to Sutpen indicates that), and that in the end he achieves dignity and manhood.

The final and incontrovertible evidence that Snopes is not to be equated with poor white comes in *The Hamlet* (though actually most of the characters in the book, though they may be poor, are not, strictly speaking, "poor whites" at all, but rather what uninstructed reviewers choose to call by that label). The point of the book is the assault made on a solid community of plain, hard-working small farmers by Snopeses and Snopesism. Ratliff is not rich, but he is not Flem Snopes. And if the corruption of Snopesism does penetrate into the community, there is no one here who can be compared in degradation and vileness to Jason of *The Sound and the Fury*, the Compson who has embraced Snopesism. In fact, Popeye and Flem, Faulkner's best advertised villains, cannot, for vileness and ultimate meanness, touch Jason.

The Negro—In one of Faulkner's books it is said that every white child is born crucified on a black cross. Remarks like this have led to a gross misconception of the place of the Negro in Faulkner's work, to the notion that Faulkner "hates" Negroes. For instance, we find Maxwell Geismar exclaiming what a "strange inversion" it is to take the Negro, who is the "tragic consequence," and to exhibit him as the "evil cause" of the failure of the old order in the South.

This is a misreading of the text. It is slavery, not the Negro, which is defined, quite flatly, as the curse, over and over again, and the Negro is the black cross in so far as he is the embodiment of the curse, the reminder of the guilt, the incarnation of the problem. That is the basic point. But now and then, as a kind of tangential irony, we have the notion, not of the burden of the white on the black, but the burden of the black on the white, the weight of obligation, inefficiency, etc., as well as the weight of guilt (the notion we find in the old story of the plantation mistress who after the Civil War, said: "Mr. Lincoln thought he was emancipating those slaves, but he was really emancipating me"). For instance, we get hints of the notion in "Red Leaves": one of the Indians, sweating in the chase of the runaway Negro who is to be killed for the Man's funeral, says, "Damn that Negro," and the other Indian replies, "Yao. When have they ever been anything but a trial and a care to us?" But the black cross is, fundamentally, the weight of the white man's

372

guilt, the white man who now sells salves and potions to "bleach the pigment and straighten the hair of Negroes that they might resemble the very race which for two hundred years had held them in bondage and from which for another hundred years not even a bloody civil war would have set them completely free." The curse is still operative, as the crime is still compounded.

The actual role of the Negro in Faulkner's fiction is consistently one of pathos or heroism. It is not merely, as has been suggested more than once, that Faulkner condescends to the good and faithful servant, the "white folks' nigger." There are figures like Dilsey, but they are not as impressive as the Negro in "Red Leaves" or Sam Fathers, who, with the bear, is the hero of "The Bear." The fugitive, who gains in the course of the former story a shadowy symbolic significance, is told in the end by one of the Indians who overtake him, "You ran well. Do not be ashamed," and when he walks among the Indians, he is "the tallest there, his high, close, mud-caked head looming above them all." And Sam Fathers is the fountainhead of the wisdom which Ike McCaslin finally gains, and the repository of the virtues which are central for Faulkner—"an old man, son of a Negro slave and an Indian king, inheritor on the one hand of the long chronicle of a people who had learned humility through suffering and learned pride through the endurance which survived suffering, and on the other side the chronicle of a people even longer in the land than the first, yet who now existed there only in the solitary brotherhood of an old and childless Negro's alien blood and the wild and invincible spirit of an old bear." Even Christmas, in *Light in Aguust,* though he is sometimes spoken of as a villain, is a mixture of heroism and pathos. He is the lost, suffering, enduring creature (the figure like Sam Fathers, the tall convict of *The Wild Palms,* or Dilsey in *The Sound and the Fury),* and even the murder he commits at the end is a fumbling attempt to define his manhood, is an attempt to break out of the iron ring of mechanism, to lift himself out of "nature," for the woman whom he kills has become a figure of the horror of the human which has surrendered the human attributes. (We may compare Christmas to Mink Snopes in *The Hamlet* in this respect: Mink, mean and vicious as he is, kills out of a kind of warped and confused pride, and by this affirmation is set off against his kinsman Flem, whose only vaues are those of pure Snopesism.)

Even such a brief comment on the Negro in Faulkner's work cannot close without this passage from "The Bear":

"Because they will endure. They are better than we are. Stronger than we are. Their vices are vices aped from white men or that white men and bondage have taught them: improvidence and intemperance and evasion—not laziness: evasion: of what white men had set them to, not for their aggrandizement or even comfort but his own—" and McCaslin

"All right. Go on: Promiscuity. Violence. Instability and lack of control. Inability to distinguish between mine and thine—" and he

"How distinguish when for two hundred years mine did not even exist for them?" and McCaslin

"All right. Go on. And their virtues—" and he

"Yes. Their own. Endurance—" and McCaslin

"So have mules:" and he

"—and pity and tolerance and forbearance and fidelity and love of children—" and McCaslin

"So have dogs:" and he

"—Whether their own or not or black or not. And more: what they got not only not from white people but not even despite white people because they had it already from the old free fathers a longer time free than us because we have never been free—"

And there is the single comment under Dilsey's name in the annotated genealogy of the Compsons which Faulkner has prepared for the present volume: "They endured."

Technique—There are excellent comments on this subject by Cowley, Conrad Aiken, Warren Beck, Joseph Warren Beach and Alfred Kazin, but the subject has not been fully explored. One difficulty is that Faulkner is an incorrigible and restless experimenter, is peculiarly sensitive to the expressive possibilities of shifts in technique and has not developed (like Hemingway or Katherine Anne Porter—lyric rather than dramatic writers, artists with a great deal of self-certainty) in a straight line.

Provisionally, we may distinguish in Faulkner's work three basic methods of handling a narrative. One is best typified in *Sanctuary*, where there is a tightly organized plot, a crisp, laconic style, an objective presentation of character—an impersonal method. Another is best typified by *As I Lay Dying* or *The Sound and the Fury*, where each character unfolds in his own language or flow of being before us—a dramatic method in that the author does not obtrude, but a method which makes the subjective reference of character the medium of presentation. Another is best typified by "Was," "The Bear," or the story of the tall convict in *The Wild Palms*, where the organization of the narrative is episodic and the sense of a voice, a narrator's presence (though not necessarily a narrator in the formal sense), is almost constantly felt—a method in which the medium is ultimately a "voice" as index to sensibility. The assumptions underlying these methods, and the relations among them, would provide a study.

Cowley's emphasis on the unity of Faulkner's work, the fact that all the novels and stories are to be taken as aspects of a single, large design, is very important. It is important, for one thing, in regard to the handling of character. A character, Sutpen, for instance, may appear in various perspectives, so that from book to book we move toward a final definition much as in actual life we move toward the definition of a person. The same principle applies to event, as Conrad Aiken has pointed out, the principle of the spiral method which takes the reader over and over the same event from a different altitude, as it were, and a different angle. In relation to both character and event this method, once it is understood by the reader, makes for a kind of realism and a kind of suspense (in the formal not the factual sense) not common in fiction.

The emphasis on the unity of Faulkner's work may,

however, lead to an underrating of the degree of organization within individual works. Cowley is right in pointing out the structural defect in *Light in August,* but he may be putting too much emphasis on the over-all unity and not enough on the organization of the individual work when he says that *The Hamlet* tends to resolve into a "series of episodes resembling beads on a string." I think that in that novel we have a type of organization in which the thematic rather than the narrative emphasis is the basic principle, and once we grasp that fact the unity of the individual work may come clear. In fact, the whole subject of the principle of thematic organization in the novels and long stories, "The Bear" for instance, needs investigation. In pieces which seem disjointed, or which seem to have the mere tale-teller's improvisations, we may sometimes discover the true unity if we think of the line of meaning, the symbolic ordering, and surrender ourselves to the tale-teller's "voice." And it may be useful at times to recall the distinction between the formal, forensic realism of Ibsen as opposed to the fluid, suggestive realism of Chekhov.

Symbol and Image—Cowley and O'Donnell have given acute readings of the main symbolic outline of Faulkner's fiction, but no one has yet devoted himself to the study of symbolic motifs which, though not major, are nevertheless extremely instructive. For instance, the images of the hunt, the flight, the pursuit, such as we have in "Red Leaves," *The Wild Palms,* the episode of "Peter Grimm" in *Light in August,* "The Bear," "Delta Autumn," "Was" and (especially in the hordes of moving Negroes) in *The Unvanquished.* Or there is the important symbolic relationship between man and earth. Or there is the contrast between images of compulsion and images of will or freedom. Or there is the device of what we might call the frozen moment, the arrested action which becomes symbolic, as in the moment when, in "An Odor of Verbena" (from *The Unvanquished*), Drusilla offers the pistols to the hero.

Polarity—To what extent does Faulkner work in terms of polarities, oppositions, paradoxes, inversions of roles? How much does he employ a line of concealed (or open) dialectic progression as a principle for his fiction? The study of these questions may lead to the discovery of principles of organization in his work not yet defined by criticism.

The study of Faulkner is the most challenging single task in contemporary American literature for criticism to undertake. Here is a novelist who, in mass of work, in scope of material, in range of effect, in reportorial accuracy and symbolic subtlety, in philosophical weight, can be put beside the masters of our own past literature. Yet this accomplishment has been effected in what almost amounts to critical isolation and silence, and when the silence has been broken it has usually been broken by someone (sometimes one of our better critics) whose reading has been hasty, whose analysis unscholarly and whose judgments superficial. The picture of Faulkner presented to the public by such criticism is a combination of Thomas Nelson Page, a fascist and a psychopath, gnawing his nails. Of course, this picture is usually accompanied by a grudging remark about genius.

Cowley's book, for its intelligence, sensitivity and sobriety in the Introduction, and for the ingenuity and judgment exhibited in the selections, would be valuable at any time. But it is especially valuable at this time. Perhaps it can mark a turning point in Faulkner's reputation. That will be of slight service to Faulkner, who, as much as any writer of our place and time, can rest in confidence. He can afford to wait. But can we?

(1946)

REBECCA WEST

Poor Relations

It was not that one really disliked Mr. Compton Mackenzie's previous books. But they were so much more like expensive cushions than like books that it seemed a social solecism, like drinking out of a finger-bowl, to be reading what was so obviously meant to be sat on. They appeared not to be created out of separate sweatings of the spirit, as books should be, but to be made up from bales of rich materials, gleaming with stiff inorganic gorgeousness, which were stored in Mr. Mackenzie's brain as gold tissue and the like might be stored in a draper's warehouse. Plumply written descriptions of scenery lay embedded in the glittering general texture even as padded fruits on the modern plutocratic cushion. Queer characters of queer trades and queer crimes hung round the edge of each like a tinsel fringe; and each was weighted as by a heavy gilded tassel with the enormous elaborated egotism of some Michael Fane or Sylvia Scarlett. There was no doubt but that Mr. Mackenzie had a bright vitality which was not always wholly febrile, and a real gift for reproducing those Cockney idioms, those rich fantasies of speech, which are the modern city people's way of singing at their work; and it seemed probable that under a style sodden with excessive literacy he concealed a certain power of descriptive writing. But he seemed to have chosen to build his literary nest in the furnishing department.

But *Poor Relations* is all right. It is a real book. It is a coherent and beautiful farce. And one of the reasons that Mr. Mackenzie has at last got his talent going is that he has ceased to handicap himself by cramming his books with reverential and copious representations of intolerable people. The doctrine that he prayeth best who loveth best all things both great and small is one attractive to the emotional mysticism of our day, but it cannot be stretched beyond certain limits. It is possible that St. Columba, who preached to the seals, and St. Francis, who preached to the birds, could take an interest in the spiritual life of Oxford undergraduates of the type who publish poems at Blackwell's with terms of reference including chrysophrase and strange sins, but after all that is what saints are for. Those of us who have no canonized position to keep up cannot be interested in Michael Fane and his friends.

But John Touchwood, the chirping, strutting little Robin-Redbreast of a man who is the hero of *Poor Relations,* does interest us; and Doris Hamilton, who is a subtle and graceful picture of the kind of nice woman who is so sensible and dignified herself that she need not fear to marry an ass, holds the attention much more firmly than Sylvia Scarlett. It is not, of course, that Oxford undergradutates are in themselves less suitable subjects for art than elderly romantic dramatists. Adolescence, if it be treated from an adult standpoint, so that distemper is not reckoned as the chief of cosmic conflicts, may be matter for a very fine book, as Dostoievsky showed in *A Raw Youth.* But the drama of a book about adolescence must be a thing of spiritual developments, and Mr. Mackenzie is never right about the interior workings of the spirit. There is no reason why he should be, when he is so intensely sensitive to the exterior manifestations of life and so unquenchably gay in recording

them. It is only the curious convention of our time that if a
novel is to be dignified its interest must be psychological
which has blinded him to the knowledge that he can achieve
a clear and joyous beauty all his own provided he works on
the surface of life. That achievement is entirely conditional
upon his choosing subjects whose interest lies on the surface
and this book fulfils that condition as none other of Mr.
Mackenzie's books have done. The tubby, benevolent John,
sitting under the cherub-haunted ceiling of his library at
Church Row, his toe on the rose-wreathed Aubusson carpet,
his head in a rosy mist of foolishness and vanity and
goodwill, while his perverse relations perpetually invade his
calm with demands and villainies that wrinkle the surface of
the optimism that lies in his open little mind like cream in a
saucer, and Miss Hamilton, pasting at his direction
presscuttings about him and his work into a large scrap-book,
preserving a docile and maternal air and yet murmuring
faintly from time to time about "lack of dignity" and even
"lack of humor," are thereby showing their essences. They
are types whose reactions to spiritual adventures would be so
simple that we do not need an artist of spiritual wisdom to
disclose them to us; their charm and value lie in just such
physical attitudes, such individualities of speech and
manners, as Mr. Mackenzie's talent can beautifully convey.
This sudden light ascent into delightfulness by one who
seemed doomed to the ponderous celebration of egotisms
gives us an intimation of what we lose by our obsession,
which has been made a thousand times worse by the
influence of the Russian novelists, with the psychological
novel. The comedy of manners has as much right to exist as
the tragedy of souls.

Poor Relations shows, moreover, that recognition of how
strange people really are which has always been one of Mr.
Mackenzie's virtues. He has resisted that persistent
underwriting of character and circumstance which has been
the curse of refined English literature ever since the days of
Gissing, and has not been afraid to allow fantastic people to

do fantastic things. This is a move towards true realism. The older one gets the more one realizes that for a plain matter-of-fact account of life as it is one must go to *Alice in Wonderland*. On some other sphere life may build itself out of solid blocks of normality on a splendid logical plan, as it does in the novels of Mrs. Humphrey Ward, but not in this. In the present volume Mr. Mackenzie is sometimes inclined to exaggerate variability of life. When he takes up a minor character and wonders with what violent characteristic to daub it into distinction he is a little like a child turning over a painting book and saying, "I will paint this horse green with pink spots." There is no reason why he should give the normal and charming Miss Hamilton a mother like a mad clown, and it was not necessary, when conducting the reader through a boarding-house, to diagnose one of the resident spinsters as having exophthalmus.

But most of the minor characters—most notably Laurence, John's parson brother-in-law, "suave and heavy like a cornflour shape," who gives up his living in order to compete with John in the art of playwriting ("Thomas, A Play in Four Acts. Act the First. Scene the First. The shore of the Sea of Galilee. Enter from the left the Virgin Mary . . .") —are done with a richness of invention and a power of dramatic dialogue which prove, what one had hitherto felt unusually plucky in suspecting in the face of Sinister Street and Sylvia, that here is an imagination altogether Dickens-like in its abundance.

(1920)

REED WHITTEMORE

Henderson the Rain King

The New Republic was the only major weekly or monthly in the country (approximately) not to review Saul Bellow's new novel in its first week of publication. A fortunate occurrence. Now I can sit down and be among the first to review the reviews.

I surveyed nine reviews. In them Saul Bellow's hero was compared to Don Quixote (thrice), Tarzan (twice), Gulliver, Everyman, Huck Finn, Daniel, a Connecticut Yankee (twice), Odysseus and Captain Ahab. Bellow's prose was found to be masterly, exemplary, supercharged (this was bad), vivid, turbulent (this was good), brilliant and labored. Bellow's story was characterized as fantastic, melodramatic, unrealistic, ironic, anarchic, frenzied (this was good), and "not essentially parodic." It was concrete for some, abstract for others. The whole performance was approved by four, disapproved by five.

Well, now, Bellow himself stepped into this phrase factory a week before it opened. He wrote a lead piece for the Sunday *Times* Book Section in which he explained that he was much interested in the matters about which the reviewers, as it turned out, were about to talk, and particularly in that little matter of the abstract *vs.* the concrete. In a judicious moment he observed that "while our need for meanings is certainly great our need for concreteness, for particulars is even greater." Indeed, he went to some lengths to ridicule meaning-hunters for being snobbish, idolatrous of culture, and excessively solemn. The piece was titled "Deep Readers of the World, Beware."

It is not often that a writer has a chance to tell his reviewers what they should argue about. I say this without irony; I mean simply that I think we are fortunate in having Bellow on the scene here. I doubt that he would have said what he said in the *Times,* just before the publication of his new book, if he had not had in the back of his mind the notion that meaning-hunters would soon be descending upon it. And what could have given him this notion but a reading of his own book? "Henderson" is one of those books clearly constructed for the delight and despair of meaning-hunters. One simply can't read it—even after reading Bellow in the *Times*—without looking at its story and its characters with an English Department's suspicion. What is the story *really,* about?

The story has been summarized at some length in all the reviews I have read, so I will forego here the pleasure of describing in detail how the middle-aged Henderson bombed the frogs and wowed the lions on his African junket. I cannot, however, neglect so readily the significance of these activities; it seems to me important to observe that the story *is* allegorical (though it is also massively concrete) and that, therefore, its readers probably ought to sit down and figure out what it is an allegory of. Most of the reviewers took a stab at this, and there seemed to be general agreement that hero Henderson was on a spiritual quest (like Don Quixote and all those others) for greater Fullness of Being; further, that he achieved a measure of success in his search, while living among the Wariri. There, as *Time* put it, he was helped to "break the cycle of Becoming for the Serenity of Being."

What was it that the Wariri provided him with?—"a shot in the arm from animal nature." This "shot" had been prescribed earlier by references to the prophecy of Daniel which, Henderson said, he "had never been able to shake off—'They shall drive you from among men, and thy dwelling shall be with the beasts of the field.'" Nebuchadnezzar, to whom the prophecy was originally addressed, didn't believe the prophecy; but when it came to pass he submitted to it gracefully and discovered that the results were excellent:

I Nebuchadnezzar lifted up mine eyes unto Heaven, and mine understanding returned unto me, and I blessed the Most High. . . .
At the same time my reason returned unto me; and for the glory of my kingdom, mine honour and brightness returned unto me; and my counsellors and my lords sought unto me; and I was established in my kingdom, and excellent majesty was added to me.

Like Nebuchadnezzar, hero Henderson was rejuvenated at the end. As we left him he was looking forward to meeting the girl he had discouragedly left a while back; he felt healthy and ready to take on his "kingdom" again:

Laps and laps I galloped around the shining and riveted body of the plane, behind the fuel trucks. Dark faces were looking from within. The great, beautiful propellers were still, all four of them. I guess I felt it was my turn now to move, and so went running—leaping, leaping, pounding, and tingling over the pure white lining of the gray Arctic silence.

In other words Henderson had had the shot in the arm he needed out there in Bellow's curious Africa, and was headed back, as the curtain fell, to tell us all, or at least friend Lily, that it would be good for modern civilization to go live with the beasts of the field for a piece. Amen.

Now it is always disconcerting and depressing to come upon the bare bones of some hopeful organic unity in a bumbling review, to see the remains of the great or small creation all stretched out helplessly before a laboratory man whose primary interest in them is in getting some sort of a grade for his naming of parts. The "Henderson" occasion is especially disconcerting because Bellow has left us instructions, both in

384

the book and in the piece in the *Times,* that his cadaver should not be so treated. Why?—because "Henderson" is a story against laboratory men and laboratory procedures, is against, in an odd way, what it is. The novelist who doesn't like meanings writes an allegory; the allegory means that men should not mean but be. Ods bodkins. The reviewer looks at the evidence and wonders if he should damn the author and praise the book, or praise the author and damn the book. And is it possible, somehow or other, to praise, or damn both?—he isn't sure.

We see the results of this dilemma among those reviewers who were uncertain about how "serious" the book was. Charles Rolo (the *Atlantic)* put the confusion most plainly when he observed that although he didn't think the novel was intended as a parody it certainly read that way. What is involved here, I think, is the nature and extent of Bellow's commitment to his story. Nobody can deny that the particulars are there, that Henderson's world has been, as Paul Pickrel (*Harper's)* put it, "vividly and brilliantly imagined." But the particulars are so clearly hokum that one is hardly disposed to reckon with them except as jokes, sometimes very good jokes:

And I began to drink, harder than ever, and was drunk in every one of the great cathedrals—Amiens, Chartres, Vezelay, and so on.

To break up the tension, however, I said, "Would anybody like to visit my pistol range downstairs?" There were no takers and I went below myself and fired a few rounds. The bullets made a tremendous noise among the hot-air ducts. Soon I heard the visitors saying good-bye.

From here we took a plane to Baventai, an old Ballanca, the wings looked ready to drop off, and the pilot was an Arab and flew with bare feet.

I built an igloo with a knife and during zero weather Lily and I fell out because she wouldn't bring the kids and sleep with me under the skins as the Eskimos do.

As I ate the cocoons and the larvae and ants crouching in the jockey shorts with the lion lying under me for shade, I spoke oracles and sang...while I fondled the animal, which had made a wonderful adjustment to me.

Thus it may be true, as Granville Hicks *(Saturday Review)* said, that Bellow's lions are lions and his pigs pigs, rather than pale symbols; but it is also true that they are curious lions and pigs—or, to bring out the big word for the day, fantasy lions and pigs. The reader is amused by them but not taken in by them. How can he be?—Bellow is not taken in by them; Bellow is busy making the pigs and lions as eccentric and extravagant as he can. And yet, strangely enough, he is asking us—as, say, Max Shulman and S. J. Perlman would not ask us—to imagine that his parody does not extend as far as his theme. He is telling us to be amused by Henderson's shenanigans in a thoroughly shenaniganed Africa, but at the same time to believe—and of course empathize with—Henderson's "Problem." Under such conditions I do not find it surprising that several of the reviewers tended to discount the concreteness of Bellow's story, to discover that "Henderson's moral dilemma is more real than Henderson" *(Time)*.

To be ponderous and impressive let me say that Bellow's procedure in "Henderson" is probably attributable to our modern incapacity to take myth, romance, all the really radical kinds of literary artifice as we perhaps ought to (ought to, at least, for the health of literature). Shakespeare, for example, could put before his audience a completely hoked-up woods in *Midsummer Night's Dream,* point out that it was "airy nothing," and have characters like Bottom undermine it regularly, while at the same time allowing Puck, Oberon, Titania and the lovers themselves to speak and act in the old somber, heroic way. This mixture of *motifs* is not possible for Bellow apparently; and since I am confident that it would not be possible for me either, I sympathize. My sympathy, though, doesn't make me like "Henderson" any better. I am amused for a while, then fatigued, but never involved. The artifice simply isn't earnest any place; only the mind behind the artifice is earnest. A good many of the reviewers pointed, either happily or unhappily, to the imaginative qualities of the book, and I am impressed by them too—one doesn't, for example, run into a frog-bombing every day. But of this quite marvelous imagination I think it is necessary to say that its owner discounted it before I did.

(1959)

C. VANN WOODWARD

The Confessions of Nat Turner

In the annals of American slavery two figures stand out with unrivaled prominence among the very few who resorted to armed rebellion—John Brown and Nat Turner, one white and one black. The historical importance of their roles is roughly comparable and there is as much reason for enduring curiosity about the one as about the other. Of the two, Turner's rebellion was far more bloody, both in the lives it took and in the reprisals it evoked. As a threat to the security of a slave based society, Turner's conspiracy was more momentous then Brown's. John Brown's raid never had the remotest chance of success.

Yet there is a remarkable disparity in the amount that is known and in what has been written about the two men and their deeds. On John Brown there exists a vast library, forty-odd biographies, massive monographs, scores of poems, plays, and works of fiction. This is partly explained by the relative abundance of source materials. Brown left extensive (though misleading) accounts of himself and a large mass of correspondence. He was acquainted with some of the most prominent writers of his day. A few intellectuals were personally involved and many were passionately interested in his conspiracy and left their own records. Two congressional hearings and a mountain of archival material multiply the sources.

In striking contrast, the sources on Nat Turner and the scholarly as well as creative writing about him are minuscule. Since there were no white participants in the rebellion and the life of no white witness of the massacres was spared by the rebels, the information about the conspiracy boils down largely to twenty-odd pages of Turner's "Confessions" in the stilted prose of the Virginia lawyer to whom he dictated them in prison. Mainly on this and on a pedestrian monograph or two rests all we know of the only slave rebellion of consequence in the largest slave society in the nineteenth-century world.

If there were ever a free hand for a novelist, this was it. Yet the obstacles were formidable. There were no models. The only major American novelist to treat a slave rebellion was Melville, and *Benito Cereno* is viewed entirely through the eyes of the white man. Nat's story would have to be seen from behind the black mask. That was the boldest decision William Styron made. There was little to go on beyond the author's imagination. What history tells us about slavery is mainly the white man's experience, not the black man's—what it was like to *have* slaves, not what it was like to *be* slaves. No one has more than an ill-informed guess about why the greatest slave republic in the New World had by far the fewest rebellions; why smaller and allegedly more benevolent slave societies bred vast insurrections, blood baths involving many thousands of slaves that lasted scores of years, and America had one that recruited seventy-five and petered out in three days; why servility and submission were the rule and Sambo the stereotype and heritage of American slavery. And most of all, what explains the terrible enigma of Nat Turner, the other-worldly young carpenter of obscure origins and apocalyptic visions who at the age of thirty-one took the road to Jerusalem, Va., martyrdom, and immortality.

To complicate the enigma, the rebellion took place not in

the brutal Delta cotton fields or the Louisiana sugar cane, but in mellowed, impoverished tidewater Virginia, where even Nat Turner thought there was "still an ebb and flow of human sympathy—no matter how strained and imperfect—between slave and master." And Nat himself was a product of benevolent, if unusual, paternalism at its best—fondly educated, trained in a craft, and promised liberation. The picture of Nat's life and motivation the novelist constructs is, but for a few scraps of evidence, without historical underpinnings, but most historians would agree, I think, not inconsistent with anything historians know. It is informed by a respect for history, a sure feeling for the period, and a deep and precise sense of place and time.

Nat was the child of a house servant and grew up in the big house, familiar with "the chink of silver and china" as well as his "black Negro world" of the kitchen, but not with the toil of field and mill. His mistress taught him to read and gave him a Bible, of which he learned great parts by heart and knew better than the white preachers of the parish. He discovered his intelligence and his ability to charm, grew accustomed to love from all sides, and never encountered harshness or brutality. "I became in short a pet, the darling, the little black jewel of Turner's Mill. Pampered, fondled, nudged, pinched, I was the household's spoiled child." Toward his master, Samuel Turner, he felt a regard "very close to the feeling one should bear only toward the Divinity." Between them were "strong ties of emotion," in fact, "a kind of love." The master responded by giving encouragement, careful training, flattering responsibilities, and, three years before Nat came of age, the intoxicating promise of freedom. Toward the field hands beyond the big house perimeter little Nat felt a contemptuous disdain, regarding them as "a lower order of people—a ragtag mob, coarse, raucous, clownish, uncouth." He identified completely with his master and looking back later realized that had this life continued he would have achieved in old age "a kind of purse-lipped dignity, known as Uncle Nat, well loved and adoring in return, a palsied stroker of the silken pates of little white grandchildren," But that life came to an end when

Samuel Turner went bankrupt and moved to Alabama when Nat was twenty. Before leaving Virginia he placed Nat in the care of a poverty-ravaged, fanatical Baptist preacher under legal obligation to free his charge in a stated time. Instead, after giving Nat a year's taste of how degrading slavery could be, the preacher sold him for $460 to an illiterate brute named Moore, from whom he eventually passed into the hands of his last owner, Travis. Among the many harsh lessons these experiences taught Nat was "how greatly various were the moral attributes of white men who possessed slaves, how different each owner might be by way of severity or benevolence." They ranged "from the saintly," such as his first owner, "to a few who were unconditionally monstrous." Nat never fell into the hands of the last type, and his owner at the time of the rebellion generally behaved "like every slave's ideal master." Whatever accounts for Nat's rebellion, it was not the irrepressible rage of the intolerably oppressed. Instead, he observed, "the more tolerable and human white people became in their dealings with me, the keener was my passion to destroy them."

Nat was twenty and on the threshold of freedom before he suddenly realized what slavery was, "the *true* world in with a Negro moves and breathes. It was like being plunged into freezing water." A year later came his betrayal, the final shattering of the dream of freedom, and his submission to a master he knew to be his moral inferior, stupid, brutal, swinish. For nearly ten years his disciplined defense was to become "a paragon of rectitude, of alacrity, of lively industriousness, of sweet equanimity and uncomplaining obedience," the ideal slave. He had learned never to look a white man in the eye, how to smell danger, how like a dog "to interpret the tone of what is being said," how to assume "that posture of respect and deference it is wise for any Negro to assume" in the presence of a strange white man, and how to "merge faceless and nameless with the common swarm." He learned how, when necessary, to shuffle and scrape and adopt the egregious, gluey cornfield accents and postures of niggerness.

He became a discriminating connoisseur of Sambo types, those given to "wallowing in the dust at the slightest provocation, midriffs clutched in idiot laughter," those who "endear themselves to all, white and black, through droll interminable tales about ha'nts and witches and conjures," and at the other extreme those who "reverse the procedure entirely and in *their* niggerness are able to outdo many white people in presenting to the world a grotesque swagger," a posture suited to the black driver or the tyrannical kitchen mammy and butler, who were skilled in keeping "safely this side of insolence." For his own part, Nat "decided upon humility, a soft voice, and houndlike obedience." Yet he was always conscious of "the weird unnaturalness of this adopted role," always counseling himself "to patience, patience, *patience* to the end," biding his time.

As he watched the potential recruits for his divine mission of vengeance and liberation he often despaired. His black brother, "half drowned from birth in a kind of murky middlessness," drifted before him "mouths agape or with sloppy uncomprehending smiles, shuffling their feet." They would suddenly seem to him "as meaningless and as stupid as a barnful of mules," and he would "hate them one and all." But this hatred would alternate with "a kind of wild, desperate love for them." The ambivalence came out in his feelings about Hark (originally named Hercules) whom he intended to make one of his lieutenants. Hark had "the face of an African chieftain," a godlike frame and strength, and a mortal grievance against his master for selling his wife and child. "Yet the very sight of white skin cowed him, humbled him to the most servile abasement." He drove Nat to incoherent rage when in the presence of any white he unconsciously became "the unspeakable bootlicking Sambo, all giggles and smirks and oily, sniveling servility," Hark's defense was that he was overcome by "dat black-assed feelin'," and Nat admitted to himself that the expression perfectly expressed "the numbness and dread which dwells in every Negro's heart."

Nat labored desperately to quell this fear in his recruits and to install pride and confidence and blind faith in their leader. He clung to his faith that in every Sambo was a Nat Turner, that while "most Negroes are hopelessly docile, many of them are filled with fury," and that servility was "but a form of self-preservation." In the more desperate of them he counted upon the common postulate that "nigger life ain't worth pig shit"—they had nothing to lose.

It is one mark of William Styron's genius that he deliberately threw away the Christ symbol, which would have been irresistible to many novelists. For Nat was strictly Old Testament, the stuff of Ezekiel, Daniel, Isaiah, and Jeremiah, the blood-stained righteousness of his somber Hebrew heroes, Joshua and David. He thought and spoke in the rhetoric of the Prophets and the Psalms and scriptural poetry weaves in and out of his ruminations. He fasted and prayed in the wilderness and waited for a sign. And the sign came: "Then swiftly in the very midst of the rent in the clouds I saw a black angel clothed in black armor with black wings outspread from east to west; gigantic, hovering, he spoke in a thunderous voice louder than anything I had ever heard: *'Fear God and give glory to Him for the hours of His judgment is come. . . .'* "

Against the hour of the bloodbath Nat had steeled himself in apocalyptic hatred, "hatred so pure and obdurate that no sympathy, no human warmth, no flicker of compassion can make the faintest nick or scratch upon the stony surface of its being." He had achieved this exaltation, he thought, by "knowing the white man at close hand," by becoming "knowledgeable about the white man's wiles, his duplicity, his greediness, and his ultimate depravity," and most of all by "having submitted to this wanton and arrogant kindness." Then when the moment came and the dread axe was poised over his master's head, Nat's hand palsied and the blow missed. Again and again between violent seizures of vomiting he tried to kill and failed. Initiative fell to a demented black monster maddened by a master's brutality. The only life Nat was able to take, among the scores slaughtered, was that of the one white person he still loved, a simple-hearted and sympathetic girl.

393

This is the most profound fictional treatment of slavery in our literature. It is, of course, the work of a skilled and experienced novelist with other achievements to attest his qualifications. It is doubtful, however, if the rare combination of talents essential to this formidable undertaking, a flawless command of dialect, a native instinct for the subtleties and ambivalences of race in the South, and a profound and unerring sense of place—Styron's native place as it was Nat Turner's—could well have been found anywhere else.

(1967)